BM

On Global War

Studies in International Relations
Charles W. Kegley, Jr., and Donald J. Puchala,
Series Editors

Marvin S. Soroos
Beyond Sovereignty: The Challenge of Global Policy

Manus I. Midlarsky
The Disintegration of Political Systems:
War and Revolution in Comparative Perspective

Lloyd Jensen
Bargaining for National Security:
The Postwar Disarmament Negotiations

Lloyd Jensen
Negotiating for Nuclear Arms Control

Yale H. Ferguson and Richard W. Mansbach
The Elusive Quest:
Theory and International Politics

On Global War:

Historical-Structural Approaches to World Politics

William R. Thompson

UNIVERSITY OF SOUTH CAROLINA PRESS

Copyright © University of South Carolina 1988

Published in Columbia, South Carolina, by the
University of South Carolina Press

Manufactured in the United States of America

First Edition

LIBRARY OF CONGRESS
Library of Congress Cataloging-in-Publication Data

Thompson, William R.
  On global war: historical-structural approaches to world politics
  William R. Thompson.—1st ed.
    p. cm.—(Studies in international relations)
  Bibliography: p.
  Includes index.
  ISBN 0-87249-562-0
  1. War. 2. International relations. 3. Cycles. I. Title.
II. Series: Studies in international relations (Columbia, S.C.)
U21.2.T465 1988
355'.02—dc19   88-14786
                                                          CIP

For Karen

*who has this strange idea that you can't use the word
"structure" four times in one sentence*

Contents

Tables

Figures

Editors' Preface

The pace of global change has accelerated greatly in the last decades of the twentieth century, and new problems occurring under novel conditions are challenging the academic study of International Relations. There is today a renaissance in scholarship directed toward enhancing our understanding of world politics, global economics, and foreign policy. To examine the transformed structure of the international system and the expanded agenda of global affairs, researchers are introducing new concepts, theories, and analytic modes. Knowledge is expanding rapidly.

Our goal in this series of books is to record the findings of recent innovative research in International Relations, and make these readily available to a broader readership of professionals and students. Contributors to the series are leading scholars who are expert in particular subfields of the discipline. Their contributions represent the most recent work located at the discipline's research frontiers. Topics, subjects, approaches, methods and analytical techniques vary from volume to volume in the series, as each book is intended as an original contribution in the broadest sense. Common to all volumes, however, are careful research and the excitement of new discovery.

The present volume by William R. Thompson meets the ambitious objectives for the Studies of International Relations series. The author—a leading theoretican in the study of international relations—brings together under one cover the most extensive set of empirical materials dealing with the long cycle of world leadership in international politics. Recently, the concept of "long cycles" has risen to a prominent place in the literature, in part because of the increasing awareness of the need to look at the unfolding of the structure of the international system from a historical perspective, and in part because of expanded awareness that many patterns that characterize international relations are subject to temporal variation across epochs. Indeed, the study of cycles in social and political inquiry has received increasing attention generally, as it would seem that any elongated time-series of sufficient historical duration has embedded within it cyclical processes. In the study of world politics as new longitudinal data have been generated, the presence of cyclical patterns has been detected, whereas heretofore these cycles were not recognized. These cyclical changes comprise phenomena in international relations that require description and explanation. Among these long-term attributes of world politics subject to cyclical fluctuation, none is more salient—or as obtrusive in its impact—than the repetitious regularity with which war has occurred since the advent of the state system.

In this ambitious empirical and theoretical work, Thompson makes the case of moving away from one-size-fits-all theorizing about warfare, and instead focuses on a specific type of war: global war. His book examines the diverse historical-structural writing about systemic warfare (as well as the literature derived from nonhistorical and structural approaches to international relations), in order that the main strands of historical-structural theorizing about systemic warfare might be summarized and compared. Discussions of the seminal work of Robert Gilpin, George Modelski, and Immanuel Wallerstein, among others, are rendered understandable and interpretable through empirical investigations that pinpoint areas of divergence and convergence among these three representative approaches to the study of the long cycle of world leadership in world politics. The analysis constructs bridges across the three main approaches by focusing on leading sector concentration/diffusion and by building upon our empirical understanding of global war through the testing of a variety of hypotheses on long-term economic fluctuations, polarity, transitional crises, and uneven development.

Moreover, this volume expands and elaborates on the long-cycle approach to world leadership by introducing ideas from other frameworks and by pursuing some questions in greater depth than has been provided previously. What makes this contribution significant and distinctive is that the analysis suggests new solutions to some of the major puzzles in international relations theory; among them are the questions surrounding the polarity controversy, the reciprocal relationship between economic and military power, and the consequences of power concentration for global stability. Equally important, this book creates the basis for offering some alternative forecasts of when a new global war might occur, based upon different extant assumptions. The importance of this work is punctuated by its ability to rest the conclusions on empirical measurement and reproducible evidence wherever possible, and on the interaction of history and structure over a span extending 500 years. No reader of this book should be able to walk away without obtaining appreciation of the important differences that separate these approaches to long-term macro trends and cycles in international politics. This contribution to the literature illuminates the gray area of international relations which can make a respectable claim for being one of those "research frontiers" on which this series is focused.

Charles W. Kegley, Jr., and Donald J. Puchala

Preface and Acknowledgments

This book is a study of five hundred years of global war behavior. In that period of time, only a very few global wars (fought in 1494–1517, 1580–1608, 1688–1713, 1729–1815, and 1914–1945) have been waged. We know them by a variety of individual names, such as the Napoleonic Wars, World War I, or World II. It is customary to think of them in this way, with each war representing a unique, major event. What is much less customary is to think of each global war as belonging to a specific category of warfare that decides leadership succession/macro policy-making conflicts for the global political system.

As a unique category with immense significance for how world politics operate, global wars deserve special theoretical and empirical attention. They must also be placed within the context of political-economic structural change. Global wars and structural change are greatly intertwined processes. At the risk of oversimplifying, structural change and the deconcentration of power in the system lead to global war. Global war, in turn, facilitates systemic change and the reconcentration of politico-economic and military power. To study global war then means that we must also come to grips with the phenomenon of the rise and fall of the major powers in the world political arena.

Such an undertaking is undeniably ambitious. It is also unorthodox in a number of respects. Unorthodoxy is not something that requires an apology, but readers, I suppose, do deserve some warning. The mainstream approach to the study of war behavior has been to view wars as belonging to a general class of interstate violence that does not require much differentiation beyond the more obvious distinctions of duration or amount of carnage achieved. The argument here will be that global wars are sufficiently distinctive to deserve to be in a class of their own. Closely related to this first deviation is a second departure from the norm. Most scholars focus on one specific war at a time. A few are interested in looking at all wars over long periods of time. The argument here will be that the global war emerged as a systemic mechanism for resolving policy/leadership disputes in the late fifteenth century. Since then, the mechanism has continued to evolve although it is fair to say that it continues to represent a political institution that is too crude and dangerous to tolerate any longer. Global wars thus need to be studied as both a historical institution and a historical process that despite its primitive nature manages to persist.

A third semi-unorthodoxy is traceable to the author's training as a behavioral political scientist. About a decade ago, my uneasiness about many of the assumptions and procedures of "quantitative international politics" led me to cast about for different ways to approach the study of world politics. In the process of casting about, I "rediscovered" history and gradually strengthened my earlier instinctive appreciation for the influence of systemic structures. Unlike many other historical-structural analysts, though, I have retained a hearty appreciation for hypotheses, relevant data, and empirical evidence. Where possible and pertinent, I will, therefore, attempt to test generalizations about global war and structural change. This makes me, I suppose, what might be termed a behavioral historical-structuralist. Needless to say, this label does not encompass a large number of international relations students. Hopefully that may change.

A final unorthodoxy to which I will admit concerns my involvement with a particular brand of historical-structural analysis, the long cycle of global leadership model. Despite the fact that I do prefer this theoretical framework to many of its rivals, I have this peculiar notion that long-cycle theory can be enriched by remaining open to ideas from other schools of thought. Accordingly, this study spends a great deal of time talking about other people's work and, in doing so, violates the implicit academic norm that it is acceptable for you to read what other people are saying but you are not supposed to admit it. An even greater academic sin is to admit it in writing other than in a perfunctory literature review or an obscure footnote.

Fortunately or unfortunately, another behavioral element that I retain is a concern for cumulative knowledge. I may be missing the point, but I fail to see how cumulation can progress if the ideal remains one of constantly demonstrating how completely independent or autonomous one's own ideas are from those of everybody else. Whatever ideas I may claim, or with which others may associate me, have not emerged *sui generis*. The truth of this statement should become abundantly evident in the chapters that follow. I only hope I have been fair to the people whose ideas I have used as stepping stones in order to construct my own arguments.

Returning briefly to a more orthodox approach, I must acknowledge my thanks to a number of colleagues for comments on earlier versions of various chapters: Al Bergesen, Chris Chase-Dunn, Suzanne Frederick, Chuck Kegley, Robert Keohane, Jack Levy, Dan Mazmanian, Pat

McGowan, George Modelski, Dave Rapkin, Karen Rasler, Mark Rupert, Bruce Russett, Randy Siverson, and a bevy of the usual cast of anonymous referees. I could also name a few others whose comments have so vexed me at times that I simply had to write another chapter as a form of response. While I would be quite happy to blame any or all of these individuals for any analytical blunders I may have committed in this study, too often, I must admit, I was simply not clever enough to follow their advice. Suzanne Tappe proved quite helpful, as is the norm, in forcing a respectable portion of the first draft fodder into the word-processing machine. A 1985–1987 grant on Systemic Leadership Decline from the National Science Foundation helped fund some of the work reported in chapters 6 and 7.

Parts of chapters 3 and 4 are taken from "The World-Economy, the Long Cycle and the Question of World System Time," pp. 35–62 in *Foreign Policy and the Modern World-System,* edited by Patrick J. McGowan and Charles W. Kegley, Jr. (Beverly Hills, CA: Sage Publications, 1983) and "Interstate Wars, Global Wars and the Cool Hand Luke Syndrome: A Reply to Chase-Dunn and Sokolovsky." *International Studies Quarterly,* Vol. 27, No. 3 (September 1983), pp. 369–274. An earlier version of chapter 5 was published as "Cycles of General, Hegemonic, and Global War," pp. 462–488 in *Dynamic Models of International Conflict,* edited by Urs Luterbacher and Michael D. Ward (Boulder, CO: Lynne Rienner Publishers, 1985). Much of chapter 9 may be found in "Polarity, The Long Cycle and Global Power Warfare." *Journal of Conflict Resolution,* Vol. 30, No. 4 (December 1986), pp. 587–615. An earlier version of chapter 10 appeared as "Succession Crises in the Global Political System: A Test of the Transitional Model," pp. 93–116 in *Crises in the World-System,* edited by Albert L. Bergesen (Beverly Hills, CA: Sage Publications, 1983). Chapter 11 first appeared as "Uneven Economic Growth, Systemic Challenges, and Global Wars." *International Studies Quarterly,* Vol. 27, No. 3 (September, 1983), pp. 341–355. My thanks to Sage Publications, Butterworths, the International Studies Association, and Lynne Rienner Publishers for permission to reprint this material.

On Global War

1

An Introduction to Structural Change and Global War

Throughout much of the nineteenth century, American decision makers preferred to adopt a relatively low profile on the international scene. By the middle of the twentieth century, however, the United States had emerged as the world system's undisputed number one power in political, military, and economic terms. Yet a mere forty years after the global war from which the United States emerged triumphant, its leadership status can hardly be said to be undisputed any longer.

Economically, traditionally important industries within the United States are in serious trouble. Steel towns are dying. Detroit continues to find it difficult to compete with the price and performance of foreign autos. The semiconductor industry, though hardly a traditional one, complains bitterly that it has problems marketing its chips and other products in Japan while, at the same time, it accuses Japanese semiconductor firms of engaging in dumping practices within the American market. As a consequence of these developments, a variety of domestic industries are seeking governmental protection against their foreign competition—behavior that would have been most unlikely and even less necessary in the devastated aftermath of the Second World War.

In other spheres, the United State, once virtually self-sufficient in petroleum, has become increasingly dependent on uncertain foreign sources. Once reasonably well insulated from the vagaries of the world marketplace, exports as a proportion of gross national product (GNP) more than doubled between 1970 and 1981. Once the major source of new loans as the center of the international financial system, the United States officially became the world's largest debtor country in the mid-1980s. More fundamentally, between 1950 and 1980 the United States' share of world GNP declined from 40 percent or higher to 21.5 percent. Its proportion of world trade fell from 20 percent to 11 percent.

The American share of holdings in gold and foreign exchange reserves plunged from 32 percent to 6 percent (Scott, 1985a:18). As part of this general process, the number of American firms among the world's largest corporations also has fallen. In 1956, forty-two (84 percent) were headquartered in the United States. By 1980, the number had declined to twenty-three (46 percent) (Bergesen and Sahoo, 1985:597).

Militarily, the United States emerged from World War II as the leader of the winning coalition. Although there were larger standing armies in 1945, the quality of U.S. firepower, its monopoly of atomic weapons, and its ability to move forces throughout the globe were so superior to the capabilities of other armed forces that the United States literally was in a class by itself. Some twenty-five years later, the United States had acknowledged a position of rough nuclear parity with the Soviet Union. Within a few more years, American decision makers were engrossed in withdrawing from Indochina.

Politically, the United States once could expect strong support for its positions in the United Nations General Assembly. This is no longer the case and has not been the case for a number of years. Now the United States ignores International Court of Justice decisions, withdraws from U.N. agencies it can no longer control, and reduces its financial contribution to the international institutions it had created as a cornerstone of the new American world order. On a more bilateral level, the United States had been able to topple regimes antagonistic to it in various parts of the world such as Iran and Guatemala. Two or three decades later, the same United States appeared to be relatively impotent in its inability to rescue forty-four diplomatic hostages held captive in Tehran. Little more success has been obtained in altering the complexion of the post-Somoza regime in Nicaragua. Nor is this loss of influence restricted to the Third World—as suggested by New Zealand's decision in 1986 to discontinue its participation in the ANZUS alliance.

It would be easy to exaggerate the United States' loss of economic, military, and political influence. But while it might be tempting, hyperbole, most likely, would not be very accurate or useful even for heuristic purposes. The argument here is not that the United States has lost all vestiges of its once predominant position in world politics and economics. Yet it clearly has experienced the erosion of some of that former standing—and some of the influence that goes with losses in the international hierarchy of relative position. Just how much positional and influence loss has been incurred over the past few decades is an interesting question in its own right.[1] But it is not the focus of this study.

The relative decline of the global system's current leading actor should be viewed first and foremost as the most recent instance of a much larger, long-term, regularized process of structural change in the world system. A macrotrend is evident: power in the world is in the process of becoming increasingly less concentrated. While deconcentration processes are apt to seem appealing to many observers—in the sense that pluralism is often equated with such desirable ends as democracy, justice, and human welfare—there are fairly compelling reasons for believing that deconcentration at the global level may ultimately lead to intensive, life and death struggles on a planetary scale. That is, deconcentration may accelerate to the point where it is probable (and some would say, necessary) for the leading power to engage in warfare to preserve its position, while other contenders will be inclined under conditions of deconcentrating power to contest the old structural hierarchy and order.

Such a struggle for systemic leadership evolves or, more aptly put, degenerates into *global war*—an infrequent type of warfare that nevertheless has accounted for some 79 percent of the casualties brought about by great-power warfare in the past five hundred years.[2] The next global war—World War III—could well prove to be the last one if nuclear weapons are employed. And, despite the wishful thinking that the next major-power war will be fought on a conventional basis, there seems little reason to think that nuclear weapons would not be employed once global warfare erupted. Obviously, it is desirable that we improve our understanding of the linkages between structural change and global wars as soon as possible if we are to avoid such a catastrophic outcome. To achieve this improvement in understanding the linkages, it will be argued, it is necessary to modify the analytic procedures and routines through which we habitually interpret world politics.

GLOBAL WAR

One of the more important assumptions upon which this study is predicated is the contention that all wars are not equal in terms of their theoretical significance, let alone in terms of their impacts on the societies in which they are fought. This assumption may not seem all that unorthodox. After all, who would wish to argue against the generalization that some wars last longer, kill more people, consume more resources, or involve more disputants than other wars?

The available evidence clearly supports such a statement. For example, Jack Levy's (1983a:96) analysis of 119 wars involving one or more great powers over the 1495–1975 period establishes the following means for the length of duration, the number of great-power participants, and the number of battle deaths:

	Mean
Duration in years	4.4
Great-power participants	2.2
Battle deaths	280,000.0

Of the 119 wars, only 12 wars (10.1 percent), listed in table 1.1, exceed the mean values on all three characteristics.

Yet while table 1.1 serves to demonstrate rather quickly that all wars are not created equal, even the wars that are identified as most noteworthy, on the basis of the selected characteristics, are not of equal interest for the purposes of the present study. The number of years of fighting, the number of great-power participants, or the number of battle deaths do not constitute the only indicators for differentiating between the wars that are most or less theoretically significant. In this sense, the wars listed in table 1.1 are not equally interesting. World War II is much more theoretically salient than a seven years' war or a war of the Austrian succession. Moreover, some unlisted wars—wars that failed to meet the mean threshold criteria—such as World War I, (with a duration of 4.3 years)—possess more significance than some of the wars that are listed.

The absence of World War I from the "Big 12" war list, despite the fact that only World War II brought about more battle deaths, underscores the arbitrariness of the ad hoc criteria utilized. Granted, other thresholds might have been employed that would have caused World War I to be included. The point to be made, however, is that the most obvious indicators of war "magnitude," "severity," or "intensity" are not necessarily the best instruments to isolate the phenomenon of theoretical interest. If a theory of war specifically addresses duration or participation as principal subjects of inquiry, that is one thing. Most do not. If instead, the primary theoretical concern centers on wars that are fought over who will lead in the global system or wars that bring about a significant reconcentration of capabilities in the system, the number of battle deaths may not prove to be a very good discriminator.

Global wars, the principal subjects of this study, do encompass both

Table 1.1

Most Severe Wars according to Selected Criteria

War	Years	Duration in Years	Number of Great Powers	Battle Deaths
1. Thirty Years' War—Bohemian	1618–1625	7.0	4	304,000
2. Thirty Years' War—Danish	1625–1630	5.0	6	302,000
3. Thirty Years' War—Swedish	1630–1635	5.0	4	314,000
4. Thirty Years' War—Swedish-French	1635–1648	13.0	5	1,151,000
5. Dutch War of Louis XIV	1672–1678	6.0	6	342,000
6. War of the League of Augsburg	1688–1697	9.0	5	680,000
7. War of the Spanish Succession	1701–1713	12.0	5	1,251,000
8. War of the Austrian Succession	1739–1748	9.0	6	359,000
9. Seven Years' War	1755–1763	8.0	6	992,000
10. French Revolutionary Wars	1792–1802	10.0	6	663,000
11. Napoleonic Wars	1803–1815	12.0	6	1,869,000
12. World War II	1939–1945	6.0	7	12,948,300

Data Source: Levy (1983a:88–91).

leadership struggles and capability reconcentration. They are wars fought to decide who will provide systemic leadership, whose rules will govern, whose policies will shape systemic allocation processes, and whose sense or vision of order will prevail. In all of these respects, global wars are similar to the critical realignment elections and civil wars that decide similar issues at the national level.

For these issues of leadership and political management to be resolved, even if only for a finite period of time, a lead state must emerge, at the head of a victorious coalition, from the struggle. One of the chief prerequisites for assuming the leadership role is control over a sizeable proportion of the capabilities that enable states and other actors to exert influence at and over great distances. To lead or even to act successfully on a global scale, actors must possess capabilities of global reach. Part of the global war process, therefore, is the facilitation of a concentration of these resources (historically sea and, more recently, aerospace power financed by the system's most dynamic economy). In the possession of a single state, global reach capability concentration creates the material foundation for systemic leadership.

Leadership struggles are not all that common. Significant episodes of systemic capability reconcentration are even more rare. Scholars of war are not in full agreement on their identity just as other students quarrel about the status of critical realignment elections and how genuine some civil wars are. Yet the candidates for the global war category are not all that numerous. They certainly number less than a dozen—a subject that will be discussed in more depth in chapter 5—and the more recent candidates (the Napoleonic Wars and World Wars I and II) do enjoy a respectable amount of consensus. The 1688–1713 fighting at the end of the seventeenth and the beginning of the eighteenth century (League of Augsburg [1688–1697] and Spanish Succession [1701–1713] also enjoys a fair amount of support as an era of global warfare. More in dispute are the qualifications of the mid-eighteenth century wars (Austrian Succession [1739–1748] and Seven Years' [1755–1763]), the Thirty Years' War (1618–1648), the Dutch War of Independence (1580–1608), and the even earlier combat over control of Italy and the Indian Ocean (1494–1517). One of the goals of this study will be to assist the movement toward greater consensus on this question of which wars deserve the global war level and which do not.

The importance of these wars is not captured very well by their small number. A more revealing number is the estimate noted earlier that global wars have been responsible for nearly four-fifths of the battle casualties in great-power warfare. An even more frightening number could be generated by estimating the potential number of casualties that could be anticipated if a future global war is fought.

Is there any need to spend time justifying a focus on global war and structural change? The answer is yes. Until relatively recently neither topic has been all that common in the annals of international relations. Wars have been treated more or less as if all instances of fighting between states belonged to the same general category. Similarly, it has been easy to bypass structural change processes within a "system" that has been viewed as a residual category for any interactions external to the nation-state, as the aggregation of all activity external to the nation-state, or simply as a figment of the theoretical imagination.[3]

Some brief examples of what might be described as "mainstream" approaches to the subject of war in a systemless world may help to illustrate the claim that studies of structural change and global war have been forced to "swim against the current" of conventional international relations. Nevertheless, the reader should keep in mind that the following discussion of the more conventional examples cannot possibly do full justice to the individual merits or liabilities of the models that are mentioned. They are introduced here only for the passing purpose of contrast.

MORE CONVENTIONAL, ASYSTEMIC APPROACHES TO THE SUBJECT OF WAR

Geoffrey Blainey's (1973) approach to explaining war stresses the nature of disputes over relative power. If they are given the opportunity to exhibit their superior bargaining capabilities, states tend to win disputes without bloodshed. It is quite possible, however, that one side may not be able to accurately assess the opposition's capability. It is also conceivable that both sides will simply disagree about which side is the stronger. Should these conditions prevail, assuming the usual conflicts of interest as well, war becomes a device for resolving the initial conflict of interest and determining which side is the stronger one. The more quickly the secondary question is settled, the sooner the war is likely to end.

Blainey's model encompasses seven additional considerations: local theater military advantages, the likelihood of third-party intervention, estimates of domestic conflict propensities as well as the ability to pay for a war, the length of time that has transpired since the last war, the nationalistic and ideological factors, and psychological idiosyncracies of the pertinent decision makers. Viewed as potential influences on capability perceptions, they may interact in such a way so as to convince both sides of their capability edge. When this occurs, the probability of war will be high. If both sides are left uncertain about their relative positions, the probability of peace continuing remains strong.

This model is regarded as equally applicable both to the duels of two-state dyads and to the more complicated affairs involving the participation of a number of states, which Blainey calls general wars:

. . . a general war is a series of wars happening simultaneously and entangled with one another. The kind of reasoning which can explain why two countries begin to fight will also explain why a third, fourth, or even a tenth country joins in the fighting.

War began when two countries had contradictory ideas of their own bargaining position and therefore could not solve peacefully an issue which vitally affected them. The spread of war to other countries was the result of the same kind of conditions which began the war . . . Decisive fighting in the early phase of some wars not only raised issues that were vital to adjacent nations but it led to contradictory perceptions of military power. A country which was decisively winning the first phase of a war—France in 1792 or Germany in 1940—usually became more confident and enlarged its war aims. But its heightened sense of power was not shared equally by adjacent nations. Some agreed with this perception and either became fighting allies of the temporary victor or offered peaceful concessions. Some disputed the assessment and, confident of their own might, declared war on the temporary victor. . . . (Blainey, 1973:241).

Blainey thus interprets World War II as inherently no different than any other war. The participants may be more numerous than in a number of other wars, but there is no reason to treat it any differently from an explanatory point of view than wars between, say, two Latin American states quarreling over a disputed piece of territory.

Bruce Bueno de Mesquita's (1981) expected utility model is remarkably compatible, as models go in international relations analysis, with Blainey's relative capability calculations. In the expected utility model, it is assumed that war decisions are made by a single, rational leader. War is probable if one of these leaders perceives the net gain of fighting to be greater than the expected value of remaining at peace. The net gain is in turn a function of the likelihood of winning as opposed to losing something of value. Since success or failure is considered primarily to be a function of relative strength, other things being equal, a leader should be expected to opt for war as long as the net gain exceeds zero or as long as the leader's side possesses a relative capability advantage.

If the participants in the conflict are aligned with other states, the decision calculations become more complex. The way in which utility is estimated remains much the same. Only now, the would-be war participant must also contemplate the alliance commitments, the relative capabilities, and the policy preferences of potential third parties. Other model components—uncertainty, risk adversity, and physical distance between disputants—also can be introduced to make the decision calculus even more complicated.

Despite the greater explicitness of the underlying assumptions, the predictions of the expected utility model resemble Blainey's. In circumstances in which alignment is not a factor, weak states are not likely to attack strong states. But, war is most likely when both sides anticipate victory. One of the new elements stemming from the expected utility calculations, however, is that war may erupt even though both sides agree on which side is expected to win. They may still disagree on what it might take to resolve their differences short of war. Nonetheless, combat is expected to continue as long as at least one participant expects to benefit by avoiding negotiations.

To test this expected utility model (another notable departure from Blainey's approach), Bueno de Mesquita requires information on a number of variables that include evaluations about who initiated each war, against whom, and with what outcome. While it must be granted that such identifications are frequently debatable, the treatment (Bueno de Mesquita, 1981:209) of the twentieth century's two world wars is particularly revealing for our interest in systemic warfare:

	Initiator	Opponent	Winner
1914	Austria-Hungary	Serbia	Serbia/Yugoslavia
1939	Germany	Poland	Poland

In other words, World War I is reduced to a clash between Serbia and Austria-Hungary just as World War II is regarded as a German attack on Poland that Poland eventually won. Contrastingly, Small and Singer's (1982:89–91) compilation of basic war data lists fifteen participants for World War I and twenty-nine for World War II.

How is Bueno de Mesquita's coding justified? In both cases, the timing of war entries by states categorized as third parties is thought to be crucial. On World War I, Bueno de Mesquita argues,

> . . . Austria did not initiate combat against any other states at the outset. Russian troops engaged Austrian troops because of the Russian third-party decision to aid the Serbians. While Germany declared war on Russia, the Russians initiated the first combat between their army and the Germans. France's declaration of war was only a response to the Russo-German situation, which itself was a response to the already unfolding conflict. Indeed, only Austria and Serbia were at war on July 29, 1914, the first day of fighting. Germany and Russia did not enter the war until August 1, France not until August 3, and Britain did not until

August 5. These entries are more appropriately viewed as
third-party decisions to join an ongoing war. . . . (Bueno de
Mesquita, 1981:100)

Much the same is said in reference to World War II:

> . . . When Hitler's armies invaded Poland on September 1, 1939,
> no other nation was attacked, nor was any other nation at war
> with Germany. Indeed, we know that Hitler hoped that the attack
> on Poland would not prompt Britain (or France) to declare war
> on Germany. The decisions by Britain and France to enter the
> war on September 3, 1939, as well as the decisions in numerous
> other capitals, was prompted by the German initiation of war
> against Poland. Those decisions represent third-party choices,
> thus making those states not amongst the initial opponents for
> my purposes. . . . (Bueno de Mesquita, 1981:100).

For Bueno de Mesquita's specific purposes, it is quite plausible to
accept his coding of who initiated the two world wars. A very narrow
interpretation of the identity of the opposition is also conceivable for
assessing initial relative capabilities. Identifying Serbia and Poland as
the respective winners of the wars begun in 1914 and 1939, however, is
an entirely different matter. While they may be included among the
members of the winning coalition for some purposes, to relegate what
transpired within days to the residual category of third-party intervention grossly alters the nature and meaning of the two world war events.

Whether states choose to fight or not, no doubt as both Blainey and
Bueno de Mesquita suggest, does have something to do with decision-
maker assessments about who is expected to win and lose. Without
getting into the problem related to assumptions of unitary, rational decision making, it is also worth observing that neither Blainey nor Bueno
de Mesquita claims that he is fully specifying the context of war decisions. Their intention is to seize upon only the most immediate
context—the minimal set of necessary conditions that must be satisfied
prior to the onset of war. Excluded variables are not necessarily irrele-
vant, but they clearly do not enjoy the same analytical priority.[4]

From the perspective of someone interested in structural change and
global war, it is difficult, then, if not impossible to avoid being disap-
pointed by these woefully incomplete, primarily actor-centered perspectives. To assume that actors are free to choose or do precisely as
they please ignores what Philip Abrams (1982:2–3) once called the
"two-sidedness" of the social world:

... a world in which we are both the creators and the creatures, both makers and prisoners; a world which our actions construct and a world that powerfully constrains us ... The two-sidedness of society, the fact that social action is both something we choose to do and something we have to do ...
    ... What we choose to do and what we have to do are shaped by the historically given possibilities among which we find ourselves.

As Abrams suggested, structures developed over time do not fully determine actor choices. But, they are likely to exert strong influences on the choices that are taken. Accordingly, systemic structures constrain actors from attaining some goals just as they may enable the same or other actors to realize other ends. Nor are these structures simply analytical artifacts imposed on the ostensibly more concrete state actors. On the contrary, the structures are patterns established over time by the nature of actor interactions and relationships. Precisely the same thing can be said about the structure of the ostensibly more concrete nation-state. In either case, the structures can be and are modified or influenced by actors. Yet the reciprocal nature of the causal arrows is definitely asymmetrical. The structures are more likely to influence actor behavior more consistently than the other way around. Or, as Bennett and Sharpe (1985:10) have expressed it with more subtlety:

... structures are historical products of past human actions and, in certain circumstances, are susceptible to marginal change or transformation by the concerted efforts of the actors.

An emphasis on systemic structure should not obscure the fact that national decision makers have interests that they wish to pursue. But even these interests have been shaped and conditioned historically by structures and by the states' positions within the structures. Actors may thus choose between options but never entirely freely. Relative strength is also important but not so much for simply identifying who will fight whom when but also why. Moreover, the "why" is not Blainey's or Bueno de Mesquita's relatively narrow disagreement about relative capabilities in the midst of a generic conflict over incompatible interests. Rather, the "why" of systemic warfare suggested by analysts of historical structure is linked to change and actors' incentives for striving to improve or defend their relative positions within various types of networks.
All conflicts, disputes, and wars are not meant to be explained

equally well by an emphasis on systemic structure. Why should we expect all conflicts to be accounted for by a single, "one-size-fits-all" model? From a systemic point of view, there is no denying Austro-Hungarian-Serbian conflict in 1914 or German-Polish antagonism in 1939. Yet there was so much more going on in 1914 and 1939 than is suggested by a shortsighted fixation on dyadic conflict or even a multiple chain of dyadic conflicts. What are sorely missing in these asystemic models are the structural rhyme and reason underlying major-power confrontations.

A STRUCTURAL INTERPRETATION OF MAJOR-POWER CONFLICT

The world system is composed of actors with different resource bases and varying levels of ambition. As in other political systems, there is a power hierarchy or pecking order that is wide near the bottom and narrow at the top. Accordingly, most states will play only marginal roles. A few elite actors, however, possess great influence and, from time to time, one of these elite actors enjoys a sufficiently commanding lead after an intensive struggle over the nature of the global system's constitution that it climbs to the top as the system leader.

World politics, in this view, is not characterized by the persistent randomness or anarchy assumed by classical analysts of international relations. Structures, order, rules, and some degree of regulative capability influence foreign policy behavior. To the extent that a structural set of rules affects who gets what, when, and how, systemic orders are inherently biased. Some actors win (lose) more than others. Older power contenders, especially if they fought on the winning side of the last succession struggle, have the opportunity to shape international interactions and relations in their own favor. Since the benefits tend to be allocated long before latecomers have achieved competitive positions in the pecking order, the prevailing order tends to discriminate against their goals and aspirations. Improvements in relative capability position for some actors thus go hand in hand with the confrontation with structural constraints—a situation that is rendered all the more frustrating because the goals are apt to be in the process of becoming more ambitious. In the absence of some type of cooptation by the established elites, latecomers are prone to becoming challengers of a systemic status quo which they see as biased against them. To ameliorate some of the structural constraints imposed on them by a previously established order, challengers may be encouraged to attack the prevailing order.

A good many domestic political systems normally handle structural reforms, elite circulation, and leadership succession struggles through legislative, judicial, and electoral formats. While we should keep in mind that they are not always successful at the national level, the same procedures are likely to require more forceful approaches in systemic arena. Declining elites are unlikely to surrender their positions and their advantages without a struggle. Ascending challengers are equally unlikely to obtain all of their goals entirely peacefully.

Challengers are not only confronted with the customary elite intransigence, systemic folkways dictate that newcomers demonstrate their claims to movement up the pecking order. A perceived improvement in relative capability position often will not suffice. What needs to be demonstrated is the ability to effectively mobilize capability and to apply it successfully. Such rites of passage can be accomplished by defeating weaker opponents in the regional neighborhood. The Germans (Prussians) fought Denmark twice and Austria once before taking on France in 1870. Japan defeated China in 1895 and, in some respects, did the same to Russia a decade later. The 1898 Spanish-American confrontation represents one more manifestation of the graphic exhibition of status mobility at the expense of a weaker neighbor.

Systemic conflict is characterized by occasional and very intensive warfare involving many if not all of the elites fighting over who and whose rules will govern the system (global war). A second type of conflict behavior is displayed by upwardly mobile states that become embroiled in disputes with their neighbors and downwardly mobile powers. A third, not completely mutually exclusive, type of conflict behavior is represented by elite powers probing and testing the positional claims of other elite actors.[5]

This form of conflict may take the form of bilateral crises that end with one or both sides backing away from full-scale warfare. If the probes suggest exploitable weaknesses, more extensive tests may be forthcoming that in turn, may lead to the first two types of systemic conflict. Alternatively, the outcomes may be less than fully conclusive as in the three Anglo-Dutch wars of the seventeenth century or the repeated Anglo-French contests of the eighteenth century. One side may do better than the other side in the combat but not quite well enough to suppress the likelihood of subsequent tests and probes.

This structural interpretation of systemic conflict cries out for greater elaboration. As an outline, it glosses over a number of extant differences of opinion in the historical-structural literature that need to be explicated at greater length (see chapters 2 through 4). There are promising convergences across analytical paradigms that need to be exploited just as there are significant divergences that will need to be treated cautiously lest they be ignored or dismissed too readily as unimportant. But even in outline form, a host of substantive questions is suggested. Why do the relative positions of states rise and fall? Is this process cyclical? Is it subject to recurring phases that operate like systemic conflict seasons? Are multipolar distributions of power, a favorite topic of conventional international relations, really any more stable than bipolar distributions? What is the role of uneven economic growth patterns? To what extent do rising challengers catch up with declining system leaders before a global war becomes probable? How likely are the variously positioned actors to fully comprehend the structural shifts going on around them? If the level of structural awareness tends to be less than ideal, does this make global wars more or less likely?

All of these analytical and substantive questions will be pursued to varying extents in the chapters that follow. And though the history of studying global wars is not all that lengthy, enough information is available to provide answers, or at least their first approximations, as well.

Chapters 2 through 4 concentrate on what might be thought of as analytical preliminaries. Chapter 2 describes the structure of international relations analysis in order to pursue further why the subjects of structural change and global war are still somewhat alien to the tradition of study in this field. Particular attention is paid to the case for, and the problems associated with, the argument that the field can be reduced to three main paradigms: classical realpolitik, global society, and neo-Marxist. These main paradigms are then linked to three specific models (structural realist, long cycle, and world economy) that are representative of the historical-structural mode of analysis in world politics and world political economy.

Chapter 3 continues this exposition by describing the three specific models in sufficient detail to permit comparative statements about convergences and divergences. Chapter 4 then concentrates on examining one important area of convergence/divergence, the question of *system time* or how analysts go about gauging the extent of structural change, systemic transformation, and movement toward global war.

Chapter 5 presents a critical review of previous efforts to model cycles of war and peace. A historical-structural approach that focuses on global war impacts on the level of concentration in the system is advanced as a way to overcome some of the limitations of the earlier examinations. Shifting attention away from the timing of global war, chapter 6 considers one of the basic motors of change that are responsible for cycles of global war. Technological innovation and leading sector development/diffusion, it is contended, constitute crucial explanatory factors in all three of the principal historical-structural frameworks reviewed in chapter 3.

Chapter 7 continues this line of inquiry by empirically examining the historical pattern of interaction among an index of leading sector concentration developed in the preceding chapter, the distribution of sea power as a primary vehicle of global reach, and the onset of global war. Global war is demonstrated to be a critical influence, albeit more so in terms of sea power than for leading sectors, in concentrating these capabilities as the resource foundation for post-systemic war leadership.

Leading sectors also possess a direct connection to the controversy of how and whether long-term cycles of economic fluctuations, referred to as Kondratieff long waves, influence cycles of war. That possibility and the likelihood of a reciprocal influence, the impact of global war on long-term cycles of economic oscillations, is the subject of chapter 8.

Chapter 9 returns the focus to the classical structural question pertaining to the influence of distributions of military power. Are global wars any more or less probable in multipolar as opposed to bipolar systems? Or does it make any difference as long as both types of distribution ultimately give way to global war? Chapter 10 pursues the related, if less macroscopic, question of power transition. What is the relationship between the crossing trajectories of ascending challengers and declining system leaders and the probability of global war? Do challengers tend to be patiently prudent and wait until after the transition to launch their assault? Or do they strike too soon? If they tend to attack prematurely, does this factor help to explain why they lose repeatedly? Chapter 11 draws on the answers developed in chapters 9 and 10 to discuss the role of uneven economic growth in producing challenges as found in world-economy (but also in other) explanations of systemic warfare.

Finally, chapter 12 returns explicitly to the question of timing structural change by considering the merits of recent arguments suggesting that the contemporary system is entering a "1914" condition and comparing them to scenarios that project a possible future global war to the middle of the next century. Do these arguments square with what is known about the developments leading to global war—particularly in terms of the conclusions developed in the preceding eleven chapters? While the contention that the 1914 syndrome is recurring is viewed as a premature perception, the arguments do permit us to consider to what extent a future global war is probable. The implications of these forecasts will be explored in order to underscore the importance of global war to the future of the world system and its prospects for survival.

2

Systemic Structure and the Development of International Relations Theory

The professional study of international politics and international relations in general is neither particularly old nor all that well ordered. It often seems difficult, in fact, to describe the general state of international relations analysis as anything else but in a considerable state of disarray. Despite the stakes involved, observers seem to agree on very little. It sometimes seems as if every analyst lives in his or her own small universe replete with a unique analytical vocabulary and an invisible set of theoretical principles. Of course, these statements are exaggerations. Every observer is not his or her own school of thought. There are also some positive signs that some of the disarray is beginning to be supplanted, however tentatively, by patches of agreement and convergence with respect to particular issues. The linkages between structural change and global war comprise one conspicuous example of such an area of convergence.

To explore this optimistic statement further and to set the stage for the chapters that follow, we need to first consider the paradigmatic development of theory about international relations. To improve our comprehension of the structure of world politics and its various implications, we must first come to grips with the structure of thought about world politics.

THE ANALYTICAL STRUCTURE OF INTERNATIONAL RELATIONS

Blind Men, Waves, and Fads

The analytical development of international relations, and its concommitant disarray, is often portrayed in metaphorical fashion. A familiar analogy is the reference to the fable involving a group of blind men groping their way around different portions of an elephant's anatomy (Jervis, 1969; Puchala, 1972; Kegley, 1986). Quite naturally they make different identifications of the beast's identity based on their non-overlapping probes. In one sense, the metaphor equates the lack of sight with different analytical perspectives. Not only do analysts of international relations view matters with vastly different interpretative assumptions, they also arrive at widely varying conclusions. Since the conclusions are so closely linked to the assumptions, genuine communication across perspectives frequently requires something akin to an act of theological conversion.

It would be unrealistic to hope that some external agency could grant a common set of lenses to the international relations community of analysts. But it is not utopian to wish that somehow we might learn to grope our way around the international relations beasts in a more coordinated fashion. Whether the forced unification of the various explanatory approaches in international relations would really advance our understanding remains an open question. But, certainly, the aspiration of unification is a noble one—not unlike Arthur's knights seeking the Holy Grail. Even so, there is no circumventing the static nature of the blind men metaphor. The elephant and the groping analysts are taken as givens captured at a specific point in time and space. But how did this troublesome state of affairs come about in the first place?

The study of international politics possesses still another popular metaphor for its dynamic of evolution as well. Usually attributed to Karl Deutsch (McClelland, 1972; Starr, 1974), the metaphor is one of progressive waves of analytical improvements:

> . . . the first was the rise of interest in international law,
> symbolized by the two Hague Conventions of 1899 and 1907,
> and the many legal agreements and scholarly studies that
> followed. The second wave was the rise of diplomatic history
> after the opening of many government archives after World
> War I, and the simultaneous rise of interest in international
> organizations. . . .
> A third wave of advance has been under way since the 1950's.
> It has consisted in the reception of many relevant results and
> methods from the younger of the social and behavioral sciences,
> such as psychology, anthropology and sociology, together with
> demography and the newer economics of development and
> growth. While this wave is still continuing, a fourth wave has
> begun to reinforce it. This is the rise of analytic and quantitative

research concepts, models and methods, a movement toward the comparative study of quantitative data and the better use of some of the potentialities of electronic computation (quoted in McClelland, 1972:23).

The wave metaphor is useful because it suggests that the study of international politics is subject to periodic change in the foci that receive attention, the assumptions that are adopted, and the techniques that are brought to bear on what is often regarded as one of the more intractable fields of analysis. But the international law-diplomatic history-eclectic social science borrowings-behavioral analysis chain highlights only some of the waves. Late nineteenth-century geopolitics and the early twentieth-century interest in imperialism were two waves of sorts that preceded and overlapped with the interest in international law. The interwar dispute between "idealists" and "realists" (Carr, 1946/1962; Keohane, 1986) also is oddly neglected by the wave treatment.

More recently, substantive interests in regional integration (Deutsch et al., 1957; Haas, 1964; Hansen, 1969; Haas, 1975); comparative foreign policy (Rosenau, 1966; McGowan and Shapiro, 1973, Rosenau, 1971), transnational actors and issues (Keohane and Nye, 1972; Modelski, 1979), bureaucratic politics (Allison, 1971; Levy, 1986), alliances (Holsti, Hopmann, and Sullivan, 1973; Job, 1981; Ward, 1982), international political economy in general (Staniland, 1985; Gilpin, 1987) and international regimes in particular (Krasner, 1983; Strange, 1981; Rosenau, 1986) could be viewed as topical waves or enthusiasms of varying magnitudes. Continuing in the metaphorical vein, these topics might be described more accurately as splashes and occasional undertows that nonetheless contribute to and shape the ways world politics are studied and the images of international reality that emerge from using these analytic lenses. "Islands of theory" is still another way (Guetzkow, 1957) of describing them.

There also is no denying that the study of world politics is inherently faddish by nature. Nor are analysts of world politics immune to changes in their environment. Geopolitical analysts (Mahan, 1890; Mackinder, 1962) in the late nineteenth and early twentieth centuries were responding to general changes in their perceived environment and, in particular, to the relative and shifting power of Britain, Germany, and Russia, and the other major powers just as geopolitical scholars do today (Brzezinski, 1986). Early twentieth-century students of imperialism (see Brewer, 1980) were either anticipating to some extent or else attempting to explain the advent of World War I. International law and organization benefited from the post-war optimism of the war to end all wars. Realists triumphed over the short-lived ascendancy of the idealists in the disappointing era leading up to the Second World War.

The study of post-war regional integration, another approach to reducing the probability of war, flourished as long as European integration appeared to be making headway. But as European integrative progress seemed to falter and the integration plans of other regions rarely advanced beyond vague treaties, analytical interest diminished. Similarly, transnational actors had always been on the scene. International economics and politics had long been intertwined. Yet it required the 1960s–1970s prominence of the multinational corporation and the dramatic activities of such actors as the Palestine Liberation Organization (PLO) and the Organization of Petroleum Exporting Countries (OPEC), to facilitate the growing interest in transnational actors. The difficult-to-avoid economic vicissitudes of this period also facilitated the rekindling of the interest in international political economy. The interest in the transnational actors seems to have ebbed a bit as the political fortunes of such actors as the PLO and OPEC, relative to the durable nation-state, have waxed and waned. But the political-economic problems, not surprisingly, continue to enjoy a high profile as significant subjects of study.

The Case for Three Basic Perspectives

Despite all the environmental changes, the waves, the islands, and the inherent fickleness, the basic perspectives brought to bear on explaining international relations have not experienced quite as much flux as the various metaphors would appear to suggest. Most commentators on the prospects of paradigmatic shifts in this field concede a hegemonic position to the classical, "billiard ball" perspective, exemplified by the arguments of Blainey and Bueno de Mesquita discussed in chapter 1, which has an intellectual pedigree extending back at least, if not farther, to the seventeenth-century arguments of Hobbes and Rousseau.[1]

There is less agreement on the identity of the classical perspective's main rivals. Some scholars curiously insist on granting paradigmatic status to Deutsch/McClelland/Starr's behavioral wave (Lijphart, 1974; Alker and Biersteker, 1984). Yet it is reasonably easy to demonstrate that the bulk of quantitative research in international relations has been conducted following classical realpolitik assumptions (Vasquez, 1981). It would certainly be an error to equate "behavioral" with "quantitative." Nevertheless, there is considerable overlap. And one of the other principal hallmarks of the behavioral wave—eclectic borrowing from other social sciences—is no more likely than a penchant for enumeration to qualify as a paradigmatic shift in the Kuhnian sense (Kuhn, 1970) of that term.

Two other candidates, however, offer more promise as genuine alternatives. Both are discussed by two of the more persuasive epistomological essays (Rosenau, 1982, and Holsti, 1985a) devoted to classifying the rival perspectives in international relations. In a field often characterized by the previously discussed tendency for every analyst to represent a distinctive framework, it is always reassuring to find a modicum of agreement and overlap.

Rosenau's (1982) discussion is limited primarily to a brief outline of what he views as the three main approaches to studying world affairs. His discussion focuses on three features outlined in table 2.1: images of system structure, images of the nature of the underlying order, as well as the link between assumptions and "methodological impulses." His state-centric approach can be equated readily with the classical position. The system structure is highly fragmented. The underlying order is an anarchic one in which states are predominant. Accordingly, emphasis is placed on studying events bound by time and place, unfolding within limited time frames.

At the other end of the spectrum is the perspective that Rosenau calls the global-centric approach. The image of system structure from this angle is based on the premise of a highly integrated, world capitalist economy based on a pronounced division of labor. The underlying order is remarkably stable yet subject to long-term shifts in the distribution of productive power. As a consequence, global-centric analysts prefer longitudinal case studies to best capture the *longue durée* of the world political economy.

Intermediate between the state and global-centric approaches in a number of ways lies the multicentric perspective. Power is possessed by states and nonstates alike. The structural emphasis is placed on interdependence, change, and complexity. In contrast to the two other approaches (and contrary to the evidence reported in Vasquez, [1981]), Rosenau describes multicentric analysts as the ones most likely to engage in quantitative inquiry because their approach stresses the probability of recurring patterns.

This assertion linking "quantitative analysis, theory development, (and) hypothesis testing" with the multicentric approach is one of the more debatable generalizations found in Rosenau's trichotomy. Another

Table 2.1

Rosenau's Three Major Approaches to World Politics

Characteristic	State-Centric	Multi-Centric	Global-Centric
Structure of the global system	Fragmented, with power distributed among nation-states	Interdependent, with power distributed among nation-states and a variety of non-state actors	Integrated, with power distributed in terms of centuries-long patterns that are global in scope
Nature of underlying order	Anarchic, because all actors respond to different stimuli	Mostly orderly, because most actors are performing functions necessary to system maintenance or transformation	Very orderly, because a capitalist world economy locks actors into their circumstances
Essential manifestation of underlying order	Predominance of nation-states	Complexity, because old patterns of interdependence become obsolete and new ones become salient	Production, trade, and distribution patterns of goods and services
Time frame in which relevant phenomena unfold	Limited	Varied	Extensive
Phenomena to be clarified through inquiry	Time- and place-bound events, situations, issues, policies, conflicts, crises	Recurring patterns, their shifts and their breakpoints within and among systems, issue-areas, and structures of authority	Long-time continuities, deep structures

Source: Based selectively on Rosenau (1982:3).

one pertains to the identification of the global-centric approach that seems to describe only some of the analyses that might be said to fall within this categorization. On the other hand, Rosenau advances a proposition (not explicitly expressed in table 2.1) that many readers will find far less dubious. In response to the question of to what extent each of the approaches or its adherants is open to new data supporting alternative approaches, Rosenau's answer is the same for all three of the centricities—virtually nil.

Holsti's (1985a) labels are different from Rosenau's, and his evaluation is more extensive. But essentially the two scholars converge in painting a very similar picture of the analytical propensities practiced by the international relations community of scholars. Of the many versions of the "paradigm" concept, Holsti is interested in sets of questions or problems that a theoretical perspective uses to establish boundaries of inquiry.[2] He contends that international relations theory has tended to focus on three questions that may be generalized in the following way:

1. What is identified as the central problem of international relations?
2. Who are the essential actors and/or what are the fundamental units of analysis?
3. What image(s) best portrays the milieu in which international relations are conducted?

Applying these questions to the contemporary literature yields three distinctly different theoretical perspectives that Holsti labels: the classical, the global society, and the neo-Marxist. Holsti is quick to add that each perspective encompasses several variations on the themes that characterize and differentiate the main approaches. Put another way, in order to describe the three perspectives in general terms, it is difficult, if not impossible, to give full credit to all the idiosyncrasies and creative deviations from the modal approaches that have been introduced by a number of scholars.

To distinguish the three approaches, table 2.2 focuses on Holsti's answers to the three key questions. The classical approach envisions international relations as a system of states, lacking any central authority, and therefore compelled to compete in their pursuit of security. The anarchic character of the system, however, implies that states will need to resort to war from time to time in order to best protect and advance their national interests. Warfare and the security dilemma provides the core theoretical interest.

Holsti's "global society" perspective is the most amorphous of the three. One of the principal reasons for this vagueness is that advocates of a global society approach are more or less uniform in their rebellion

Table 2.2

Three Theoretical Perspectives on International Relations

Characteristic	Classical	Global Society	Neo-Marxist
Problématique	War and the pursuit of security/order	Global change and transformation	Inequality
Unit of analysis/ analysis/essential actors	States/system of states	Variable	Class/world capitalist system
System's key feature	Anarchy/absence of central authority	Complexity	Division of labor
Examples	Morgenthau (1973)	Modelski (1972)	Wallerstein (1974)
	Bueno de Mesquita (1981)	Mansbach et al. (1976)	Frank (1978)

against the adequacy of the classical perspective, but they are less likely to agree precisely on how best to proceed beyond the rejection, or at least the partial dismissal, of the traditional assumptions. Representative works that illustrate the analytical diversity would include Burton's (1972) cobweb model of world society, Modelski's (1972) geocentric perspective, Keohane and Nye's (1972) transnational model, the many writings associated with the World Order Models Project (Falk and Kim, 1983), and Mansbach and Vasquez' (1981) argument for issues areas and nonstate actors.[3]

Nevertheless, the second perspective does stress that the world is far more complex and variegated than the classical image permits or is able to accommodate into its vision. The interaction of states is only part of the picture and needs to be elaborated by investigating the increasing interaction of individuals and nonstate organizations. Moreover, the growing complexity of interactions and interdependence of the actors are seen as promoting the potential for the creation of a genuinely global society. As a consequence, problems require global, as opposed to national, management. War remains an important problem, but it is only one of a number of problems brought about by past and ongoing systemic change and transformation.

The third perspective, the neo-Marxist approach, emphasizes the inequalities stemming from the world capitalist system's division of labor between a dominant core and an exploited periphery. Typically, this perspective has tended to place less emphasis on what the other two perspectives regard as international relations, and more emphasis on the barriers to Third World development in the absence of radical change in the basic nature of the capitalist world economy.

Indeed, the relatively little attention paid by neo-Marxist analysts to conventional international relations topics leads Holsti to a rather blunt conclusion on the prospects of interparadigmatic synthesis:

> The only conclusion I can derive from reviewing the two literatures [classical and neo-Marxist] is that there is no possibility, and probably no desirability of synthesis . . .
> The main reason for taking this position is that the two paradigms are concerned with fundamentally different problems, the one with peace, war, and order, the other with inequality, exploitation, and equality. The empirical connection between war and inequality remains problematic . . . There is thus no more reason to seek synthesis between these two topics than there is for the dental researcher to integrate work with someone doing research on cancer of the colon. Because both study a human affliction is not sufficient reason to claim that the intellectual tools, concepts, and research agendas of the two should be integrated (Holsti, 1985:74).

On the other hand, Holsti gives the impression that the classical perspective is capable of adapting to changing conditions (e.g., increasing complexity and interdependence) and thereby could eventually incorporate the more telling criticisms from the global society school of thought.[4] Some synthesis is then possible and desirable between the classical and global society perspectives but neither possible nor particularly desirable with the neo-Marxist approach.

THE PROSPECTS FOR SYNTHESIS: STRUCTURE, POWER CONCENTRATION, AND SYSTEM-SHAPING WARFARE

As stated earlier, Holsti and Rosenau's identifications of the major interpretative approaches and their analyses of their differences are among the more persuasive attempts to categorize the heterogeneity of international relations analysis. One or the other may also be right about the likelihood of synthesis across paradigms. But their examinations do miss one of the more encouraging developments in current analytical trends—namely, the emergence within each perspective of partially complementary or overlapping interpretations of the significance of systemic structure, intermittent concentrations of power, and system-shaping warfare. The overlap may not make synthesis either more desirable or more probable, but it does diminish both the costs of, and resistance to, the possibility of synthesis. It is also a welcome development for those concerned about whether the blind men's groping can be more closely coordinated so as to bring some measure of cumulation, consensus, and closure to the representation of international reality. But before this argument can be pursued properly, it should be helpful to pause and consider some other features that differentiate the three major perspectives.

In some respects, table 2.3 can be viewed as an elaboration of Holsti's third question—the world image dimension. Seven dimensions are featured. The first two focus on the theoretical significance of national boundaries and the potency of the nation-state. In the classical perspective, states (subsystems) are the principal actors. An international system exists in principle but, lacking any central authority, it serves primarily as a constant, anarchic backdrop. As a constant, its explanatory value is considerably limited and subordinated to the dominant actions of the subsystems. But because the system is so unstructured and unruly, states are and must be ever vigilant in the protection of their sovereignty. They must be vigilant in the protection of their sovereignty. They must also be prepared to engage in self-help whenever expedient. The emphasis on the virtue of sovereignty facilitates the enshrinement of the dichotomous distinction between foreign and domestic policies and activities that, in turn, are subject to different rules and explanations of behavior.

The other two perspectives are ambiguous on the first characteristic and much more firm on the second. The ambiguity on the question of system/subsystem dominance is not necessarily applicable to all of the analyses that might be assigned to the global society and neo-Marxist categories. The problem is that, in some works, the system is clearly more important than the state actors. In others, the explanatory role of the system versus the state and other actors is not at all clear. But when a topic such as this is not addressed explicitly, one can only infer that the system is seen as a vague environmental background, not unlike the view most common in the classical perspective.

In marked contrast, the three perspectives are divided on the internal/external distinction. Most analyses falling under the global society and neo-Marxist rubrics place much less emphasis on this distinc-

Table 2.3

Selected Characteristics of Classical, Global Society, and Neo-Marxist Analysis

Characteristic	Classical	Global Society	Neo-Marxist
System/subsystem dominant	Subsystem dominant	Variable	Variable
Internal/external distinction	Independent	Increasing interdependence	Interdependent
Structural hierarchy	Great vs. small powers	Emphasis on disparity	Emphasis on disparity
Power concentration	Prevented by balance of power	Variable	Variable
Focus on Wars	Interstate wars	Variable	Variable
Temporal scope	Usually limited	Variable	Variable
Use of history	Anecdotal/ episodic	Variable	Variable

tion than is found in the classical approach. The analytical boundaries of key processes and problems may only sometimes be coterminous with state boundaries. The distinction between what is "foreign" and "domestic" thus is often blurred.

Structural hierarchy and the concentration of power are two other important components of analytical world views. In the classical mode, two subapproaches prevail. Either all states are treated as more or less equally sovereign, as international law prescribes, or a distinction is made between relatively strong and relatively weak state actors. Curiously, though, once such a distinction is made, there is an assumption, often implicit, that the members of each class are more or less equal with the other members of their class. Hence, disparities in actor strength or capabilities, for the whole or within parts of the whole, are largely deemphasized or ignored.

As indicated in table 2.3, global society and neo-Marxist analyses are far more likely to establish a clear sense of hierarchy in which actors, not merely states, can be ranked according to their unequal capabilities. The problems associated with inequality, after all, constitute the central *problématique* of the neo-Marxist framework.

The power concentration feature takes the notion of structural hierarchy one step further. If stratification in social systems is usually portrayed by the triangular metaphor (a small elite at the top and the majority at the bottom or base), the basic question is how sharp is the triangle's peak. The most pronounced situation would occur if one actor predominated in the system. This question of power predominance is central to classical analyses but in a unique way. One of the main explanatory tools in this approach is the balance of power concept. When one state threatens to become hegemonic, other states in the system coalesce to prevent it. Preponderance or the preponderance of a single actor, therefore, is significant by its absence or suppression.

A much different point of view can be found within the two other perspectives. Rather than a constant absence of preponderance, the intermittent hegemony or leadership of the system's most powerful actor is a crucial element in explaining how the world works. As a consequence, what has been an important constant in one perspective is a crucial variable in the other two approaches. While we will return to this topic repeatedly, it must again be pointed out that the intermittent power concentration element is not found in all global society and neo-Marxist works—only in some.

A fifth characteristic that is closely tied to the power concentration element concerns distinctions made about different types of war. All three approaches categorize wars differently depending on who is fighting whom (e.g., wars between states, wars within states, wars between states and nonstate groups). But the question is whether all wars of a given type are equal in significance. For classical analysts, interstate wars are the most important category. Those wars that are fought between coalitions of great powers are the most important for they illustrate the workings of the crucial balance of power mechanism.

A number of global society and neo-Marxist works evince little interest in wars as a central topic of inquiry. But for those that do, the classical treatment of interstate wars or great-power wars fails to appreciate that some wars have more significance in terms of their consequences for the system than do others. A few wars (hegemonic or global wars) reorder the system's structure and usher in a new period of power concentration. As such, these special wars serve as critical benchmarks in explaining the process of concentration and in determining where the system is at given points in time.

The last two characteristics—temporal scope and use of history—illustrate once again the difficulty of making sharp generalizations about interperspective differences. Classical analysts tend to focus on more contemporary events. Historical anecdotes are used to illustrate how some processes such as the balance of power or alliance formation have changed or remain the same. As a rule, classical analysts are also likely to view the advent of nuclear weapons as a critical watershed in international relations. Pre-1945 events therefore are difficult to compare with post-1945 events. Although the topical emphasis may vary, much the same can be said of numerous global society and neo-Marxist analyses. However, some works within these two approaches diverge quite explicitly from the tendency to make limited use of history. They have adopted instead the principle that key systemic processes, as well as the system itself, began to take shape some five hundred years age. Accordingly, to best understand how the system operates, a long view of structural development is not only helpful but also vital. A sensitivity to the history of the system or, at least, specific interpretations of systemic evolution are crucial to the process of creating generalizations about how the system functions.

Table 2.3's elaboration of the world-image dimension reinforces an appreciation for some of the different points of view entertained by the three approaches. Yet it also underscores some very real difficulties inherent in the effort to reduce the number of competing perspectives to three. The closer one's examination of a particular framework, the more awkward it is to make uniform generalizations. The world-image assumptions associated with global society and neo-Marxist analyses tend to be different from those adopted by classical analysts. Unfortunately, it is easier to say that they are different than to be precise in how they differ. The problem is not so much that the two alternative perspectives are fuzzy. But they definitely are not as homogenous as the classical framework has become after hundreds of years of development. Indeed, given the heterogeneity, it may be more fruitful to search for converging points of view across the three perspectives than to belabor the extent of divergence. At the very least, a more specific focus on analyses falling under the umbrella of global society and neo-Marxist approaches is warranted.

Structural Realist, Long Cycle, and World-Economy Models
Holsti (1985:37) inadvertently suggests a point of entry for the search for specific convergences when he argues that:

> The most recent international relations research agenda, which seeks to identify the relationship between economic cycles, leadership in the diplomatic system, and the incidence of war, blends all the components of the classical tradition; states as the essential actors, the normative concern with locating the sources

of war and the conditions of peace, and an image of a community of states in which there is perpetual movement upwards and downwards in cycles of leadership, rise and decline. The focus on economic explanations of cyclical patterns, combined with much quantitative research, does not render this work either new or indicative of a paradigm shift. It carries forth the work of several centuries, albeit with new emphases and insights.

Holsti is quite right to reject economic explanations of cycles and the investigation of enumerated data as evidence of paradigmatic shifts. But it can be argued that he errs in assigning all of these recent analyses to only one of the research traditions in international relations. Some of the recent cyclical analyses most certainly do belong to the classical paradigm. Yet similar or overlapping analyses may also be discovered within the realm of global society and neo-Marxist studies. And therein lies an extremely interesting possibility for greater convergence across the three frameworks. In a number of cases, the appropriate analogy is not that of researchers of dental and colonic disorders—although even here the discrepancies may be exaggerated. Rather, to the extent that researchers investigate topics that differ only in terms of the labels assigned to them by various conventions (e.g., systemic power concentration, leadership decline, the consequences of system-shaping wars), the more appropriate analogy is to researchers who investigate similar or related disorders with a mixture of somewhat different and sometimes similar assumptions. The point to be stressed is that the assumptions are not always that radically different nor are the ultimate conclusions.

Table 2.4 repeats the seven characteristics listed in table 2.3 for three specific schools of thought—structural realism, long cycle, and world-economy—located respectively within Holsti's classical, global society, and neo-Marxist frameworks. In contrast to the dissimilarities emphasized in table 2.3, these three subapproaches have much in common, despite their diverse paradigmatic provenance.

Chapter 3 will discuss these three approaches in much more detail. For now, it should suffice to point out that the three models overlap to a considerable extent on the seven characteristics outlined in table 2.4. Naturally, there are other paradigmatic characteristics, such as the assumptions pertaining to the basic motors propelling actor behavior, that are less convergent. But of the seven listed in table 2.4, structural realism, long-cycle, and world-economy analyses agree in particular on the structural hierarchy and power concentration features. Different labels and concepts are employed for distinguishing system leaders

Table 2.4

Selected Characteristics of Structural Realism, Long Cycle, and World-Economy Analysis

Characteristic	Specific Approach		
	Classical: Structural Realism	Global Society: Long Cycle	Neo-Marxist: World-Economy
System/subsystem dominant	Subsystem dominant	System dominant	System dominant
Internal/external distinction	More interdependent	Interdependent	Interdependent
Structural hierarchy	Hegemon vs. nonhegemons	World power, global powers, others	Hegemon, core powers, periphery
Power concentration	Intermittent	Intermittent	Intermittent
Focus on wars	Variable/ hegemonic warfare	Global warfare	Hegemonic warfare
Temporal scope	19th/20th centuries	From late 15th century	From late 15th century
Use of history	Qualified stress on continuity	Stress on continuity	Stress on continuity

from nonleaders. Different indicators of power concentration may also be preferred. Yet all three approaches do stress the significance of intermittent power concentration and a consequent structural hierarchy.

On the other five characteristics, long-cycle and world-economy approaches demonstrate somewhat greater affinity with each other than they do with structural realism. Summarily, one might describe this matter of affinities by generalizing that long-cycle and world-economy analyses are more eager to embrace—while structural realist analysts are more hesitant—these five other characteristics.

Consequently, one can find formal acknowledgment of the system dominance assumption in structural realist work, but much of the discussion is likely to be couched in subsystemic units of analysis. Typically, the emphasis is placed almost exclusively on the hegemonic state. Benchmark wars may be recognized as watersheds, but very little attention is likely to be given explicitly to the consequences of the wars. Moreover, most structural realists are quite reluctant to push the application of their analytical framework farther back than the nineteenth-century Pax Britannica—and even that era's qualifications tend to be suspect. In marked contrast, long cycle and world-economy students envision a modern system beginning to emerge in the late fifteenth century.

Even so, the general point remains that, in spite of the differences of interpretation, these three approaches constitute currently evolving analytical points of view that are interacting with changes in the real world. Partially as a consequence, they share important points of convergence. Indeed, at times, it seems as if they have more in common with one another than they do with other schools of thought that can be placed within each of the paradigmatic rubrics.

What is being suggested here is that our collective concerns with the possibility of Kuhnian paradigmatic shifts may be misleading if it facilitates our overlooking the evidence for simultaneous programmatic shifts (Lakatos, 1970) within the principal research frameworks. It is true that the programmatic shifts do not involve large numbers of analysts stampeding to overhaul the thrust of their research agendas. The shifts are much more tentative and incremental. Whether the number of defecting analysts expands will no doubt depend on levels of dissatisfaction with the conventional assumptions of each tradition and the level of attraction of the revised sets of assumptions, the degree of empirical support obtained, and the perceived potential for new analytical payoffs. Thus whether minority revisionist viewpoints will ever be adopted by the respective majorities remains very much an open question and one that need not concern us at the present time.

What is of concern here is whether, and to what extent, we can exploit these shifts and convergences to produce better explanations of structural change and global war. Pursuing this question is a central purpose of the eleven chapters that follow.

3

Three Models of Structural Change

In the past decade or so, relatively new, explicitly historical-structural forms of analysis have emerged in the analysis of world politics. Some of the distinguishing characteristics of historical-structural analyses include the presumptions that (a) the present world system is the product of evolutionary and discontinuous historical developments, (b) the system's past must be taken into explicit account in unraveling the system's present and future, and (c) a major key, if not *the* major key, to understanding the historical development process and the operational principles of the world system is linked to structural fluctuations in the distribution and concentration of power.

More specifically, the fundamental systemic dynamic is the structural movement to and from concentration and deconcentration as reflected in the rise and decline of a system leader. Periods of systemic leadership are followed by phases of increased competition that, in turn, devolve into periods of intensive and extensive warfare. War resolves the question of systemic leadership and ushers in a new period of unipolarity and systemic rule creation that once again erodes into multipolarity and, eventually, a renewal of war.

The linkages between structual change and war are a common denominator of what is being referred to somewhat loosely as historical-structural analyses of world politics. But the existence of gross common denominators does not imply the absence of a great deal of diversity within the historical-structural formats. There is ideological diversity. Left, right, and center are all represented. Terms of reference will differ. For example, the system leader may be labeled the hegemonic power, the dominant power, or the world power. The connotations overlap, but they also conceal different perspectives on what systemic leadership entails. Emphasis on the nature of the motors that drive systemic processes will also vary. How far back in time one can trace the continuity of these systemic processes also varies as do the different frameworks' clocks for telling system time—that is, for establishing "where" the system is in structural as opposed to chronological terms.[1]

In order to clarify where the divergences and convergences exist (as well as to elucidate the entries in table 2.4), this chapter will concentrate exclusively on describing the principal arguments and orientations of the three schools of thought (structural realism, long cycle of world leadership, and world economy) outlined in the preceding chapter. After each of the three major perspectives has been surveyed, chapter 4 will explore some of the principal differences of opinion, with particular attention being paid to the questions of system time and the probability of global war.

STRUCTURAL REALISM, CHANGE, AND WAR

In some respects, it is extremely difficult to provide a brief overview of the work that might be located under the structural realist banner. A major reason for making this assertion is the polarization in this group's topical interests. One set of analysts is interested primarily in international political economy questions. A central focus is the effort to relate structural change with foreign economic policy behavior. For example, a lively quarrel continues over the appropriate relationship between hegemonic stability decline and protectionist tariffs.[2] By and large, however, these analysts have shown little interest in questions pertaining to global warfare. It should also be noted that many of the "hegemonic stability" analyses have been executed as foils for promoting some other model or interpretation.[3] Such analytical behavior is hardly uncommon, but it does seem fair to say that hegemonic stability analysts have unusually ambivalent feelings about the efficacy of the basic hegemonic stability thesis. One result of this ambivalence is that the thesis is more likely to be criticized for its shortcomings than it is to be improved or elaborated.

The other set of analysts largely ignores international political economy questions and concentrates instead on the classical war and peace *problématique*. Analyses that might be forced into this grouping, albeit with considerable effort in some cases, would include Waltz (1979), Organski and Kugler (1980), Doran and Parsons (1980), and some of the work of Midlarsky (1986), Levy (1985), and Singer (Singer, Bremer, and Stuckey, 1972). These are analyses that express a strong interest in system structure.[4] There is also a variable interest in systemic history. In general though, a substantial proportion of these works seems much closer in paradigmatic spirit to classical realism than is the case with the structural realism found in the hegemonic stability analyses.

The divergence within the structural realism camp creates a minor dilemma for the surveyor. The literature that is most relevant for those interested in global war frequently is not all that representative of the general approach under review. The literature that is more representative is not all that germane to global war. Fortunately, a convenient compromise can be arranged readily. Some of the analyses in the second, more war-oriented grouping have either been discussed earlier (Thompson, 1983) or will receive further attention in later chapters (especially chapters 5, 9, and 10). Moreover, while it is true that most of the hegemonic stability analyses the first grouping) have bypassed the war and peace questions, there is one prominent exception—Robert Gilpin's (1981) analysis of system stability and hegemonic war—that can provide a representative illustration of the structural realism approach.

Gilpin's Interpretation of Hegemonic Stability[5]
One way to view Gilpin's approach is to compare it to a three-legged stool. One leg consists of a microscopic consideration of how the most powerful actors in a system rationally pursue their perceived interests. A second, interdependent leg focuses more macroscopically on the dynamics of the social system created by the most powerful actors. Finally, the third leg is a three-stage simplification of world history that is useful for interpreting how the first two legs are integrated differently at various points in time.

Cost and Benefit
The armature of the approach is provided by five generalizations that relate systemic equilibrium and stability, within a rational actor, cost-benefit calculus:

1. An international system is stable (i.e., in a state of equilibrium) if no state believes it profitable to attempt to change the system.
2. A state will attempt to change the international system if the expected benefits exceed the expected costs (i.e., if there is an expected net gain).
3. A state will seek to change the international system through territorial, political, and economic expansion until the marginal cost of further change are equal to or greater than the marginal benefits.
4. Once an equilibrium between the costs and benefits of further change and expansion is reached, the tendency is for the economic costs of maintaining

the status quo to rise faster than the economic capacity to support the status quo.
5. If the disequilibrium in the international system is not resolved, then the system will be changed, and a new equilibrium reflecting the redistribution of power will be established (Gilpin, 1981:10–11).

The first statement equates systemic stability with the absence of incentives to change the system. If these incentives are perceived to exist, the second statement asserts, states will seek systemic change. And the third postulate adds only that change will be sought through territorial, political, and economic expansion. Implicit then to the second and third statements is the assumption that states will try to expand if they believe they can do so with some expectation of profit. The urge to expand—a drive that is considered to be universal in both time and space—is in fact a basic motor within Gilpin's perspective. Furthermore, a large number of factors can tip the cost-benefit calculus in favor of perceived net gain. Gilpin's list includes societal experiences with previous gains in security derived from warfare; opportunities to expand the nature of state revenues; societal mechanisms for distributing the domestic costs and benefits of expansionary efforts; technological innovations in transportation, communications, weaponry, tactics, and economic productivity; and the nature and distribution of the external opposition. Nevertheless, the fundamental factor behind expansionary attempts, according to Gilpin, is the tendency for economic, military, and technological capabilities to grow unevenly.

Relative advantage is thus a necessary, although not sufficient, causal factor in efforts to transform the status quo. An advantage in relative power encourages and facilitates expansion attempts. Successful expansion, in turn, enhances relative advantages and, in the process, facilitates the generation of the economic surplus needed for political control. Eventually, a state may accumulate a sufficient relative power advantage and economic surplus to be able to dominate its entire system.

At some point, however, the expanding state will encounter a juncture at which the escalating costs and diminishing returns of further expansion interact to restrain the expansionary urge. The restraints on expansion are nearly as numerous as the factors promoting it. Depending on the era involved, natural barriers have provided the most obvious obstacles. Boulding's (1962) "loss-of-strength gradient"—or the difficulty in utilizing capabilities effectively as the distance from the home base increases—serves as another restraint. But it is also one that needs to be qualified according to the available technological resources for overcoming geographical and logistical problems.

Still another salient obstacle is the tendency for expansion to generate both opposition and imitation—which, of course, may or may not prove to be effective. A fourth consideration, and one that is difficult to pin down with precision, is the argument that economic, technological, and other factors interact to restrict the optimum size of political organizations in given historical eras. Therefore, as the size of a political entity expands beyond some limit, overhead costs tend to increase faster than the returns derived from political control. The burden of protection costs may also be aggravated by rising consumption propensities in other spheres as well. Investment then suffers at the expense of future productivity. The likely result is the undermining of the state's relative advantage foundation and its ability to maintain its position vis-à-vis the external competition. Whether cause or effect, a final restraint on expansion is provided by the internal transformations that seem to accompany a deteriorating competitive position. A lack of innovation and risk-taking, corruption, and reactionary attempts to preserve traditional privileges are illustrative symptoms.

Gilpin summarizes the relative decline syndrome as follows:

> Once a society reaches the limits of its expansion, it has great difficulty in maintaining its position and arresting its eventual decline. Further, it begins to encounter marginal returns in agricultural or industrial production. Both internal and external changes increase consumption and the costs of protection and production; it begins to experience a severe fiscal crisis. The diffusion of its economic, technological, or organizational skills undercuts its comparative advantage over other societies, especially those in the periphery of the system. These rising states, on the other hand, enjoy lower costs, rising rates of return on their resources, and the advantages of backwardness. In time, the differential rates of growth of declining and rising states in the system produce a decisive redistribution of power and result in disequilibrium in the system (Gilpin, 1981:185).

Thus, when the costs of dominance begin to exceed the revenue derived from the dominant position (statement 4), the economic surplus that is required to underwrite the dominating position begins to erode as well. If this situation of escalating costs and diminishing surplus cannot be turned around, the relative position of the dominant powers will begin to decline. As the decline progresses, the gap between the prevailing status quo and the newly emerging distribution of power continues to grow.

Systemic Change

The heart of Gilpin's systemic outlook on international political change is summarized by the following passage:

> . . . actors enter social relations and create social structures in order to advance particular sets of political, economic, or other types of interests. Because the interests of some of the actors may conflict with those of other actors, the particular interests that are most favored by those social arrangements tend to reflect the relative powers of the actors involved. . . . Over time, however, the interests of individual actors and the balance of power among the actors do change as a result of economic, technological, and other developments. As a consequence, those actors who benefit most from a change in the social system and who gain the power to effect such change will seek to alter the system in ways that reflect the new distribution of power and the interests of its new dominant members. Thus, a precondition for political change lies in a disjuncture between the existing social system and the redistribution of power toward those actors who would benefit most from a change in the system. (Gilpin, 1981:9).

Gilpin breaks with the classical perspective quite clearly by declining to make the customary distinction between internal and external politics. Actors may have different names (see table 3.1) for the social arrangements entered into at various levels of analysis, but the basic processes of political-economic control remain similar. To the extent that the processes do differ, it is primarily in terms of the comparative ambiguity found at the international level. The structure and rules of the international political system tend to be less institutionalized and overt than those that characterize many domestic systems. Nevertheless, the fundamental process of government, regardless of the level of analysis, hinges upon the distribution of power—whether it be distributed among groups, classes, or states.

As the distribution of power changes, Gilpin emphasizes, one may anticipate some amount of systemic disequilibrium and crisis until or unless the system's structure is brought into realignment with the new distribution of military, economic, and technological capabilities. This is the fundamental problem of international change in Gilpin's view. A system begins in a state of equilibrium with a given power distribution. Authority, property rights, and law or the hierarchy of prestige, the

Table 3.1

Political-economic Control Mechanisms in Gilpin's Framework

Domestic Systems	International Systems
Government	Dominance of the great powers
Authority	Prestige hierarchy
Property rights	Division of territory
Law	Rules of the system
Domestic economy	International economy

Source: based on Gilpin (1981:28)

division of territory, and the rules of the system are developed to reflect the interests of the initial set of dominant actors. When the relative capabilities of these actors decline and a new set of strong actors emerges, the constitutional foundations of the existing system and its legitimacy are undermined. Presumably, the greater the disjuncture between the existing system's governance pattern and fundamental changes in the distribution of power, the greater too the incentives for states that are growing stronger to seek change in the systemic status quo.

Historically, hegemonic war has provided the primary mechanism by which these phases of systemic disequilibrium and crisis are resolved. Such wars represent direct contests between the once dominant power(s) and the rising challenger(s). Since the fundamental issue at stake is the nature and governance of the system, the intensity, scope, and duration of these conflicts are apt to be great. A victory on the part of challengers will lead to a radical change in the way the system is governed and one that more accurately reflects the prevailing power distribution. Hegemonic war and its accompanying peace settlement, therefore, establish a new status quo that restores the system to an equilibrated state.

The more pronounced and unambiguous the postwar hierarchy of prestige, as reflected in the dominance of the leading power, the more likely the system is to enjoy a period of peace and stability. This observation reflects Gilpin's argument that power and prestige ultimately depend on the perceptions of other states. Unfortunately, the most accurate assessment of a state's ability and willingness to achieve its objectives continues to be the trial by arms of war. Hence, a victory in the last hegemonic war not only provides an unsubtle demonstration of the victor's capabilities, it also enhances the dominant state's prestige (reputation for power) and legitimacy as a system governor. The legitimacy may be further enhanced by the provision of public goods (military and economic order for the most part) and/or by the sanctioning influence of reigning ideological or religious values.

The problem remains, however, that power, prestige, and legitimacy are not constants in the international system. Changes in the distribution of power are likely to change more quickly than changes in the hierarchy of prestige. Eventually, the perceptual changes catch up with the international realities. The governance of the system begins to break down at this point. "A weakening of the hierarchy of prestige and increased ambiguity in interpreting it" ushers in a new era of conflict and struggle as the cycle of change continues.

Dominant powers provide systemic order and stability. Their decline, however, creates situations of conflict and instability. The rules for systemic governance no longer correspond to the existing distribution of power among the principal actors. War becomes the primary mechanism for correcting systemic disequilibrium. The explanatory trick then is to account for the rise and fall of the dominant powers, for therein lie the causes of systemic change. Yet while there may well be a number of timeless elements in the rise and fall dynamics, the general process is subject to contextual change. To appreciate the significance of the contextual changes, one needs to consider the Gilpin approach's third leg—the simplified interpretation of world systemic history.

Systemic History

The year 1648—the birth of the Westphalian era at the conclusion of the regional/religious wars that preoccupied Europe for much of the preceding half/century—is Gilpin's modernity watershed for the international system. This point of demarcation assists in establishing three historical eras: a pre-1648 imperial cycle period, a transitional (1648–1815) period characterized by the European balance of power, and a post-1815 hegemonic power succession period (Britain and the United States).

The premodern era witnessed a variety of attempts by one state to conquer its neighbors and to dominate its system through imperial rule. The principal political ordering mechanism, territorial control, is seen as a function of the predominately agrarian economy of the pre-modern era. Economic surplus generation was dependent upon a combination of the exploitation of peasant and slave labor, imperial tribute, and, to a lesser extent, the taxation of trade. The more territory that could be controlled, the greater the wealth that might be generated. The greater the economic surplus, the more extensive was the potential reach of imperial power. Yet the overhead costs of empire, and especially the costs of military technology and warfare, invariably escalated faster than the economic surplus could be expanded in a time characterized by slow or little economic growth. As the financial problems of empire became increasingly burdensome, centrifugal tendencies would emerge. Processes of imperial revolt, fragmentation, and decline would then ensure the continuation of the cycle of empires.

The sixteenth and seventeenth centuries introduced three interacting developments that interrupted the premodern imperial cycle. The nation-state became the principal organizational format for participation in the international system. The primary impact of this development was to alter the optimal size of the most efficient and competitive political organization. As the Hapsburgs learned belatedly in the long-running feud with the Valois, the Dutch Revolt, and the Thirty Years' War, empire was no longer a feasible proposition within the transformed European environment.

A related, second development, the advent of sustained economic growth, facilitated the nation-state's organizational triumph. On the one hand, growth helped to meet the rising military costs of international competition in a way that premodern empires frequently had found beyond their fiscal grasp. Sustained growth also diminished the influence and inherent limitations of agrarian economies. Most important, the generation of wealth was no longer as dependent upon the expansion of territorial control as it once had been. Technological advancements and productive efficiency became the new primary sources of economic wealth. This shift, in turn, was greatly facilitated by a third development—the emergence of a world market economy. To the extent that trade became an engine of growth for some states, the relative significance of domestic productive efficiency over territorial expansion increased.

All three developments worked to change the international political landscape in Europe. In the second half of the seventeenth century, the last of Gilpin's premodern empires had been defeated in the Thirty Years' War (1618–1648). Two different types of major competitors emerged in the wake of the Hapsburg defeat and decline. Some states, such as France and Sweden, continued to specialize in the cultivation of traditional military power for European warfare. Other states, most notably the Netherlands and England, preferred to emphasize the development of their commercial capabilities. The dualism in power bases, as well as the number of genuine competitors, facilitated the development of the balance of power mechanism. Its basic purpose was to ensure that no single state could establish imperial control over the European region. Gradually, however, the number of principal contenders declined, in part as a consequence of the extra-European struggle over the exploitation of American and Asian territory. Portugal, Spain, and the Netherlands were eliminated one by one until only France and Britain remained.

Gilpin describes France as the dominant but declining European power in the late eighteenth century. The French defeat in the Napoleonic Wars, by the rising British challenger, further reduced the number of real contenders for dominance to one state. The concentration of economic and military power in that one state, thanks in large part to the Industrial Revolution, signaled an end to the transitional era and initiated a new phase of hegemonic succession.

As the most efficient and technologically advanced economic power, the hegemonic power has the most to gain from participation in the world market economy. It also has the most to gain from a smoothly functioning international economic system. The consequent provision of public goods thus is hardly an act of altruism on the part of the hegemon. In return for the benefits it reaps, the hegemonic leader supplies the economic rules of the game, investment capital, an international currency, and the protection of property rights on a world scale. The hegemon also champions the principle of free trade to further improve the efficiency of the world market's functioning and, not coincidentally, the hegemon's own ability to seek profit in foreign markets that might otherwise be closed.

LONG CYCLES, CHANGE, AND WAR

Long-cycle analysis is sometimes erroneously depicted as neo-realist in orientation (e.g., Ashley, 1986; Viotti and Kauppi, 1987). Such miscategorization typically stems from overlooking the very close and evolutionary connections between George Modelski's (1970, 1972) work on the construction of what he termed a geocentric perspective in the early 1970s and the long-cycle material that began to emerge in the mid-1970s. For instance, much of the contextual background for long-cycle analysis is articulated in Modelski (1972)—a study that clearly fits within Holsti's "global society" category. Presumably, it is the stress on the significance of the military power of a few major states—only one aspect of the perspective but one that does overlap with the more classical emphases on great-power oligopoly in the international system—that most misleads categorizers.

To some extent, the problem of misinterpretation is also traceable to two other, related features of long cycle analysis. First of all, the perspective is very much an evolving one. It began with a few core ideas (Modelski, 1978) and continues to be expanded almost with each new study. The second feature is related to the first in the sense that the perspective's thrust encompasses quite a few conference papers, journal articles, and book chapters but no mongraph-length studies prior to the mid-1980s.[6] To have monitored the development of this perspective over the past decade, one would have had to engage in rather careful reading of widely scattered papers. This state of affairs should be modified in the mid- to late 1980s with the publication of Modelski (1987a, 1987b), Modelski and Thompson (1988), and Modelski and Modelski (1988).

Modelski's Long Cycles of World Leadership

Modelski's approach to historical-structural analysis is basically in agreement with the realist contention that the modern (post-1500) world system has always lacked an institutionalized central authority capable of ruling the system. But Modelski is quick to point out that the absence of a world state or empire does not preclude the existence of some form of political organization or order. That is to say, one may still have a political system whether or not one has a specific and concrete legal framework of centralized authority or sovereignty, as in the case of the familiar nation-state. In fact, Modelski asserts that the world system has not one but three principal structures: the global political system, the world economy, and the world cultural subsystem.

Global Political Management

Not surprisingly for a political scientist, Modelski's primary emphasis, so far, has been placed on discussing the theoretical nature of the global political system. This structure is defined as encompassing the institutions and more subtle arrangements for the management of global problems and interdependence. Unlike the multiple layers of political system found at the local, national, and regional levels, the global political system is not territorially based. It is concerned with long-range transactions (of global reach) that frequently tend to be intercontinental, oceanic, and, more recently, extraterrestrial in nature. More specifically, the global political system constitutes an exchange structure in which the transactions are focused on the interactions between producers and consumers of the goods and services of global order and justice—although it seems fair to say that states have placed more emphasis on the former than on the latter.

Within this system of transactions, the issue areas of international order and security, territorial rights, and the stability of international trade have constituted the primary concerns. Nevertheless, the extent to which the global system's political arrangements have been effective is subject to regular fluctuations. At times, the management of global problems is left almost entirely to the care of a single powerful state. At other times, the attempt to manage or regulate global problems is either shared among several units or simply not attempted in situations bordering on anarchy.

These fluctuations in the level and nature of global governance are described as the long cycle of world leadership, the principal process mechanism of the global political system. The basic format of the long cycle begins with a major global war that can be interpreted as a fight to determine the constitution or authority arrangement of the global political system. During and immediately after the war, a single state (see table 3.2) emerges as the system's new world power and legitimizes its preponderant position through the postwar peace settlements. The political functions of the new world power are to serve as the

Table 3.2

Long Cycle of Global Leadership

Long Cycle	Formative Global Conflict	World Power	Other Global Powers
I	Italian/Indian Ocean Wars (1494–1517)	Portugal	England, Spain, France, Netherlands
II	Spanish Wars (1580–1608)	Netherlands	England, Spain, France
III	French Wars (1688–1713)	Britain	France Netherlands, Russia, Spain
IV	French Wars (1792–1815)	Britain	France, Russia, United States, Germany, Japan
V	German Wars (1914–1945)	United States	Soviet Union

system's principal supplier of security and to establish the frameworks of the new global order as manifested in international organizations and international economic relations. The world power is able to serve these functions because, by definition, it essentially monopolizes or controls more than one-half of the resources available for global order keeping.

The Strategic Role of Sea Power

Long-cycle theory places considerable emphasis on the significance of sea power as a principal resource for creating and maintaining global reach capabilities. The emphasis is justified partially in terms of geographical necessity—for so many years in modern world history, ships have provided the most efficient means of intercontinental transportation and efforts to extend influence—and partially in terms of the importance of maritime orientations and capabilities in the development of winning strategies in global politics.

This emphasis on sea power is hardly unique to long-cycle theory. What is unique is the creation of a five-hundred-year (1494–1993) indicator system that is able to track the concentration and deconcentration of naval power, depicted in figure 3.1, as a leading index of long-cycle fluctuations.

As one might imagine, sea power has experienced considerable evolution over the past five hundred years. Its modern development began with the introduction, roughly in the late fifteenth/early sixteenth centuries, of armed sailing vessels capable of undertaking oceanic voyages. As Cipolla (1965) and others have noted, guns and sails were critical in the expansion of European power throughout the world. They were also crucial in many of the intra-European competitions of the emerging nation-states. In time, specialized vessels for war were developed and became, among other things, indicators of national military strength that were utilized by state decision makers in calculating comparative strategic standings. The standardized ship of the line eventually gave way to the iron and steel battleship, which, in due course, has given way more recently to aircraft carriers, nuclear attack submarines, and sea-based ballistic missiles. Throughout these technological transitions, the estimation emphasis of decision makers has been placed on those ships capable of serving in the first line of battle and so too is long-cycle theory's approach to measuring sea power capabilities.

To create a 500-year sea-power-capability series that captures a variety of changes in naval technology requires some amount of flexibility in measurement principles. As the detailed description and justification for these changes in measurement rules are elaborated elsewhere (Mo-

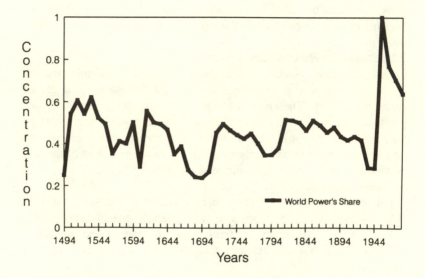

Figure 3.1   The Long Cycle of Global Leadership
Data Source: Modelski and Thompson (1988: 110–112)

delski and Thompson, 1988; Thompson and Rasler, 1988), the basic
capabilities are only briefly outlined in table 3.3.

To qualify as an eligible global power (see table 3.2), a state must
control a minimum of 10 percent of the global reach naval capabilities
and demonstrate as well genuine oceanic-scale naval activity (as opposed to regional sea such as the Mediterranean or Baltic). However,
once a state qualifies, the initiation of its capability count is begun as
soon after the preceding global war as possible. Similarly, its capabilities are no longer counted after the next global war that follows the
state's failure to meet the minimal entry qualifications. Finally, the
specific indicator utilized to measure systemic capability concentration
is the proportion controlled by the world power if it emerges from a
global war with 50 percent or more of the global powers' total sea
power capabilities. This world power designation is maintained, even
when the leader's share no longer approximates the 50 percent threshold, until a new world power emerges.

Table 3.3

Indicators of Global Reach Capability

Years	Indicators
1494–1654	The number of state-owned, armed sailing vessels capable of undertaking oceanic voyages.
1655–1859	The number of ships of the line, subject to an escalating minimal number of guns carried to qualify as front-line fighting vessels.
1860–1945	The number of first-class battleships, subject to escalating minimal attributes in terms of ship and gun size (e.g., as in the case of pre- and postdreadnought battleships).
1816–1945	The level of naval expenditure that is used to smooth the several abrupt technological changes experienced in the nineteenth and early twentieth centuries and that is given equal weight with the appropriate ship counts in a combined index.
1946–present	The number of heavy or attack aircraft carriers and, after 1960, the number of nuclear attack submarines and the number of sea-based nuclear missile warheads weighted according to equivalent megatonnage (EMT) and counter military potential (CMP)—with carriers, attack submarines, EMT, and CMP given equal weight in a combined index.

World Power and the Decay of Order

Initially, then, the long-cycle process determines who will be preponderant in global affairs. However, the status of world power is neither omnipotent nor permanent. World power does not necessarily mean world hegemony or total control of world affairs, for the role of world power is basically oriented to the global layer of interaction. To what extent a given world power has influence over the affairs of the various regional, national, and local levels is always an open question.

The problem with world power is that order tends to deteriorate over time. The world power position may be maintained more or less effectively for as long as a generation, but eventually the energy that went into establishing the new order begins to run down. Rivals are always present and increasingly prepared to challenge the decaying authority of the world power as it loses its monopolization of global capability resources. The coalition put together in order to win the last global war

Table 3.4

Fracturing of Winning Coalitions

Wars	Winning Coalition	Primary Challenger
Italian/Indian Ocean Wars (1494–1516)	Portugal + England + Burgundy + Spain	France
Spanish Wars (1580–1608)	Netherlands + England + France	Spain
French Wars (1688–1713)	England + Netherlands	France
French Wars (1792–1915)	Britain + Russia + Prussia	France
German Wars (1914–1945)	United States + Britain + Russia/USSR	Germany
—	—	USSR?

Source: Based on Modelski (1984:23).

also has a tendency toward fracturing. As sketched in table 3.4, one member of each winning coalition changed sides and became the primary challenger in the next succession struggle.

Consequently, the initially unipolar concentration of resources gives way to multipolarity, and the rivalries among the global powers increasingly take on the characteristics of oligopolistic competition. As global order deteriorates, the system gradually moves toward its minimal order point of departure and eventually another global war. It is in this sense that the pattern of world leadership is cyclical. Over a period of time (roughly 100 years) a world power emerges from a global war only to experience a gradual decay in its position of preponderance. Global order decays at a parallel rate until a new global war occurs and facilitates the emergence of a new world power.

Modelski explains the relative regularity and continuity of the long-cycle pattern as the product of an urge to impose a global order and four properties of the global political system. The desire to create a global order requires only that decision makers be aware that there is a globe to regulate and that they develop the capabilities to regulate its processes. Both of these minimal requirements began to be realized about the time the Portuguese forced their way around the southern tip of Africa and into the Indian Ocean spice trade.

The four systemic properties refer to (1) the importance of global war, (2) power monopoly, (3) the functional narrowness of the subsequent order, and (4) the tendency for world powers to drift toward territorial control policies. Of the four, the observation that global wars do not produce the most conducive settings for establishing new political orders is probably the most obvious. If major wars are necessary for imposing new global orders, the most probable expectation is more war at some future date. This expectation is made all the more probable because the new global order is based to a large extent on a world power's initial monopoly of global military capacity. The monopoly position, in turn, bestows its possessor with very real and fairly exclusive advantages in terms of security, bargaining power, and general influence. Since these advantages are desired by other states, the monopoly foundation is likely to erode as rivals improve their own global military capacities. Monopoly thus gives way to oligopoly with a number of global powers seeking to maximize short-run considerations at the expense of the more long-run global interests.

Oligopolistic competition and hostilities are accentuated by the relatively narrow scope of the global order. Material motives (for example, gold, spices, trading monopolies) have always played a highly significant role in terms of the types of rules established by world powers. Might may not make right, but it is certainly useful in obtaining and exploiting economic advantages. In addition to magnifying prevailing inequalities, this third characteristic of global order is viewed as increasing the instability and fragility of order.

Finally, the challenges of oligopolistic rivals encourages the world power, and other global powers as well, to seek direct imperial control over territory as opposed to the more flexible and mobile strategy of maintaining global communication networks that require outposts or bases but not extensive territorial control. For Modelski, the essence of global power is the accomplishment of maximum global functions with minimum territorial burdens. Increasing the volume of territorial burdens in order to preserve the illusion of control only drains resources away from the management of global problems in preference for newly acquired national and local problems. Moreover, the rivalries between the global powers can only be magnified by increasing conflict over exclusive claims to territorial control. These conflicts are certainly more likely to produce greater disorder than they are to contribute to the existing level of global order.

The Phases of the Long Cycle and Global War

The timing or prevalence of these systemic properties is neither simultaneous nor randomly distributed. Modelski argues that the central process of the global political system, the long cycle, experiences four successive stages: (1) global war, (2) world power, (3) delegitimation, and (4) deconcentration. The first phase is characterized by drastic decline in the net availability of global order and the political resources necessary to maintain order. But in the ensuing, intense, and bloody struggle for succession to the leadership position, global order priorities begin to receive greater attention.

> The macrodecision that takes the form of global war has
> certainly played a major role in the long cycles of the modern
> world and in the dynamics of the global political system. . . . It
> is noteworthy, however, that its function is not that of global war
> as such, but rather a more generalized one of systemic
> decision-making—an opportunity for a political system to make a
> decisive choice, one that commits the global system on two
> crucial points: (1) the character of its political leadership and the
> occupancy of its chief offices, and (2) the priority program of
> public policy for global problems to which the global system
> (although not really the world as a whole) will be committed for
> the next two to three generations. (Modelski, 1987b:125–26)

The second phase is ushered in by a wide-ranging, post-global-war peace settlement. Power has been reconcentrated and the legitimacy of the new global order is at a peak. It is during this second phase that the greatest amount of political goods and services (an order surplus) are provided by the world power. As memories of the previous global war fade, the priorities attached to global order are reduced, and a shortfall in global order is experienced.

During this third phase (delegitimation), the world power's monopolistic position is questioned increasingly by nationalistic challenges to the global order. The decay of the world power's position continues in the fourth phase (deconcentration), substantially reducing the resource base on which the global order is dependent. However, challengers are not yet fully prepared to press their respective succession claims to the position of world power. As a consequence, the supply of global order will tend to exceed the demand for order in the fourth and prewar phase.[7]

Global Politics and the World-Economy: Linkage Mechanisms

Modelski has few doubts that the global political system and the world economy are closely related even though he regards the "chicken-egg" question of whether economics calls the political tunes or the other way around as a relatively open question. Modelski sees two specific linkages between the political and economic systems at the world level. As noted earlier, one of the primary functions of an incumbent world power is to provide stability and many of the transactional rules for the world economy. In this respect, the world power supplies or facilitates the provision of much of the political basis for worldwide economic relations.

This first linkage mechanism should not be perceived as particularly burdensome by world power decision makers, for world powers tend also to have the most dynamic national economy characterized by high industrial productivity, economic growth, and international trade and investment centrality. Therefore, the stability of the world-economy is a very natural concern.

It is quite possible for a state to become a "globally active economic zone" without ever assuming the mantle of world power, but it is doubtful that a state can become the world power without also becoming the economic system's lead economy. Global reach and global wars are expensive propositions and thus require the support of an extensive economic base, as is provided by access to the world's leading economy. Alternatively, the advantages that come with world power status, such as political stability and a high degree of external protection, are necessary for the continued functioning of a lead economy.

These intertwining linkages between the global political system and the world economy suggest the strong possibility that the fluctuations and movements in their respective processes are also closely related. The political and the economic structures both draw on the same population and resource base. The more that wealth creation is a high priority, the fewer the resources that are left for political purposes. The reverse of this relationship should hold as well. Consequently, Modelski argues that periods of expansion in the global political system alternate with periods of growth in the world economy. More concretely, he links the controversial Kondratieff long-price waves to the previously described long-cycle phases. Very briefly, Kondratieff (1935, 1979) argued that the advent of industrial capitalism in the late eighteenth century initiated a sequence of rising and falling prices, with each rising or falling price period lasting twenty-five to thirty years. Modelski partially adapts Rostow's (1978) interpretation of this phenomenon as movements in terms of the relative scarcity and abundance of food and raw materials that are reflected in the periods of rising (scarcity) and falling (abundance) prices.[8]

Given the linkages between the global political system and world economy, it is reasonable to expect that instabilities in one structure will be transmitted to the other and vice versa. Modelski expresses this as a matter of both structures "listening to the same drummer." When the demand for political goods and services increases, resource scarcity and price levels are likely to increase as well. Alternatively, as the political demands decline, resource scarcity and price levels will also decline. The long-cycle phases of world power and deconcentration thus are viewed as periods of declining prices, relative resource abundance, and the rise of new leading economic sectors. The delegitimation and global war phases are seen as periods of rising prices, relative resource scarcity, and relatively little economic innovation. Fluctuations in the world economy, therefore, parallel fluctuations in the global political system.

THE WORLD-ECONOMY, CHANGE, AND WAR

Structural realism has been depicted here as a school of thought that is bimodally distributed according to the subject of inquiry. One group specializes in war and peace. The other concentrates on international political economy questions. Alternatively, long-cycle analyses place great stress on the critical role of global warfare in the dynamics of the global political system. At the same time, a gradually growing amount of attention has been directed to questions of international political economy. The third perspective to be reviewed here, world-economy analysis, focuses largely on questions pertaining to inequality and political economy. An interest in conflict has always been present, but any demonstration of specific concern with international relations' conventional interest in war/peace questions has been limited.

World-economy analysts have an annual conference of their own, a yearbook, and a specialized journal (*Review*). As a consequence, a large number of analyses have been produced covering a wide range of topics. Nevertheless, a standard core set of ideas has emerged and is usually associated with the writings of Immanuel Wallerstein. The emergence of a uniform core set of ideas hardly means that there is little or no dissent or deviation from theoretical orthodoxy. The assumptions and conclusions of Fernand Braudel (1984) and Andre Gunder Frank (1978), to name but two, are not always the same as Wallerstein's or those of others in this theoretical camp. Yet they are certainly similar enough to treat their writings as a single school of historical-structural thought. And since Wallerstein is very much at the center of this outlook, it is appropriate that our review center on his perspective.

Wallerstein's World-Economy Perspective[9]

For Wallerstein, there are but two types of world systems: world empires and world economies. If a single political system should gain control over most of a world-system's economy, the system becomes a world empire by definition. If no single political system exercises some level of control over the pertinent economic arena, the system is considered a world economy. Throughout history, "world empires" of limited scope (such as the Roman, Incan, and Chinese versions) have been organized successfully for significant periods of time. However, the past five hundred years or so have witnessed the emergence of a European-based world economy that gradually expanded its boundaries to encompass the entire world. Despite successive efforts to create a world empire, the world economy continues to be characterized by multiple political and cultural systems linked together through an extensive division of labor based on economic exchange and specialization.

The Emergence of a European World-Economy

The historical development of the world economy from an initially European base to its current manifestation has gone through four broad stages, according to Wallerstein. The first stage (1450–1600/50) was made possible by the conjuncture of such processes as the disintegration of Western European feudal arrangements, climatic/demographic/technological changes, the political multicentricity of the European region, and the economic need for geographic expansion. The first stage may have presented the best opportunity to transform the emerging world-economy into a Spanish world empire, but the very same processes that made the first stage possible are said to have also made world empire extremely difficult and expensive to achieve. In any event, Spain and its rulers found that they were not up to the task. Consequently, by the end of the first stage, the core of the new world economy had been established in northwestern Europe. The economic significance of the older Mediterranean power—Spain and the Italian city-states—had declined. Baltic Europe and parts of Latin America (notably the Caribbean, Mexico, and Peru) had become the primary targets for exploitation.

The second stage (1600/50–1730/50) was marked by a systemwide stagnation that brought about consolidation and retrenchment in the world economy. As part of this consolidation process, the economic and political rivalries of the northwest European core were made more intense. England triumphed over the Netherlands only to be confronted with repeated challenges from France.

The third stage (1750/1815–1917) was characterized by a noticeable shift away from an emphasis on agricultural production toward industrial production. In the process, the increased need for raw materials and the technological availability of the means to acquire them led to the expansion of the world economy to encompass the entire planet. While Great Britain was able to withstand the last French attempt to achieve primacy (1793–1815), it was less successful in coping with the American and German challenges toward the end of the nineteenth century. Stage three gave way to stage four (1917–), an ongoing period that Wallerstein associates with revolutionary turmoil and the full consolidation of the industrially based world economy. By 1945, the United States had replaced Great Britain as the system's strongest state or hegemonic power, only to find its position significantly eroded after only two decades of dominance.

World Capitalism and Political Multicentricity

Wallerstein primarily attributes the continued maintenance of the world-economy structure to its capitalist mode of production. Contrary to the conventional Marxist emphasis on the sale of labor and the subsequent loss of the ownership of the means of production by laborers, Wallerstein defines capitalism as the striving for increased efficiency of production in order to achieve a maximum price and profit for sales in a world market. In a capitalist world economy, various groups compete within a single world market. But they also attempt to bias the market in their favor by organizing to exercise influence through their respective political systems in order to obtain and to accommodate the most favorable proportion of the world-economy's economic surplus. This process results in what Wallerstein considers to be the distinctive feature of a capitalist world economy. Economic decision making is oriented principally to the larger world arena, while political decision making is directed toward the legal structures (states) that claim control over smaller pieces of space. Since, by definition, the economic arena is not controlled totally by any single political system, capitalists tend to have great freedom of maneuver and are thus able to maintain the world economy's hierarchically skewed division of labor and distribution of rewards and, most important, to accumulate capital.

Core and Periphery

At the top of the world economy's hierarchy are the core states. These core states represent the sector in which production is the most efficient and the complexity of economic activities is greatest. Not coincidentally, core states are also characterized by the strongest state political structures (for example, centralized and efficient bureaucracies, military power) and integrated national cultures. As a result of these factors and the relatively high level of capital accumulated in the core, it tends to receive the lion's share of the system's allocation of rewards. At the other end of the hierarchical scale is the world economy's periphery. The periphery's role is to specialize in the production of much less well-rewarded goods (for instance, raw materials and labor) that nevertheless are essential for daily use. Whereas core political systems tend to be strong, peripheral states are either weak and highly penetrated or nonexistent, just as their level of cultural integration tends to be minimal.

An intermediate category is reserved for semiperipheral states that serve as collection points for important occupational skills that may be politically unpopular in the core states. Wallerstein views the semiperiphery area as vital to the continued functioning of a capitalist world economy in that, as both exploiter and exploited, semiperipheral states reduce the amount of noncore opposition faced by the core area. The final and fourth sector of the world economy is labeled the external arena. The distinguishing characteristic in this case is the existence of trade relationships between the first three sectors of the world economy and other world systems, but the trade is focused primarily on the exchange of luxury goods (goods not essential for daily use). However, as the boundaries of the world economy expanded, the external arena diminished in size until, during stage three, it ceased to exist around the end of the nineteenth century.

Just as the external arena gradually vanished as it was absorbed into the world economy, membership in the core, periphery, and semiperiphery is not constant. For example, semiperipheral states may once have been demoted from an earlier core area or they may have managed to pull themselves out of the periphery. Nevertheless, it is within the core area itself that the most important mobility processes take place. The very categories of core and periphery indicate the existence of disparities between the strength of states. These disparities are also found within the sectoral categories as well as between them. Within the core area, the critical distinction is between hegemonic powers and other core states.

Hegemony and World War

Historically, most core states have not been hegemonic powers. Occasionally and for relatively brief periods, one core state will assume a position of dominance, not only within the core but throughout the world economy. Although Wallerstein recognizes only three hegemonic states (the United Provinces of the Netherlands, 1620–1672; Great Britain, 1815–1873; and the United States, 1945–1967), he views the pattern of ascendancy to hegemonic status as remarkably simple and easily generalizable. First, candidates for hegemonic status must create and demonstrate a decisive superiority in the efficiency of their agricultural-industrial productivity. This superiority leads to the achievement of a dominant position in the distribution of world trade, with its parallel benefits in terms of the control of transportation, communication, and insurance. Commercial dominance, in turn, leads to a third important sphere of control: finance and investment.

It seems unlikely (and historically unsupported) that the dominance of any core state will emerge suddenly and simultaneously in all three spheres. Rather, Wallerstein views the achievement of productive, commercial, and financial superiority as successive (in this order) yet overlapping in time. When a core state can demonstrate that it is dominant in all three spheres, it has established its hegemony over the world economy.

More recently, Wallerstein has placed somewhat greater stress on the role of two elements that have always been prominent in long-cycle theory but much less so in world-economy analyses: war and sea power. Three world wars—thirty-year-long, land-based conflicts fought by all or most of the world system's major military powers—play the role of consolidating the newly emerged hegemon's position. The three wars, referred to as alpha, beta, and gamma by Wallerstein (see table 3.5), performed this role by restructuring the interstate system at war's end in 1648, 1815, and 1945. The wars themselves represent succession struggles between two principal contenders. One is land-based and the other is sea/air-based. The latter wins. The postwar settlement then "encrusts" the hegemonic victor's edge after the process of engaging in world war first facilitates the development of the hegemon's resource edge.

The main problem with achieving hegemony is that the role has not been (cannot be?) maintained indefinitely. Indeed, it appears to be an extremely transitory phenomenon. As the primary beneficiary of the world market, the role of hegemonic power is an attractive prize for rival core states and would-be hegemonic powers. The hegemonic role is also an extremely expensive one. To advance and defend its economic interests, the hegemonic state will require great and costly mili-

Table 3.5

World Wars, Hegemony, and Succession Contenders

World Wars	Hegemon	Succession Contenders
Alpha		
Thirty Years' War (1618–1648)	United Provinces of the Netherlands (1620–1672)	England France
Beta		
Napoleonic Wars (1792–1815)	Great Britain (1815–1873)	Germany United States
Gamma		
Euroasian Wars (1914–1945)	United States (1945–1967)	Western Europe Japan

Source: Based on information in Wallerstein (1984:37–46).

tary and bureaucratic strength; in short, it becomes imperialistic in its external relations. This requirement necessitates increased tax burdens. In addition, Wallerstein contends that rising wage levels are still another concomitant of hegemony. Given these rising overhead costs and the increasingly successful competition from rivals within the core, the hegemonic power is forced to work extremely hard merely to maintain its various superiorities, let alone to improve on them.

Instead, the hegemonic power tends to begin losing its competitive advantages almost as soon as it has achieved them. Even so, this hegemonic decline process does not usually or need not entail the loss of absolute productive, commercial, and financial power. It is more likely to be a matter of the core rivals enhancing their own economic and military strength. Thus, the immediate decline of hegemony means a loss of strength relative to the gains registered by other core states. As the core rivals grow stronger, the primacy of the hegemonic power comes into increasing question until it finds that it has been reduced to the position of being, at best, but one of several powerful core states. At the world-system level, this hegemonic cycle translates into alternating phases of power concentration (hegemony) and decreased latitude for weaker core states and phases of power diffusion and increased freedom of maneuver for core states.[10]

Expansion and Contraction
In addition to the rise and fall of hegemonic powers, a second dynamic

process of economic expansion and contraction is central to Waller-stein's perspective on world-system processes. Since the mid-fifteenth century, the world-economy's division of labor has steadily evolved toward increasingly mechanized production, marketable land and labor, and contractually regulated social relations. As a partial function of technological change (for instance, transportation and communica-tions), the boundaries of the world-economy have gradually expanded. But Wallerstein's version of the history of economic development is not characterized by monotonically linear progress. Instead, periods of economic expansion (A phases) are followed by periods of economic stagnation (B phases). Each expansionary phase encounters a point at which the capital accumulation process is blocked or slowed by the lack of interstate coordination of world supply and demand. The ensuing phase of economic stagnation is eventually overcome by the combina-tion of several processes (the expansion of the world-economy's bound-aries, the development of new products, the reconcentration of capital, the relative increase of demand, and the political restructuring of states and the interstate system).

However, prior to the onset of a new A phase, the core states attempt to avoid or to minimize the impact of economic contraction by increas-ing the extent of their political and economic control over the exploita-tion of the peripheral areas. These attempts to restructure the world market in their own favor during the stagnation phases leads to in-creased competition, conflict, and war between the core states. The most frequently cited example is the roughly forty-year period of the scramble for colonial territory and great power crises leading up to World War I. It is in this two steps forward, one step backward fashion that the capitalist world-economy has spread to encompass the geo-graphical world and to intensify the maldistribution of rewards between core and periphery.

In sum then, Wallerstein's perspective on the world-system empha-sizes the evolving structure of the world-economy. The processes that receive the most attention are the core's exploitation of the periphery, the rise and fall of hegemonic powers, and the sequential dynamics and consequences of economic expansion and contraction.

CONCLUSION

The three models outlined represent departures, in varying degrees, from the classical paradigm in international relations. There are also a sufficient number of differences across the three models to discourage anyone from confusing any one of them for another. Many of these differences are not trivial. They reflect divergent assumptions and, not surprisingly, may very well lead to conflicting conclusions about what ostensibly is the same subject matter. It is also difficult, if not epistemologically incorrect, to dismiss one school of thought's assumptions and conceptualizations as false or erroneous. Some degree of tolerance for differences of opinion must be honored if the historical-structural vantage point in world politics is to develop into full fruition. Ideally, the best ideas will win out.

In the interim, some of the disagreements—particularly those concerning system time—are more susceptible to objective empirical inquiry than others. As McGowan (1980:7) has noted, a large proportion of social science research has ignored or distorted time either by outright omission or by confusing chronological time with the temporal parameters of structural change. In contrast, an underlying premise of at least some of the models with which this chapter has been concerned is that it is both difficult and frequently misleading to interpret behavior without due consideration being given to historical-structural context. But how one asks and answers the question of what system time it is depends on the language or framework one employs. The three main historical-structural frameworks in international relations—structural realism, long-cycle, and world-economy—all approach this fundamental question of system time differently. These differences, in turn, have direct implications for explaining global war that need to be explored and clarified in chapter 4.

4

System Time and Its Phases:
Conflicting Images

The basic elements of the structural realist—long-cycle, and world-economy perspectives, as described in chapter 3—suggest areas of overlap and some of disagreement. The fundamental common denominator is the premise that the world system experiences more or less regular rhythms. In particular, one of the most significant rhythms is the concentration, deconcentration, and reconcentration of power in the system. Accompanying the fluctuations in power concentration is the intermittent leadership provided by a single state. It is an understanding of, and an appreciation for, these rhythms that is so essential to explaining a wide variety of socioeconomic and political behavior within and crossing national borders.

While there are other areas of agreement among scholars studying this dimension of world politics, it is their disagreements that are most significant for our interest in the relationship between system time and global war. By and large, the exclusive application of one perspective is likely to yield a historical timetable that is greatly different from the chronological guidelines offered by other perspectives. Since these conflicting timetables are the products of different assumptions and orientations, the discrepancies are usually understandable just as they are also compelling as objects of comparative testing. The discrepancies can also be revealing.

An excellent example is provided by the frequent, virtual absence of the idea of a system in structural realist analyses. Without a system, it is rather difficult to do much with the related idea of system time—one of the ways in which we can discern what point the system has reached in terms of its deconcentration-reconcentration rhythm. After we discuss the absence of system time and its implications in Gilpin's (1981) study, the focus will return to an empirical exploration of the conflicts in system phases found in world-economy and long-cycle analyses. Particular attention will be allocated to evaluating the predictive utility of the temporal schemes for capturing the timing of major-power warfare.

HEGEMONIC STABILITY AND THE ABSENCE OF SYSTEM TIME

Gilpin's focus on the hegemonic power as opposed to the structure of the system—a definitive characteristic of most hegemonic stability analyses—is quite representative of structural realism. In long-cycle and world-economy studies, the system leader also receives considerable attention. But in these approaches, systemic leadership/hegemonic power is viewed first as the embodiment of a systemic attribute—namely, structural concentration. In hegemonic stability analyses, it is the relative weight or clout of the hegemon vis-à-vis the other actors in the system that is emphasized first and last. For this reason, hegemonic stability analysts are apt to measure the hegemon's advantage in terms of country-to-country ratios (e.g., the hegemon versus a rival, as in a Britain:German ratio prior to 1913) of productivity or trade position advantages (see Krasner, 1976). A more systemic approach would involve calculating the leader's proportional edge over either the rest of the system or at least the system's elite.

Measurement strategies reflect underlying assumptions. There is also a difference between knowing that a system leader's edge over its most threatening rival has slipped 10 percent while its overall proportional lead, from a systemic perspective, remains unchanged or, alternatively, has slipped 20 percent. Similarly, there is a difference between knowing that one state has an edge over a number of others and knowing that the same state is the predominant state in the system. If nothing else, the minimal threshold for recognition is much lower in the former situation than in the latter. One consequence of this lower recognition threshold is that a hegemonic stability analyst is likely to ask which state is ahead at any given point in time rather than to ask which state, if any, is in a position to function as a system leader.

Since hegemonic stability analyses tend to be less than fully systemic in orientation, they also tend to have relatively lower expectations concerning leadership in the system.[1] It also makes it much less likely that they will pursue the type of phase movements associated with world-economy and long-cycle analyses. Whether readers judge these consequences favorably or not, Gilpin's specific approach to structural change suggests an additional problem. Long-cycle and world-economy analyses contend that a modern world system began to emerge in the late fifteenth/early sixteenth centuries. An implication that is quite explicit is that post-1500 systemic processes are not necessarily identical to pre-1500 processes. In particular, some attention is given to the subject of empires and the processes of imperial expansion. Prior to 1500, empires tended to dominate. After 1500, empires continued to exist and to be created, but they were much less likely to be predominant. To the extent that they did continue to predominate, as in the nineteenth-century case of the British empire, it can be argued that the empire was more of a consequence, than a cause, of the ascent to systemic leadership (Thompson and Zuk, 1986).

As Gilpin (1981:112, 131) himself points out, the imperial predilection for territorial expansion became a less efficient way for states to acquire wealth and power after the development of a world market economy—one of the factors differentiating the modern, trade-oriented system from the pre-modern, agrarian-based systems. The irony here is that Gilpin's theoretical logic for hegemonic behavior is predicated more on traditional behavior than it is on a form of systemic leadership that presumably is less imperial in flavor.

To defend this charge, it is necessary to look more closely at some of the material Gilpin relied upon in developing the perspective advanced in his 1981 study. One of the more frequently acknowledged debts is to Elvin's (1973) analysis of Chinese economic history.[2] In a discussion of the size of empires, Elvin argues that the expansion of a political unit is due to some form of organization, economic, or military superiority over its neighbors. Since these advantages are subject to diffusion, imperial size is apt to be unstable. However, the extent of its expansion tends to be determined by the balance of the empire's technological superiority versus the burdens of size. The greater the territorial size to be controlled, the more extensive are the size and costs of the bureaucracy and military. Therefore, "empires tend to expand to an equilibrium point at which they can just maintain their full extent" (Elvin, 1973:19).

This imperial-size logic resembles very closely Gilpin's cost-benefit calculus of structural change described in chapter 2. Consider, for example, two of the five generalizations that outline his hegemonic stability perspective (Gilpin, 1981:10–11):

3. A state will seek to change the international system through territorial, political, and economic expansion until the marginal costs of further change are equal to or greater than the marginal benefits.

4. Once an equilibrium between the costs and benefits of further change and expansion is reached, the tendency is for the economic costs of maintaining the status quo to rise faster than the economic capacity to support the status quo.

The point that is being stressed here is not the resemblance, a matter Gilpin fully acknowledges, but the imperial context of Elvin's argument. Elvin based his propositions on the behavior of the Chinese and, to a lesser extent, Roman empires. In contrast to Gilpin, however, Elvin cautioned readers against applying his generalizations across time indiscriminately. Discussing another generalization that is also adopted by Gilpin, Elvin (1973:20–21) states

> . . . the cost of the best military techniques tends to increase with time. In so far as a state has static revenues, or revenues rising more slowly than the cost of warfare, it will tend to fragment. . . . other things being equal, a reduction in the size of political units reduces the financial burdens of large geographical scale, and enables the resources to be saved to be put in weaponry.
>
> Now, manifestly, there is something absurd about this argument if it is applied indiscriminately to all historic periods, and thus to all states of technology. In contemporary terms, it amounts to saying that Switzerland or Mauretania should be better able to afford atomic bombs and missiles than the USA or USSR. The argument is rescued from such an unhappy conclusion by the all-important qualification that it must be limited to periods or areas where the financial burdens of scale are still significantly large relative to the cost of the best armaments. In modern times, this is no longer the case; and this fact is, indeed, one of the ways in which "modernity" may be partially defined.

A similar argument is advanced here. By extending the imperial model into the modern era (roughly post-1500 by world system standards), Gilpin unnecessarily constrains his model's motor to an anachronistic expansionist logic. Modern system leaders, whether we call them world powers or hegemonic powers, are engaged in a different sort of operation than their imperial predecessors. While some system leaders may have engaged in old-fashioned territorial expansion, this is not the principal barometer of their success. It may even be an indicator of decline. While technological superiority over neighbors may remain a consistent impulse for ascent in the world system (see chapter 6), there is a difference between the more limited edge offered by a bronze sword, a Viking long boat, a Mongolian stirrup, or a Chinese chariot and the greater complexities of more modern forms of technological superiority. The former facilitated raiding activities and conquest. The latter, which certainly encompasses military and transportation superiorities as well, made formal conquest and occupation even easier in some respects but much less necessary and, ultimately, even unfashionable. This is, indeed, "one of the ways in which modernity may be partially defined."

The place of empire is an obtrusive indicator in historical-structural analyses. If an argument is advanced for comparing Athens, Rome, or the Incas as direct analogues of post-1500 world system leaders, a faint alarm bell should be heard. The argument here is not that such comparisons are a waste of time. They need not be. Apples and oranges can be compared instructfully as long as we keep in mind which are the apples and which are the oranges. For that matter, it is fair to say that the possibilities of finding pre-1500 analogues to the post-1500 phenomenon of systemic leadership have not yet been exhausted. The study of comparative historical systems requires greater attention.[3] Until more work is completed in this area, it is premature to label everything before 1500 as one type of fruit and some of the things that happen after 1500 as another type. Nevertheless, the system time of empires is not very likely to be identical to the system time of the modern world system.[4]

WORLD SYSTEM TIME: DIFFERENCES OF OPINION

To some extent, new frameworks tend to be developed in reaction to earlier or prevailing frameworks. World-economy analysts are reacting, in part, to the modernization perspective in which the older, more industrialized states/societies are viewed as developed and the newer, less industrialized states/societies are viewed as in transit between the traditional and modern ends of the continuum. Rather than dwell on what are viewed as misleading characteristics of states and societies, the world-economy framework is a macroscopic approach that stresses instead the world system's core-periphery division of labor and the historical development of dependency and underdevelopment.

Long-cycle analysts hail from political science—a field in which the division of labor frequently segregates the examination of "comparative" (predominately within-states) and international (between-states) politics. Since development questions in political science are rightly or wrongly more often linked to within-state phenomena and since long-cycle analysis has emerged from the international side of the research enterprise, questions pertaining to societal modernization have not been of the highest priority. Indeed, the study of national development may be said to be in an arrested state of development.

World-economy and long-cycle analysts have converged on the world system from different levels of analysis (Waltz, 1959; Singer, 1961). While world-economy students are rejecting prevailing societal level assumptions and assertions, long-cycle students are reacting to studies of the international system that are characterized by a relatively ahistorical (or vastly different historical) point of view and a marked emphasis on the persistent anarchy of the interstate jungle. Structural realism, on the other hand, really represents only a modification, and often as not only a marginal modification, of the classical tradition to which long cyclists are reacting.

Systemic wars are far more important to the long-cycle framework than wars in general are to the world-economy school of thought. This difference stems from basic differences in the two alternative approaches to explaining the development of the world system. The world-economy framework focuses on capitalism and capital accumulation as the fundamental motors of systemic change. Other processes and events, as a consequence, tend to be relegated to subordinate, less central concerns.

In the case of war, world-economy analysts (Chase-Dunn and Sokolovsky, 1983) are willing to acknowledge that systemic wars perform several functions for the system. Wars provide a medium through which the struggle for dominance can be conducted. The mobility of states within the international stratification system can be facilitated. New power structures can also be developed through the agency of systemic war. Nonetheless, the principal role of systemic warfare continues to be one of functional maintenance. Systemic wars sustain the continued functioning of the capitalist world economy.

Long-cycle analysis, in contrast, is much more open ended as to the identity of the motors of systemic change. The phases of world power and global war, the respective high and low points of world order, however, are viewed as uniquely salient periods of time that reoccur. Theoretical emphasis has thus been devoted to empirically describing these periods and some of the processes that link them. Global war, especially, has immense significance as the periodic turning point in systemic transformation. It is the lever that switches the system from deconcentration to reconcentration. In view of this critical role, it would be rather difficult for long cyclists to subordinate global war to other processes. In other words, something that is secondary to the world-economy perspective is regarded as primary by the long-cycle perspective.

Basic Rhythms

These differences in origin and emphasis notwithstanding, the problem remains that the behavioral explanations and predictions that are used to evaluate the utility of the frameworks are so closely tied to the temporal phases—the hour hands of the different system time clocks. One graphic illustration of this problem is supplied in table 4.1. An important rhythm for the world-economy perspective is the expansion and contraction of the world-economy. We are told to expect increased rivalry and war among the core powers during the B phases as they

Table 4.1

Dating Phases of Economic Expansion/Contraction, Global Wars, and Long Cycles

Period	Economic Phase	Global Wars/Cycles	Period
		Italian/Indian Ocean Wars	1494–1517
		Long Cycle I	
Early 1500s– 1620/50	A		
		Spanish Wars	1580–1608
		Long Cycle II	
1620/50–1720/50	B		
		French Wars	1688–1713
		Long Cycle III	
1720/50–1814	A		
		French Wars	1792–1815
		Long Cycle IV	
1814–1849	B		
1849–1873	A		
1873–1896	B		
1896–1929	A	German Wars	1914–1945
1919–1938/45	B	Long Cycle V	
1938/45–1970	A		
1970–	B		

Note: The A and B phase dates are taken from Bousquet (1980:48).

attempt to minimize the impact of contraction. From a different point of view, however, it is the long cycle of world leadership that is the world system's primary rhythm. The most intensive period of conflict and war among the global powers, in this interpretation, occurs toward the end of each long cycle as the global powers struggle for the succession to the world power position. Is it possible that both perspectives are correct and provide accurate predictions?

Table 4.1 provides information on the dating of the world-economy's A and B phases in conjunction with the previously reported long-cycle durations and the timing of the global wars. The A/B phases and the long cycles are not too well synchronized. An A phase characterizes most of the length of the first and third long cycles, while a B phase parallels the decay of world power in the second long cycle. The fourth long cycle encompasses several A and B phases. The fifth long cycle may also experience more than one A and B phase.

Of course, neither long cyclists nor world-economists need necessarily be disturbed by the general lack of correlation between A/B economic phases and long cycles of world leadership. But a more telling divergence occurs when one matches the global wars with the lengths of the A/B phases. Of the six sets of global war, four (Italian/Indian Ocean, Spanish, second French, and the first German) apparently took place during periods of economic expansion (A phases). If one regards these six sets of wars as the most intensive and significant periods of world warfare, the assertion of a relationship between B phases and core power conflict and warfare is not particularly well supported in terms of the incidence of global wars.[5]

Systemic Leadership Differences

Turning to the subject of the rise and fall of world powers, another important world-system process, similar problems of discrepancy are encountered. As demonstrated in table 4.2, world-economy students focus on three hegemonic powers in the modern history of the world economy. Long cyclists see five world powers, if Great Britain is counted twice. Hegemonic stability analysts are apt to recognize at least one and sometimes two hegemons. The major differences of identification thus revolve around Portugal in the sixteenth century, the Netherlands in the seventeenth century, and Britain in the eighteenth century. Only after the Napoleonic Wars does anything resembling a consensus emerge.

In addition, there is substantial disagreement in estimates of the length of tenure of the world's system leaders. Essentially, these dis-

agreements, as are the differences of identification, are readily traceable to different definitions and different readings of systemic history.
The world-economy perspective's definitional focus on hegemonic
powers as leaders in terms of agricultural/industrial productivity, commerce, and finance dismisses Portugal as a spice-trading state. Spices
are regarded as a luxury item as opposed to the essential or basic
economic commodities that a dominant power must control. Just how
dispensable spices were to the European economy, however, is subject
to some debate (Parry, 1966).

Long cyclists and world-economy analysts disagree more about the
period in which the Netherlands was a systemic leader than they do
about its leader status. That is, the seventeenth-century Dutch satisfy
both camps' definitions, but the structural realism definitions that are
available are usually too stringent (see chapter 6) to admit any
seventeenth-century state. Similarly, the dispute over whether Britain
was a systemic leader before the Napoleonic Wars hinges on whether
the emphasis is placed on economic dominance or naval standing.

The long-cycle school's definition of world power emphasizes the
concentration of global military resources, especially naval force. Unlike the hegemonic powers in the structural realist and world-economy
perspectives, the long cycle definition is provided specific operationalization. A world power must control 50 percent of the global powers'
pertinent military resources immediately after a global war, even
though this is unlikely to be the case at later points in the same long
cycle. Hegemonic powers remain hegemonic only as long as they
maintain their dominance. In the long-cycle perspective, world powers
may lose their naval superiority and yet retain the systemic role designation until they are displaced during or after a global war.

Given these different definitional connotations and procedural conventions, it might seem that the contents of table 4.2 refer to dissimilar,
incomparable phenomena. Nor is there any compelling reason to expect a single state to achieve leadership in both economic and military
spheres simultaneously. Consequently, alarm is not necessarily warranted if two observers assign different respective dates to the
perceived achievement of economic and military superiority. Unfortunately for world-systems analyses, there are several problems with this
justification. First, the "incompatibility" thesis overlooks the causality
question. Which comes first? Does economic superiority precede military predominance or vice versa? Which goes first? Does economic
superiority decay more quickly than military predominance or vice
versa? Alternatively, does it make any difference which comes and/or

Table 4.2

Hegemonic and World Powers

System Leaders	Hegemonic Stability	World Economy*	Long Cycle
Portugal			1517–1580
Netherlands		1620–1672	1609–1713
Great Britain			1714–1815
	1816–?	1815–1873	1816–1945
United States	1945–?	1945–1967	1946–

*World-economy hegemonic tenure estimates vary by source. The tenure dates reported in this table are taken from the discussion in Wallerstein (1984:37–46).

goes first in terms of the decline of world power and expectations about its foreign policy behavior? These are not issues that can be readily dismissed.

Second, is it theoretically or empirically conceivable that a state can be the leading state in the world system in terms of economic (military) capabilities but not necessarily in terms of military (economic) capabilities? Wallerstein (1984), for one, implies that hegemonic powers tend to develop equally great military strength. Modelski (1981), for another, contends that world powers are likely to be strong economically if only to be able to afford to pay for their military strength. Thus, their answers to this second question are in the negative. But, if this is the case, does it make sense to argue for the superiority of one perspective's emphasis over another's? Will not the unraveling of the correlation and chronologically sequencing between economic and military power concentration provide us with roughly equivalent information about system time?

System Phases

Third, and returning more directly to the question of system time, what are we to make of the differences in system phases that key on the rise and decline of world powers? The hegemonic stability model, of course, is not very helpful in this regard. It is entirely silent on the possibility of phases within either the decline or the more rarely discussed ascent periods. Long cyclists, however, divide each interval into four phases: world power, delegitimation, deconcentration, and global war. Each phase is differentiable, at least in part, by the amount of capability decay experienced by the world power. Each phase is also characterized by expectations of different behavior on the part of both global and nonglobal actors. For instance, relatively greater amounts of conflict are theoretically anticipated and empirically found (see Modelski and Thompson, 1980, 1981/1987) in the delegitimation and global war phases than in the other two phases. In addition, we are told to expect nationalistic challenges in the delegitimation phase and intensive conflict between the global powers in the global war phase.

Although it was not discussed in the section describing the world-economy perspective, Wallerstein, with a group of other analysts (see Research Working Group on Cyclical Rhythms and Secular Trends, 1979), has also advanced a four-phase process of hegemony outlined in table 4.3.[6] As in the four phases of the long cycle, two of the four hegemonic phases are characterized by relatively greater conflict. Conflict is said to be more acute in the phases of ascending and declining hegemony than in the phases of hegemonic victory and maturity. We are also told to expect that the conflict will take place between the core rivals for the hegemonic power position. Preemptive maneuvers in the periphery are most likely to occur during the declining hegemony phase.

Nevertheless, if one tries to match the two sets of four phases over time, the same type of lack of correspondence previously encountered in table 4.1 is discovered. Table 4.4 lists the respective dates assigned to the alternative sets of phases for the periods associated with Dutch, British, and American supremacy/leadership. Several observations are

Table 4.3

Phases of Hegemony and Associated Behavioral Patterns

Hegemonic Phases	Behavioral Expectations
Ascending hegemony	Acute conflict between rivals to succession
Hegemonic victory	New hegemonic power bypasses old hegemonic power in decline
Hegemonic maturity	True hegemony—competition between the hegemonic power and other core states in free-trade, generally open system
Declining hegemony	Acute conflict of old hegemonic power versus successors—rival core powers move to preempt potential peripheral zones

Source: Based on information in Research Working Group on Cyclical Rhythms and Secular Trends (1979:498).

generated by the comparison. The most obvious comment one can make about these phase comparisons is that the world-economy perspective bypasses the 97-year period between 1701 and 1797 that encompasses much of the third long cycle (of Great Britain's first long cycle). It is not clear how we should interpret this lengthy gap. It seems most unlikely that the second leading core power in the world-economy perspective—Great Britain—made no improvement (ascendancy) in its agricultural/industrial, commercial, and/or financial/investment status during what is essentially the eighteenth century. For that matter, Wallerstein's (1980b:145–189) own description of the first two-thirds of this period hardly squares with an extended interruption of the rise and fall of the economic powers process.

Second, the phases do not overlap well. It does seem reasonable to equate roughly the phases, if not the concepts, of hegemonic maturity and world power. In the cases of the Dutch and American hegemonies/leadership, there is considerable overlap in the assigned dates. However, the two British world power phases are not matched particularly well. As noted above, there is no correspondence with the first world-power phase. By the time the world-economy perspective accords hegemonic maturity to the British, they are well into the second phase of political and military decay.

This lack of match for the nineteenth-century British case underscores a general distinction, vis-à-vis historical-structural phases, between the two perspectives. The world-economy perspective emphasizes economic ascendancy and arrival at the top in the first three of its phases. However, three phases of the long cycle perspective emphasize positional decay. Thus, it is possible to describe the same historical-structural era as characterized primarily by ascent from one perspective and decay from the other. In this respect, the world-economy perspective on hegemonic power can be described as oriented toward a future period of dominance, while the long-cycle perspective is oriented toward the movement away from a period of post-war politico-military supremacy.

Metaphorically, it is as if both schools of thought are describing the configuration of a roller coaster. However, where one view focuses on a long upward slope, the other view perceives a long downward slope. And they disagree over where in the world system's rhythmic time series a true "inflection point" (as a mathematician would term a turning point in the direction of a series) should be located. In the comparison of the two perspectives, it is not clear whether one or two dissynchronized laws of gravity are at work.[7]

THE SYNCHRONIZATION AND UTILITY OF WORLD-SYSTEM PHASES: AN EMPIRICAL EXAMINATION

Whatever the number of laws of gravity at work in the world system, one would still expect some degree of overlap between the long cycle's periods of high naval power concentration and the world-economy perspective's periods of economic hegemony. Some discrepancy might be expected if it is true that economic hegemony precedes and leads to the creation of corresponding military predominance. In such a case the underlying causal ordering would allow a period of economic hegemony to exist immediately prior to the establishment of any equivalent military leadership. It would seem unlikely that military leadership could exist in the absence of economic hegemony—at least from the perspective of the world-economy school. If the lag between economic hegemony and military preponderance is reasonably short, it might also be hypothesized that the military capabilities of future hegemons would surpass those of declining hegemons at about the same time as the passage in economic terms.

Hegemonic Phases and Naval Power Concentration

The conceptualization and measurement of hegemony is complicated and deserves treatment as a project in its own right. For present purposes, the dating scheme advanced by the Research Working Group (1979), in the absence of closure on this troublesome problem, will be utilized as an approximate guide to the coming and going of economic hegemony. This means that new hegemonic powers passed old powers in decline in the following phases of hegemonic victory: 1590–1620, 1815–1850, and 1913/20–1945. Periods of full economic hegemony (or hegemonic maturity) are found within the 1620–1650, 1850–1873, and 1945–1967 intervals.

In contrast to the hegemonic power cycle, considerable attention has been devoted to the question of operationalizing the idea of naval power in the long-cycle scheme. Capital ship and naval expenditure indicators on ocean-going sea power are available from 1494 (Modelski and Thompson, 1988). From this perspective, the naval leadership threshold is set at 50 percent of the combined capabilities of the qualifying global powers. Use of a minimal threshold does not mean that leadership necessarily is forfeited when the dividing line is not longer equalled or exceeded. Yet an explicit threshold can be useful for signaling when superiority is clearly evident just as one might employ some similar benchmark for productive, commercial, and financial superiority.

Tables 4.4 and 4.5 summarize information pertinent to the question of the extent to which economic hegemony and naval leadership are synchronized. As noted in table 4.4, each of the periods of economic hegemony tend to be coterminous with periods of high naval-power concentration. Nevertheless, two other facets of table 4.4 are of particular interest. First and not surprisingly by now, two clusters of high naval power concentration (1502–1544, 1719–1723) are not associated with corresponding years of economic hegemony. While it might be tempting to dismiss the 1719–1923 cluster as a too brief aberration, the five-year peak in concentration values is actually highly misleading. Between 1714 and 1750, the mean naval concentration value is .472, which indicates that this postglobal war period behaves much like the other four except that the concentration values tend to hover just below the .500 threshold in a good many of the immediate postwar years.

The main point is that there are three "humps" in the economic hegemony cycle while there are five in the naval power series. As expected then, it has been true historically that periods of economic superiority have also been periods of naval superiority. The two measures of power exhibit a high level of covariation. Yet there have been periods of naval power concentration that have not been identified as hegemonic in the world-economy perspective's terms.

The second interesting factor found in table 4.4 is located in the initial dates of the naval leadership clusters. Whereas the earliest asserted beginning dates for economic hegemony are 1620, 1850, and 1945, the naval power concentration threshold is first exceeded in 1608, 1809, and 1944 respectively. Two of the temporal gaps (1608/ 1620 and 1944/1945) are not all that spectacular but, in each case, it can be said that naval superiority "predates" (or is at least coterminous with) the economic hegemonic tenures advanced by the Research Working Group. Moreover, the .500 threshold is first exceeded in four of the five cases during a year of global warfare. The one exception (1719) involves only a short lag after the end of global warfare in 1713. We will return to this point in chapter 7 for it reveals something uniquely significant about the process of naval power concentration.

Table 4.5 amplifies the findings summarized in table 4.4 in several respects. Two of the rising system leaders, the Netherlands in 1602 and the United States in 1941, created global naval capabilities that exceeded the capabilities of the declining system leaders within the appropriate periods of "hegemonic victory." If we take the earliest beginning dates of hegemonic victory as givens (1590, 1815, and 1913/ 20), the implication is that a future leader passes a declining leader first in terms of economic capabilities and then in terms of military capabilities. One could view this tentative implication as offsetting the timing of economic and naval capability peaks in table 4.4. But the generalizability of power-passage timing is qualified markedly by England's 1676 development of a naval capability superior to the Dutch. Parenthetically, it is also probably worth noting that this "passage" put the English only in second place in the naval ranks of the period. France had already outbuilt the Dutch. A few more decades were to pass before the English were able to overtake the French during a subsequent period of global war.

Table 4.4

Disagreements in Dating Historical Phases of the World System

Netherlands

Ascending hegemony	1575–1590		
Hegemonic victory	1590–1620	Global War	1580–1608
Hegemonic maturity	1620–1650	World power	1609–1634
Declining hegemony	1650–1700	Delegitimation	1635–1661
		Deconcentration	1662–1713

Great Britain

		Global War	1688–1713
		World power	1714–1738
		Delegitimation	1739–1763
		Deconcentration	1764–1791
Ascending hegemony	1798–1815		
Hegemonic victory	1815–1850	Global War	1792–1815
Hegemonic maturity	1850–1873	World power	1816–1840
Declining hegemony	1873–1897	Delegitimation	1841–1872
		Deconcentration	1873–1913

United States

Ascending hegemony	1897–1913/20		
Hegemonic victory	1913/20–1945	Global War	1914–1945
Hegemonic maturity	1945–1967	World power	1946–1972
Declining hegemony	1967–	Delegitimation	1973–

Note: the dating of the phases is based on information reported in Research Working Group on Cyclical Rhythms and Secular Trends (1979:499) and Modelski and Thompson (1981/1987).

Table 4.5

Hegemonic Maturity and High Military Concentration Values

Periods of Hegemonic Maturity	Years of Naval Power Concentration*
	Portugal 1502–44
	Spain 1594–97
Netherlands 1620–50	Netherlands 1608–19, 1624, 1632–33, 1635–36, 1640–42
	Britain 1719–23
Britain 1850–73**	Britain 1809–12, 1814–34, 1843, 1854–57, 1861, 1880–81, 1889–90
United States 1945–67	United States 1944–

*Values greater than or equal to .500.

**Some world-economy analysts prefer an 1815–73 date for British hegemony.

Data Source: Hegemonic maturity dates (Research Working Group on Cyclical Rhythms and Secular Trends, 1979:499); naval power concentration (Modelski and Thompson, 1988).

The second qualification to the question of hegemonic victory passages is associated with the absence of military passage in the 1815–1850 period. Great Britain managed to succeed itself as world power in 1816 by long-cycle standards. Between the global warfare in 1688–1713 and World War I, Great Britain's naval leadership was never seriously challenged by a single rival—even if the same assertion can not be made about the eighteenth-century's sporadic coalitions of naval rivals to the British position. Hence the findings summarized in tables 4.4 and 4.5 reaffirm the mixed picture of the synchronicity of hegemonic power and naval power concentration. Juxtaposing the two perspectives yields outcomes that are only sometimes in step with one another.

Patterns of Conflict

Neither of these orientations need be considered inherently superior or inferior per se, but the contrasting orientations do make for substantial differences in recording and recognizing past and current system time. Whether either orientation is more or less useful in terms of explaining and predicting behavior, as usual, remains very much a theoretical and empirical question. Another limited example of this problem can be supplied by considering, once again, comparable predictions about when to expect more conflictual relations among the system's leading powers. Within the world-economy school of thought, we are told to expect intensive core rivalry primarily in the first (ascending hegemony) and fourth (declining hegemony) phases. Alternatively, the long-cycle approach puts forward its delegitimation and global war phases as the periods during which one is most likely to encounter conflict between the global powers.

Focusing on warfare between the global powers as one restrictive, although important, indicator of conflict, it is possible to conduct a quick test of the relative utility of these predictions. Table 4.6 provides a 412-year period of overlap (1575–the present) for the two sets of structural phases. If we then relate table 4.7's amount of warfare between two or more global powers in terms of the years associated with the two sets of structural phases, the outcome reported in table 4.8 emerges.

Two features of table 4.8 need to be underscored. While the 1575 point was selected as a mutual beginning point for information about the two sets of phases, the number of years at risk is not the same for both perspectives. The world-economy phase delineation omits the 1701–1798 period, which eliminates 98 years from its test that is included on the long-cycle side of the ledger. Secondly, proportionality in the table is computed in terms of how many war years are concentrated in each phase (as opposed to war years as a proportion of the total number of years in each phase). One of the reasons for this approach to

Table 4.6

Hegemonic Victory and Years of Military Power "Passage"

Periods of Hegemonic Victory	Year Future Leader Passed Declining Leader's Naval Power Score
1590–1620	1602 (Netherlands)
	1676 (England)
1815–1850	None applicable
1913/20–1945	1941 (United States)

Data Source: Hegemonic victory dates (Research Working Group on Cyclical Rhythms and Secular Trends, 1979:499); naval power concentration (Modelski and Thompson, 1988).

calculation is that the number of years associated with any of the eight phases is uneven. It is difficult to compare the war propensity of a phase with only 58 years with a phase with as many as 96 or 134 years. Accordingly, the fairest way to test these phase predictions is to first calculate the distribution of years and then determine whether the distribution of war years deviates from what we might expect if we only knew how many years were regarded as phase X as opposed to phase Y.

A more supportive outcome for the long-cycle phase prediction, in comparison to the world-economy predictions, is registered in table 4.8. War years are somewhat more likely to be associated with the ascending hegemony phase, but the same cannot be said for the phase of declining hegemony. In contrast, the long-cycle's global war phase is clearly the deadliest or more war-prone phase as predicted. Also as expected, the second most war-prone phase is that of delegitimation. Together the two phases account for nearly three-quarters of the 181 years of global warfare.

This sort to test is certainly less than conclusive, given the multiple forms manifested by economic and political conflict. But the test outcome does suggest that the long-cycle approach is the relatively more powerful of the two perspectives when it comes to specifying systemic phases of intensive conflict between the system's major actors.[8]

CONCLUSION

The differences between, as well as the respective advantages and disadvantages of, the world-economy, structural realist, and long cycle of world leadership perspectives could easily be pursued at greater length and in more detail. To some extent, this type of exercise will indeed continue in some of the chapters to follow, especially chapters 5, 6, and 10, where other dimensions of the conceptual and measurement problems are brought into the picture. Rather than dwell too long on this preoccupation, this seems an appropriate point to summarize some of the direct implications of the present discussion of system time for the analysis of power deconcentration, structural change, and global war.

Long cyclists would most certainly agree with one world-economist's (Wallerstein, 1980b:245) advice that "one cannot analyze social phenomena unless one bounds them in space and time." Practitioners of both schools of thought would also agree that a meaningful comprehension of current affairs requires an appreciation of the historical evolution of the world system in terms of both secular trends and cyclical

Portugal	Spain	France	England/ Britain	Netherlands
	1494–1500	1494–1500		
	1502–1505	1502–1505		
	1510–1513	1510–1516	1510–1514	
	1515–1516			
	1521–1530	1521–1530	1522–1523	
	1536–1538	1536–1538		
	1542–1544	1542–1560	1542–1546	
	1547–1559		1549–1550	
			1557–1560	
1579–1580	1579–1608	1589–1598	1585–1603	1579–1608
	1621–1659	1626–1630	1624–1630	1611–1648
		1635–1659	1652–1659	1652–1654
	1667–1668	1665–1668	1663–1667	1663–1667
	1673–1678	1672–1678	1671–1674	1671–1678
	1682–1684	1683–1684		
	1688–1697	1688–1697	1688–1697	1688–1697
	1701–1713	1701–1713	1701–1713	1701–1713
	1718–1720	1718–1720	1718–1720	1719–1720
	1727–1728	1727–1728	1726–1728	
	1733–1738	1722–1738	1739–1738	1743–1748
		1742–1748		
	1761–1763	1755–1763	1755–1763	
	1779–1783	1778–1783	1788–1783	1780–1783
	1793–1802	1793–1815	1793–1815	1793–1810
	1804–1808			
		1854–1856	1853–1856	
		1870–1871		
		1914–1918	1914–1918	
		1939–1940	1939–1945	
		1944–1945		

Source: Modelski and Thompson (1981).

regularities. From a historical-structural perspective, it is then elementary that analyses and evaluations of foreign policy, the decline of power, or the onset of global war be linked to the appropriate identification of system time as an important contextual parameter.

7

tween the Global Powers

Russia/ USSR	United States	Germany	Japan
1733–1738			
1742–1748			
1757–1763			
1799–1802			
1805–1807			
1812–1815			
1854–1856			
		1870–1871	
1904–1905			1904–1905
1914–1917	1917–1918	1914–1918	1914–1918
1941–1945	1939–1945	1939–1945	1941–1945

In addition, long cyclists and world-economists would agree that the relative positional decline of the world system's strongest power is quite probable, and perhaps inevitable, given the historical record and the nature of the world system's basic structures and processes. In terms of the analysis of the decline of systemic leadership and global war, the most appropriate question is not whether it is conceivable that the current system leader is experiencing relative positional decline. Rather, the relevant questions to be investigated are to what extent has the system leader's relative position declined and what types of policy behavior should be anticipated as a consequence of different stages of positional decline.

Nevertheless, long cyclists and world-economists disagree about how to calculate system time. This disagreement is not trivial, for it reflects central disagreements about the nature of key systemic structures and processes. So far, there have been few, if any, explicit attempts to bridge these differences over the relative significance of military-

Table 4.8

Structural Phases and Global Power Warfare, 1575–1986

Structural Phases	Number of Years	Proportional Number of Years	Number of War Years	Proportional Number of War Years
World Economy:				
1. Ascending hegemony	58	.175	35	.259
2. Hegemonic victory	100	.301	32	.237
3. Hegemonic maturity	78	.235	31	.230
4. Declining hegemony	96	.289	37	.274
5. Ascending/ declining hegemony	154	.464	72	.533
Long-Cycle:				
1. Global war	134	.326	86	.475
2. World power	101	.246	25	.138
3. Delegitimation	93	.226	47	.260
4. Deconcentra- tion	83	.202	23	.127
5. Delegitima- tion/global war	227	.552	133	.735

political and economic structures and processes. However, it would seem to be an extremely dubious proposition that foreign policy behavior, particularly foreign policy behavior associated with the decay of world power and the onset of global war, can be comprehended in exclusively military-political or economic terms. Nor is this really what is at stake in the disagreements about system time.

It is not simply or exclusively a question of military-political interpretations versus economistic interpretations. Scholars in both camps would be among the first to deny that they slight one sphere of activity in preference for another. Yet the questions that are asked, the way they are asked, and the paradigmatic origins of the two systemic perspectives do tend to tilt the consequent analyses. There may not be much that can or should be done to correct the tilt. But at the very least and regardless of perspective affinities or allegiances, we do require a better understanding of the relationship and interaction between military-political and economic structures and processes.

The divergences between the world-economy and long-cycle perspectives are particularly relevant to an understanding of the contemporary era. It may well prove to be inappropriate to argue that the current period of "hegemonic decline" is analogous to earlier periods of "hegemonic decline." Similarly, it may also prove to be inappropriate to contend that the current phase of "delegitimation" is similar to earlier periods of "delegitimation." Juxtaposing the two historical-structural perspectives' arguments and evidence, it appears that naval superiority preceded economic superiority in the Dutch and British eras of leadership. Contrarily, economic superiority preceded military predominance in the American era. However, the decay of Dutch and British military superiority appears to have been less rapid than that of their relative economic positions. While the American case is awkward because its leadership history is still in progress, it appears that the relative American economic position peaked in the 1950s, if not earlier (see chapter 6) and has continued to decline since that time. This relative economic decline either precedes the decline of relative American military power or roughly parallels the decay in military position.

The precise implications of these macrohistorical comparisons are not yet clear, but the differences between the Dutch/British and American eras may reflect important structural novelties in the current era. If so, it can be expected that the structural or decay pattern differences should bear some significant consequences for systemic leadership decline and the prospects for global war. But then the similarities may work to offset the differences and keep the system on its established structural track. System time will tell. Whose version of system time remains to be seen.

It is also pertinent to note that, with hindsight, it is fairly easy to identify the primary rivals or challengers in the Dutch (England and France) and British (France and later the United States and Germany) eras. The same identification is less easily made in the current era. The Soviet Union is, of course, the obvious military rival, but no single state has yet approximated or even approached the general American position of economic strength. Assuming continued economic gains on the part of Japan, just how long might it take for the Japanese to adopt the traditional guise of a challenger? Then too, long cyclists argue that a system leader can renew, and one did renew, its positional lead. From this point of view, there is historical precedent for the United States recreating its post-World War II position. The only problem is that is seems most unlikely that such positional improvement could be realized in the aftermath of a world war III.

However, or whether, we learn how to alter the way the system has worked, the basic point remains that we have much to learn about the structures and processes of the world system. Greater elaboration, improvement, and perhaps some degree of synthesis of the structural realist, long-cycle, and world-economy schools of thought is in order before we may expect to be able to tell system time with any degree of precision. This is precisely what is attempted in the next eight chapters. Each chapter is devoted to a specific question or set of related questions that pertain to structural changes, continuities, and global war. Each chapter seeks to elaborate our understanding of the selected topic(s) via empirical inquiry with an eye toward synthesis whenever possible or appropriate. Finally, each chapter endeavors to contribute to improving the accuracy of our ability to monitor the movement of system time.

Chapter 5 focuses on the basic timing of systemic warfare. After critically reviewing earlier efforts, largely of the classical stripe, to identify phases of war and peace in the post-1500 era, a less inductive, if equally empirically grounded, analysis of systemic war candidates will enable us to discriminate between those wars that reconcentrate the system and those that do not.

5

Looking for Cycles of War and Peace

For those who wish to make a case for repetitive regularities in the occurrence of warfare, or at least certain types of warfare, the following two passages might seem comforting:

> Confronted with what might otherwise be a mysterious conundrum or a vast buzzing welter, we have devised all sorts of models and metaphors as a means of imposing coherence. . . . When it comes to war—a type of social event that is clearly the result of complex and interdependent processes—the tendency to fall back on one or another of these simple models is particularly acute. . . . From among the inexorable trend (toward or away), the cyclical and the stochastic models, modern man seems to prefer the cyclical. The trend model seems too teleological and the stochastic model seems too nihilistic, whereas the cyclical one has a certain aura of *a priori* plausibility in the twentieth century. After all, who amongst us is eager to embrace the implicit assumption of a largely beneficent, or essentially malevolent, or utterly capricious cosmos? Somehow, the notion that war comes and goes with some regularity seems to be the assumption that is least offensive to contemporary sensibilities (Singer and Cusack, 1981:404–406).
>
> As widely held as the belief that war is on the increase is the belief that war comes and goes in some clear and recurrent cyclical pattern (Small and Singer, 1982:143).

Yet is it really true that the belief that war is cyclical is widespread? Does twentieth-century man really prefer the plausibility of the cycle to the teleology of the trend or the nihilism of the stochastic perturbation? If so, why then are empirically grounded, cyclical models and analyses of war so rare? For that matter, why is there so much skeptical resistance to the idea that certain cyclical rhythms are fundamental to the unraveling of world politics? A variety of answers to these partially rhetorical questions is conceivable. Nevertheless, cyclical analyses are hardly the norm and academic skepticism is sufficiently abundant that it is quite easy to argue that the following summary evaluation comes closer than the ones above to capturing the prevailing outlook on cycles of war and peace.

> History seems to be neither as monotonous and uninventive as the partisans of the strict periodicities and "iron laws" and "universal uniformities" think; nor so dull and mechanical as an engine making the same number of revolutions in a unit of time. It repeats its "themes" but almost always with new variations. In this sense it is ever new, and ever old, so far as the ups and downs are repeated. So much for periodicity, rhythms, and uniformity (Sorokin, 1937:359–60).

While it is possible to contend that Sorokin's view is more representative of the academic community than the views expressed by Singer, Small, and Cusack, it is equally important to point out that Sorokin's conclusion was made nearly inevitable by one of his fundamental premises. Cycles require precise periodicities according to Sorokin. A fifty-year war cycle, therefore, could not have a forty-five-year length in one period and then last for fifty-five years in the next sequence. The two waves might average at fifty years, but averages are meaningless in the Sorokin view. Yet to require such precision of social and political rhythms seems both unreasonable and naive. Most observers, for example, accept the existence of business cycles. While those same observers may disagree about their casual mechanisms, few, if any, believe that business cycles are characterized by precise periodicities.

Although Sorokin is often cited approvingly by cyclical skeptics, his insistence on unwavering precision is consistently ignored. This trait—the tendency to overlook central premises—is also characteristic of much of the literature on cycles of war and peace. On the one hand, we have a small empirical literature that has attempted to model war cycles along fairly inductive lines. If or when evidence for a cycle (or cycles) is uncovered, some effort may then be made to account for the discovery. But, generally, the support for the existence of cycles of war produced by these efforts has been uneven and often amorphous.

On the other hand, we have a small theoretical literature on cycles of what are variously referred to as general, hegemonic, or global wars. This second literature, which admittedly is of fairly recent origin for the most part, is often overlooked as a source of hypotheses, or, more simply, misinterpreted by the first group. Yet many analysts seem to think that the inductive modeling efforts somehow address the empirical validity of arguments pertaining to the repetition of systemic wars. To the contrary, as will be argued in this chapter, the evidence produced by the first group has little bearing on the claims of the second group, the inductive modeling efforts have been looking for cycles of war and peace in all the wrong places.

In order to elaborate on these assertions, we need to first review the nature of the inductive evidence for cycles of war and peace and then contrast this evidence with the types of arguments put forward by the analysts of repetitive systemic wars. It should become clear that there is an important conceptual gap between what has been modeled and what historical-structural analysts would like to see modeled.

THE INDUCTIVE MODELING LITERATURE

Wright

Any discussion of warfare can hardly overlook the work of Quincy Wright (1942/1965). As in the case of so many other war-related topics, Wright also touched upon the subject of cyclical oscillations. While his observations are often cited as justification for analyzing cycles of war, the nature of his basic generalization on this topic is less than straightforward in meaning.

> In addition to these three periods—the normal battle period of a day, the campaign period of a season, and the war period of four or five years—a longer period may be detected. There appears to have been a tendency in the last three centuries for concentrations of warfare to occur in approximately fifty-year oscillations, each alternate period of concentration being more severe. The period is not discernible in the sixteenth century and is scarcely noticeable in the seventeenth century. The War of the Spanish Succession (1701–14) occurred less than a century after the Thirty Years' War (1618–48), but there were several important wars initiated by Louis XIV between these two great wars. The War of the Spanish Succession was followed in about another century by the World War (1914–18, renewed in 1939). In the mid-eighteenth century a concentration of wars centered about the Seven Year's War (1756–63) and in the mid-nineteenth century about the Crimean War and the wars of Italian and German nationalism (Wright, 1942/1965:227).

Taken at face value, the passage seems to suggest the following sequence: the Thirty Years' War; the wars of Louis XIV; the War of the
Spanish Succession; wars centered around the Seven Years' War; the
Napoleonic Wars; the Crimean War and the Italian/German wars of
nationalism; World War I; World War II. But to accept this sequence as
meaningful, at least one of two conditions would first have to be satisfied. Either this listing would have to exhaust the system's inventory of
warfare or that of a significant group of actors such as the great powers
during the period encompassed by the observation. Or, Wright would
have to have made a case for these wars as being of special categorical
interest. It's clear that the first condition is not satisfied. Wright provides a detailed list of the warfare between 1480 and 1940 that includes
a number of nonmentioned wars for the post-Thirty Years' War period.

It seems also clear that Wright was not thinking of great-power warfare as a separate class. Elsewhere in his encyclopedic tome, Wright
presents a list of fifteen "general wars," which are reproduced in table
5.1. Wright does not define the concept of general war, but he appears
to be isolating periods of concentrated great-power warfare in which all
or most of the great powers participate for at least two years or more.
While he does specifically name the fifteen wars listed in table 5.1,
Wright also muddied the issue a bit by identifying other great-power
wars ongoing more or less simultaneously with these events—of which
only some can be linked as directly or even indirectly related.

In any event, most of the wars mentioned in the quoted paragraph can
be found in table 5.1, but not all of them are there (i.e., the Italian/
German wars of nationalism are missing). Yet there are also wars listed
in table 5.1 that are missing from the paragraph on the fifty-year periodicity (e.g., the War of the Quadruple Alliance, the War of the Polish
Succession). Upon examining the chronological sequence found in table 5.1, we also see that there is no discernible fifty-year pattern. Up to
the midnineteenth century, each successive war is separated by no more
than fifteen years and often less. Moreover, if we assign each ongoing
war to the appropriate fifty-year aggregations beginning in 1600, as is
done in table 5.1's last column, no alternating sequence of more or less
warfare is apparent.

Wright did, of course, advance a variety of other conceptual distinctions between types of warfare (e.g., balance of power wars versus
imperial wars), but most of these types would produce far greater frequencies and more continuous durations than the set of great-power
general wars. The one possible exception is Wright's (1942/1965:359-
367) discussion of "political trends" in European international politics

Table 5.1

Wright's General Wars

General Wars	Dates	Fifty-Year War Ongoing Aggregations
		1600–1649
1. Thirty Years' War	1618–1648	
2. Franco-Spanish War	1648–1659	
		1650–1699
3. First Coalition against Louis XIV	1672–1679	
4. Second Coalition against Louis XIV	1688–1697	
		1700–1749
5. War of the Spanish Succession	1701–1714	
6. War of the Quadruple Alliance	1718–1720	
7. War of the Polish Succession	1733–1738	
8. War of the Austrian Succession	1740–1748	
		1750–1799
9. Seven Years' War	1756–1763	
10. American Revolution	1778–1783	
11. French Revolutionary Wars	1792–1802	
		1800–1849
12. Napoleonic Wars	1805–1815	
		1850–1899
13. Crimean War	1854–1856	
		1900–1949
14. World War I	1914–1919	
15. World War II	1939–1945	

Source: Wright (1942/1965:647–649).

that he asserted were characterized by four successively different ways of dealing with instability (territorial sovereignty, balance of power, concert of power, and nationality). Each of these four epochal conceptions was "successively recognized in the treaties terminating the great wars." In turn, the "great wars" (also referred to as the great transitional wars) to which Wright alluded are the Thirty Years' War (1618–48), the 1688–1714 period of warfare leading to the Peace of Utrecht, the French Revolutionary/Napoleonic Wars, (1789–1815), and World Wars I and II (1914–45).

The system's great wars are, therefore, recognizable in terms of their impact on what Wright refers to as the system's constitution. Distinguishing wars according to their effect on the system's game rules is a theme to which we will return at later points in this chapter. It suffices for the moment to observe that Wright's great wars are no more subject to a fifty-year periodicity than are his general wars. The first great war is separated from the second by some forty years while the last three are separated by roughly one-hundred-year intervals.

Wright's periodicity claim evidently then is not in reference to the frequency of wars in general or of particular types of war—whether it be great-power wars, general wars, or great transitional wars. Rather, it turns out that Wright is actually referring to the intensity of war as measured by the number of battles. If the number of battles engaged in by Wright's ten principal powers (England/Great Britain, France, Spain, Austria, Prussia/Germany, Russia, Turkey, the Netherlands, Denmark, and Sweden) are aggregated by year, the following clusters of battles are said to emerge: 1618–48, 1672–90, 1701–15, 1740–63, 1789–1815, 1854–78, and 1914–41.

Since Wright (1942/1965:626) provides battle frequency data only in decennial aggregations, the precise duration of his asserted clusters cannot be replicated easily. But if one inspects the decennially plotted data (see figure 5.1), it is possible to detect spikes of varying magnitudes in the vicinity of the following decades: 1630–1649, 1670–1679, 1700–1719, 1740–59, 1790–1819, 1860–1879, 1910–1919, and 1930–1940. These decennial spikes do tend to overlap with Wright's clusters of battle concentration. It is presumably the timing of these battle clusters that led Wright (1942/1965:232) to put forward his one elaboration on the fifty-year oscillation:

> The alternating periods of predominant war and predominant peace have varied in length, but there has been a tendency for each to approximate twenty-five years during the [post-Thirty Years War era].

Given this interpretation, it is possible to visually appreciate the accuracy of Wright's assertion. But it is another matter entirely to ask whether the number of battles has a great deal of theoretical significance or operational reliability. One might consider, for example, how many land battles are equivalent in systematic significance to some of the great sea battles such as Trafalgar or Midway? In some other cases, the relative absence of battles (e.g., the small number of naval battles in which the Germans participated in World Wars I and II) may be more significant than many of the land battles that did take place. Alternatively, in an examination of any compilation of battles (see Harbottle, 1975, or Dupuy and Dupuy, 1977), one cannot avoid being struck by the subjectivity involved in deciding which battles are included or excluded. Major battles tend to be included, but so are a number of minor battles of interest for a variety of reasons (for instance, following the course of a campaign or illustrating the tactics of an individual general or admiral). Invariably, certain periods of time and/or certain regions are slighted. The sixteenth century, for example, is always poorly covered and, of course, prior to the twentieth century, non-European areas are frequently ignored unless European armies are involved in some way.

All of these threats to validity and reliability are not of equivalent significance. But they do suggest that we need to be careful in according too much importance to findings based on battle frequency data. Perhaps the most appropriate commentary is suggested in the following evaluation.

> . . . no class of military incidents has the same significance in all periods of history. The battle has been the most persistent type of military operation between armed forces on a limited terrain for a limited time, usually a day or less. At some periods,

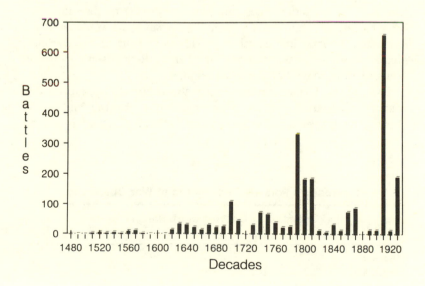

Figure 5.1 Wright's Decennial Battle Frequencies
Data Source: Wright (1942/1965:626)

however, battles have been isolated events from which flowed important political consequences. At other times a battle has been but an incident in a campaign consisting of complicated strategic operations over a season or in a siege or maritime blockade. In such circumstances political consequences cannot be attributed to the single battle but only to the whole campaign. Campaigns themselves have sometimes been but incidents in a war waged on many fronts with a number of distinct armies over a series of years. Neither the battle, the campaign, nor the war is entirely satisfactory as a unit for statistical tabulation.

The author of the above paragraph was none other than Quincy Wright (1942/1965:102).

Richardson and Moyal

Toward the end of World War II, another major name in the empirical study of conflict, Lewis F. Richardson, published his finding that the 1820–1929 outbreaks of war with magnitudes 3.5 to 4.5 were characterized by a Poisson (random) distribution. Similar results (Richardson, 1960:129), as shown below in table 5.2, were obtained when Wright's data for the 1500–1931 period were examined.

Although Richardson demonstrated little direct interest in the question of cycles and periodicities, and had even less use for the validity of Wright's data, it is frequently assumed that a war cycle would be likely to produce a nonrandom distribution with more years of frequent outbreaks of war than are expected by chance. Richardson's evidence would seem to contradict this expectation.

However, the Poisson distribution of war outbreaks appears to depend on how analysts treat calendar time. Both Richardson and Moyal (1949) demonstrated that the random distribution is observed as long as

Table 5.2

Richardson's Poisson Distribution of War Outbreaks

Data	Number of Outbreaks of War per Year:						Total
	0	1	2	3	4	5 +	
Observed Distribution	223	142	48	15	4	0	432
Poisson Prediction	216.2	149.7	51.8	12	2.1	0.3	432.1

Source: Based on Richardson (1960:129).

each year is treated separately. If years are clustered in various ways, the probability of event independence becomes more doubtful. For example, Moyal (1949) found statistically significant autocorrelations in the frequency of Wright's war outbreak data at 5- and 15-year lags. Moyal then went further and calculated a 50-year moving average of war outbreaks per year which disclosed, in Richardson's words, "a conspicuous oscillation" with peaks in 1625 and 1880 and a trough in 1745.

Moyal's finding does not seem to have inspired any further research into its implications. As Wilkinson (1980:30) has once remarked:

> What might account for such a periodicity? The question takes on additional significance in that the maximum probability of outbreak is larger than the minimum by an impressively large factor of five, which suggests that whatever accounts for the historic variation may be worth examining if we wish to minimize the probability of war outbreaks for the future. Were there fewer war crises at the bottom of the cycle? Was there a better mechanism of crisis resolution, a more pacific world view, greater general satisfaction with the status quo, a more centralized power structure? Investigation is warranted.

Further exploration may no doubt be warranted. But two factors are probably most responsible for the absence of direct reexamination to date. Although usually referred to as a 200-year cycle, as many as 255 years separate the two Moyal peaks at 1625 and 1880. How are we to account for such a long-term fluctuation? Without some substantive clue, it is difficult to know how to proceed. In addition, the finding is based on Wright's war data, which are vulnerable to a host of criticisms pertaining to debatable rules about which events are included and excluded, and for what time periods (cf., Singer and Small, 1972:17–19; Wilkinson, 1980:122). Alternative data bases of comparable length (e.g., Beer, 1974; Levy, 1983a) have only become available in the past few years.

Denton and Phillips

Denton and Phillips (1968) sought evidence for the idea that the level of violence in the international system was characterized by 25- and 80–120-year upswings. Since these upswings could be brought about by increases in either the frequency of warfare and/or the scope/intensity of warfare, a composite "amount of violence" index was created by combining information on the following indicators for the Wright war data set: (1) the frequency of war, (2) the number of belligerents, (3) the number of belligerents divided by the number of states in the system, (4) the total number of belligerent years of war per time interval, and (5) the number of battles fought. No distinction between intra- and interstate violence is made. No attempt is made to capture the number of lives lost in warfare. Nor are any distinctions made about the status of the war participants. All actors, including revolutionary groups, are treated equally.

Despite the fact that the five indicators were not all that highly intercorrelated (mean correlation = .499), a single composite index was then created employing factor analytic techniques. In addition, the 1480–1900 time period that they chose to analyze was divided into five-year-aggregations (for the 25-year cycle) and twenty (for the 80–120-year cycle) for the indicators described above. This procedure implies that (a) the emphasis is on war ongoing as opposed to war outbreaks, and (b) war duration is considered to be of some importance as well since long-running wars would be likely to be counted in successive intervals.

The reported findings for a 25-year cycle are difficult to interpret. The authors report the number of periods above and below the mean for 20-, 25-, and 30-year intervals. Their interpretation is that violence increases about every 20 years between 1495 and 1680 and about every 30 years between 1690 and 1900. However, knowing the distribution of periods above and below a mean does not tell us to what extent the temporal pattern is one of cyclically alternating periods of higher and lower levels of violence. A visual examination of their plotted data is not particularly reassuring on this score.

In contrast, the findings for the 80–120-year cycle are much more easy to evaluate. Denton and Phillips (1968:190–91) report that the data do indeed support the generalizations that

(1) Periods of high violence in the system will be followed by a decrease in the level of violence.
(2) Periods of low systemic violence will be followed by an increase in violence.
These hypotheses imply a system in which conflict (manifested in violence) grows in scale until a reaction against violence *per se* occurs. This reaction results in lower conflict in the system until conditions permit the growth of new conflict.

To test these hypotheses, the authors ask how frequently a period with high or low violence (defined in distance from the mean terms) was followed by an increase or decrease in violence. When "high" violence is defined as half a standard deviation above the mean, periods of high violence are followed by periods with a decrease in violence five of six times and periods of low violence are followed by periods with an increase in violence thirteen of fourteen times.

The statistically significant distribution of 25-year intervals may be interesting but the connection to an 80–120-year cycle is less clear. The appropriate question would seem to be not whether adjacent periods of time alternate between high and low levels of violence but whether violence builds up to a high level before crashing to a low level and then beginning anew the build-up to another high systemic level. Denton and Phillips' (1968:191) plot of the 1480–1900 intervals is reproduced in figure 5.2. The basic pattern is not quite as temporally uniform as the calculated distribution implies. The level of violence rises in successive intervals between 1481–1500 to 1561–1580, 1581–1600 to 1641–1660, 1661–1680 to 1701–1720, and 1721–1740 to 1821–1840. After the Napoleonic Wars, the direction of movement reverses itself and the level of violence declines gradually from 1821–1840 to 1881–1900. Hence, we have the following sequence: a 100-

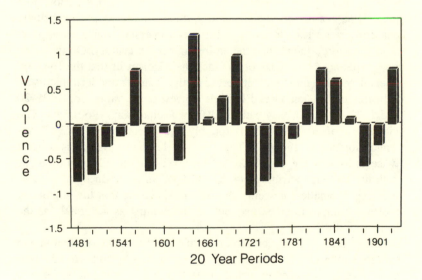

Figure 5.2   Denton and Phillips' Levels of Violence
Data Source: Denton and Phillips (1968:191)

year rise and abrupt decline, an 80-year rise and abrupt decline, a 60-year rise and abrupt decline, and a 120-year rise, and an 80-year decline.

Clearly, these findings raise a number of questions—all of which go unanswered. First, the 80- to 120-year cycle is actually a 60-to 120-year cycle. There is no need to resurrect Sorokin to wonder why the cycle is sometimes fairly short (half the length of the longest interval) while at other times it is quite long (twice as long as the shortest interval). Second, the temporal pattern that is created by twenty-year intervals is substantially different from the profile established by five-year intervals (and the cyclical findings reported for the shorter cycle). As is often the case with cyclical analysis, investigators must be sensitive to the risk of creating the very cycles they are hypothesizing through the data manipulations employed to examine a given series.

Twenty-year intervals, furthermore, are fairly broad periods of time for aggregation purposes. Consequently, it is difficult to know just what event or events in a score of years are responsible for establishing that interval's level of violence—at least without replicating the creation of the violence index. Nevertheless, one cannot help but wonder why the 1821–40 interval is twice as violent as the preceding 1801–20 interval that encompasses the Napoleonic Wars. It also seems curious that the first half of the nineteenth century, often celebrated as an unusually peaceful era (at least in terms of European interstate warfare), appears so much more violent than the entire eighteenth century. On the same note, what are we to make of an index that informs us that the 1641–60 interval was the most violent period in the system's modern history?

Interestingly, Denton and Phillips suggest some values for 1901–20 and 1921–40 which they estimated from Richardson (1960) data. The violence score for 1901–20 is roughly equivalent to the level of systemic violence in 1861–80. The 1921–40 level of violence is at least twice as high as the level recorded for 1901–20 but still only on a par with the violence attributed to the 1821–40 interval. In light of these puzzling anomalies, it seems only fair to speculate that the amount of violence composite index may not be functioning as accurately as the authors assume.

Accordingly, it is difficult to know just what to make of Denton and Phillips's long violence cycle. We are never told why an 80-to 120-year cycle should have been expected in the first place. Nor can we be sure how much of a role the techniques (e.g., the composite index or the twenty-year aggregations) have played in shaping the cyclical fluctuations that emerge in figure 5.2. In sum, Denton and Phillips's procedures and evidence are less than fully convincing. However, one is forced to concur with the authors' concluding statement: "The possible effects of improved data are, of course, not known."

The Correlates of War

Empirical analyses of war periodicities naturally require, at a minimum, information on the frequency and duration of warfare. Not surprisingly, each of the three major war data sets in the quantitative analysis of international relations has been associated with the quest for periodicity in some way. After all, periodicity is or can be treated as if it is a basic descriptive question. Having touched upon the pertinent work of the developers of the first two sets (Wright and Richardson), it is appropriate to turn to the third—the Correlates of War (COW) project headed by J. David Singer.

Many readers may already be sufficiently familiar with the various differences in data collection procedures among the three main war data sets that we need not devote time and space to that topic at this juncture. From a periodicity perspective, however, it is important to stress that the Correlates of War project's focus is limited to the post-Napoleonic Wars era (1816 on) and that much of the relevant analysis has been centered on international (excluding intranational) warfare.

Essentially, Singer and Small (1972) pick up the analysis of periodicity where Richardson and Moyal left it. Richardson's finding of a Poisson-distributed outbreak of war with one-year intervals is replicated separately for the frequencies of 1816–1965 international and interstate war, with six-month intervals. The randomly distributed outcome is quite similar to Richardson's finding. Moyal's examination of autocorrelation patterns is also replicated but this time through the technique of spectral analysis. No systematic fluctuation (limited to a periodicity of forty years or less) was observed in the annual amount of international war begun. However, some evidence suggesting twenty- and forty-year cycles is generated when the same technique is applied to international war under way (as measured in normalized nation-months). Similar results are obtained when 1816–1965 interstate and 1816–1919 central system wars are analyzed separately.

In a recent update of this analysis, Small and Singer (1982) extend their war series through 1980 and find no empirical reason to adjust their earlier findings on the Poisson distribution of war outbreaks or the absence of cyclical fluctuation traces in the international war-begun series. Moreover, the spectral analysis of war under way again generated support for a war periodicity—now described as residing in the

20- to 30-year range. But, as the authors note, the peaks of war under way for the twentieth century's two world wars (1917 and 1943) happen to be 26 years apart. The possibility that their 20–30-year cycle might be the product of the two outliers led them to recalculate the analysis without the two world wars. Once the outlier values are removed, the 20–30-year-cycle evidence tends to disappear but the reanalysis still produces support for a 14–21-year-cycle. As Small and Singer (1982:150–56) conclude:

> This range of 14–21 years is, of course, often treated as the interval between political generations, lending some modest support to certain inter-generational hypotheses built around age, learning, and forgetting.

In a related but much more complicated analysis, Singer and Cusack (1981) confine their attention to the 101 wars engaged in by major powers between 1816 and 1965. Basically, the question they address is whether any periodicity can be detected in the intervals between the termination of one war and the onset of another. Using a battery of techniques ranging from the Poisson through correlations to spectral analysis, Singer and Cusack are unable to discern any systematic periodicity that cannot be accounted for by outlier problems. Yet they do find relationships that suggest that when major powers

> suffer military defeat, and pay a high price in battle deaths per month of war, they tend to avoid war for a longer time, and the longer they wait, the more intense the next war experience will be (Singer and Cusack, 1981:417).

They are also careful to make explicit what one could say is probably the major weakness of the Correlates of War project's approach to the question of periodicity.

> Having addressed the proposition that national war experiences come at regular intervals in time with some periodicity— foreordained or otherwise—all we have demonstrated is that the probability of the major powers getting into war is independent of when and with what effects they experienced their prior wars. Does this absence of periodicity permit us to infer that there is no underlying regularity, and that war experiences are randomly occurring responses to randomly occurring conditions? Clearly not, since it is quite possible that war requires the concatenation of several conditions, each of whose appearance is cyclical, but with different intervals. This *could* produce a periodicity in the war experiences of nations, but the concatenation of as few as

three such cycles, even if they show (for example) three-, ten-, and fifty-year periodicities, would occur only once every 150 years. Thus the war cycle would be so long as to make its occurrence barely visible in the span under scrutiny here (Singer and Cusack, 1981:419).

Whether Singer and Cusack regard this qualification as a serious constraint on their analysis' ability to tap cycles of war is not a critical issue here. The fundamental point is that it is possible that the Correlates of War data set, restricted as it is to the post-1816 period, may not be capable of capturing longer-term cycles. With "only" 150 to 165 years of data, short-term, generational cycles may certainly be tackled, but cycles that require the passage of several generations are probably beyond the scope of the COW project. Evidence generated by analysis dependent on COW data, therefore, cannot be regarded as the final word on the presence or absence of cyclical periodicities in war.

Levy

Finally, some mention of one of the most recent examinations of the war cycle question is in order. Jack Levy's (1983a) assembly of data on the 1495–1975 war experiences of some fourteen great powers contributes still another data set to the realm of empirical conflict analysis. As a new data set, it possesses at least three explicit advantages over the others that have been employed in tackling hypotheses about fluctuations in warfare. It avoids Wright's legalistic biases in collecting data on war frequency and duration. It concentrates on a specific group of important actors rather than trying to encompass multiple levels of analysis. And, it offers a much longer time span than the Correlates of War data set.

However, as in the case of most of the other studies reviewed here, the question of war cycles is only one of many treated by Levy. He initiates his analysis by observing that the work done by Sorokin, Wright, Denton and Phillips, Richardson, Singer and Small, and Singer and Cusack has not generated much empirical support for the notion of cyclical trends. He then visually inspects a set of scattergrams charting the serial history of great-power warfare as measured in terms of frequency, duration, extent (the number of great-power participants), magnitude (the summary duration for all participating great powers), severity (the number of battle deaths), intensity (the number of battle deaths divided by the population of Europe), and concentration (the severity divided by the magnitude). He (Levy, 1983a:137) concludes:

There are no hints of any cyclical patterns in either the occurrence of war or in any of its other dimensions. For each of the war indicators, the highest peaks in war as well as the periods of no war appear to be scattered at random . . . In the absence of any hints of the existence of cyclical trends either in the scattergrams or in earlier studies, however, it is very unlikely that sophisticated statistical techniques could uncover any patterns that are sufficiently strong to have any substantive significance. For this reason these tests are not applied here.

THE SEARCH FOR CYCLES OF WAR AND PEACE

This selective review of the empirical literature for and against war periodicities has not been intended to examine every facet or component of the pertinent literature. Rather, it has been intended to illustrate certain distinctive features of the literature. Most clearly, the evidence for specific war periodicities is less than compelling. Each time a researcher uncovers some form of cycle, it has become customary that more questions are raised than are answered. Such a state of affairs, admittedly, is not all that uncommon in the empirical study of world politics. But in this particular case, many of the questions that are raised have to do with precisely what activity is thought to be cycling and why. Or, the questions concern whether the techniques and/or procedures utilized to detect the cycle are actually most responsible for the appearance of a cyclical fluctuation in the data. The ultimate outcome is a great deal of uncertainty about what has been found and whether what has been found has any meaning.

Should we then adopt the prudent strategy that advises that if previous empirical researchers have experienced so many problems in uncovering war cycles, they probably do not exist in any systematic fashion? No, such a conclusion would be premature—not in spite of the evidence accumulated—but, in part, because of its very nature. Prudence, as well as skepticism have crucial roles to play in the war-research process. But the often nebulous literature on war periodicity reveals several interrelated features, so far left implicit, that may actually be responsible for many of the amorphous findings.

Rules of Engagement

First of all, most, if not all, of the analyses reviewed here have violated what should be the first rule of periodicity research:

Any search for periodicity in the incidence of war is likely to be informed by some theoretical framework which seeks to account for the hypothesized or observed periodicity (Singer and Small, 1972:208).

Had Singer and Small written that the search *must be informed,* it is quite possible that the earlier research on periodicity might have produced much different results if they had followed this maxim. As it is, a peculiar empirical tradition that encourages grossly inductive searches for periodicities has been established. Only if some type of cycle emerges, with some exaggeration, is it then incumbent upon the researcher to struggle with an explanation for the finding. Indeed, the mere existence of earlier examinations of periodicity will frequently suffice as justification for continued searches in the same inductive spirit. But if the earlier examinations lacked strong justification in the first place, an entire subliterature gradually emerges on a very shaky, substantive foundation. We need to reverse the tradition and insist on the statement of specific reasons to search for periodicities in war. Without specific and *a priori* justification, it is unlikely that we or its midwives will be able to make much sense of what emerges in its absence.

Second, a veritable host of indicators—frequency, duration, magnitude, severity, intensity, number of battles, and so forth—have been examined at various levels of analysis. Rather than simply picking an indicator, several indicators to hedge our bets, or some composite index to hedge our bets even better, the specific and *a priori* justification should clarify in what form the cycle should be anticipated. If, for instance, the hypothesized cycle is predicted to exist at the systemic level, introducing information on intranational civil wars may either be essential (if the premise makes it necessary to aggregate the system's total sum of violence) or confusing (if the premise focuses only on certain major-power wars fought to settle systemic leadership struggles). Only when we know exactly what the hypothesis is about can we judge whether the data, and the tests conducted on those data, correspond to the original premise. This second rule is particularly critical if there is some reason to suspect that all wars and all actors are not of equivalent significance—to both world politics and cyclical fluctuations on war and peace.

Third, analysts of cyclical periodicities, particularly those of the long-term persuasion, need to develop a keener sensitivity for the history of the series they are examining. If one is going to examine a four- or five-hundred-year series, for example, it helps to know whether it makes sense from an historical perspective to simply divide the series into two segments of equal length. It also helps to know whether it is appropriate to give equal weight to the squabbles of Central European principalities, the frequently bloody yet peripheral clashes of Russia and the Ottoman Empire, and the major clashes of the system's strongest powers. Alternatively, if an index of systemic violence is constructed that suggests that the worst conflict occurred in the middle of the seventeenth century, the distant clamor of validity alarm bells should be heard at some point before the analysis is completed.

In sum, what are needed are theoretically and operationally justified and historically sensitive analyses. Satisfying these preconditions for the analysis of war and peace cycles will not, by any stretch of the imagination, resolve once and for all the periodicity question (or questions). But the extent to which the preconditions are satisfied should assist in narrowing the extent and nature of disagreement.

The goal of narrowing academic disputes about the periodicity of war can be taken one step further. As already noted, most of the empirical periodicity literature has treated war in a relatively undifferentiated fashion. To be sure, distinctions are sometimes made about international and intranational conflict. The wars of great powers have also been examined as a special case. Nevertheless, it has been an underlying premise of this chapter that the differentiation must proceed even further if we are to capture what historical-structural analysts regard as the most salient war periodicity in the world system. This further step requires differentiating wars according to the role(s) they perform in the system's processes. From this historical-structural vantage point, most of the wars of the past five hundred or so years are not unimportant by any means, but a few wars have far greater systemic significance than the others. It is those few wars with the greatest significance that tend to reoccur in cyclical fashion. Consequently, it is their periodicity with which we should be most concerned.

Identifying Systemic Wars

Table 5.3 provides an interesting illustration by bringing together and contrasting three different perspectives on the tempo of what is variously labeled general war, hegemonic war, and global war. Whatever the terminology, the most interesting feature of table 5.3 is the impressive degree of overlap in the asserted cyclical phases.

Of course, the overlapping phases are not addressing exactly the same systemic processes. Toynbee's (1954) perspective is closely linked to the classical balance of power conceptualization.

Table 5.3

Three Interpretations of General, Hegemonic, and Global War Cycles

Toynbee		Farrar		Modelski	
General war	1494–1525	Probing war	1494–1521	*Global war*	1494–1516
Breathing-space	1515–1536	Adjusting wars	1521–1559	World power	1517–1540
Supplementary wars	1536–1559			Delegitimation	1541–1561
General peace	1559–1568	Probing wars	1559–1568	Deconcentration	1562–1579
General war	1568–1609	*Hegemonic wars*	1568–1588	*Global war*	1580–1609
Breathing-space	1609–1618	Probing wars	1588–1618	World power	1609–1634
Supplementary wars	1618–1648	Adjusting wars	1618–1659	Delegitimation	1635–1661
General peace	1648–1672	Probing wars	1659–1688	Deconcentration	1662–1687
General war	1672–1713	*Hegemonic wars*	1688–1714	*Global war*	1688–1713
Breathing-space	1713–1733	Probing wars	1714–1740	World power	1714–1738
Supplementary wars	1733–1763	Adjusting wars	1740–1763	Delegitimation	1739–1763
General peace	1763–1792	Probing wars	1763–1789	Deconcentration	1764–1791
General war	1792–1815	*Hegemonic wars*	1789–1815	*Global war*	1792–1815
Breathing-space	1815–1848	Probing wars	1815–1848	World power	1816–1848
Supplementary wars	1848–1871	Adjusting wars	1848–1871	Delegitimation	1849–1880
General peace	1871–1914	Probing wars	1871–1914	Deconcentration	1881–1913
General war	1914–1918	*Hegemonic wars*	1914–1945	*Global war*	1914–1945
Breathing-space	1918–1939				
Supplementary wars	1939–1945				
General peace	1945–	Probing wars	1945–1973	World power	1946–1973
				Delegitimation	1973–

Sources: Toynbee (1954); Farrar (1977); Modelski and Thompson (1981) and Modelski (1984).

> . . . the most emphatic punctuation in a uniform sequence of
> events recurring in one repetitive cycle after another is the
> outbreak of a great war in which one Power that has forged ahead
> of all its rivals makes so formidable a bid for world dominion
> that it evokes an opposing coalition of all the other Powers . . .
> (Toynbee, 1954:251).

According to Toynbee, the combination of cumulative tensions and the disproportionate increase in the relative strength of one of the great powers seeking world dominion leads to the engulfing explosion of a general war. The challenger is defeated by the temporary coalition brought together by the challenger's threat. A patched-up peace, the "breathing-space," is improvised so that the system may recover from its exhaustion. But the problems that were left unresolved in the general war eventually lead to another burst of supplementary warfare that produces more constructive settlements of the outstanding issues and brings about an interlude of "general peace."

In partial contrast, Farrar (1977) assigns wars to three general categories according to their relationship with the existing distribution of power's status quo. Probing wars are the least violent and bring about little change. Adjusting wars create a moderate amount of violence and either bring about some changes in the status quo or else indicate that some changes have already taken place. Still, adjusting wars fall short of disturbing the overall structural distribution. Hegemonic wars, however, do bring about fundamental changes in the system's structure and are associated with a high level of violence. The system's essential war dynamic is thus viewed as first testing, then adjusting or modifying, and then testing again the prevailing status quo. As the pressures for change accumulate and coincide with the attempt of a great power to dominate the system, a hegemonic war establishes a new status quo.

While Farrar's view is not all that incompatible with Toynbee's, Modelski's perspective, as we have seen in chapters 3 and 4, is that a single world power emerges from the struggle for systemic leadership, the global war, with a preponderant control of the resources essential to global reach. As this resource base erodes, the world power phase, a period of systemic leadership and politico-economic rule creation, gives way to the phases of delegitimation and deconcentration. Structural power deconcentration proceeds until challengers for the role of world power are encouraged to initiate a new struggle for systemic leadership.

Systemic War Candidates

Yet even though these interpretations of Toynbee, Farrar, and Modelski

Table 5.4

Systemic War Candidates

Wars	Mowat (1928)	Wright A (1942/65)	Wright B (1942/65)	Toynbee (1954)	Farrar (1977)	Modelski (1978)	Gilpin (1981)	Wallerstein (1984)	Midlarsky (1984)	Levy (1985)
1. Italian/Indian Ocean (1494–1516/25)		X			X	X				
2. Dutch Independence (1560/85–1608/9)					X	?	X			X
3. Thirty Years (1618–1648)		X	X	X			X	X	X	X
4. Franco-Spanish (1648–1659)		X								
5. Franco-Dutch (1672–1678)		X	X		X		X			X
6. League of Augsburg (1688–1697)		X	X	X	X	X	X	X		X
7. Spanish Succession (1701–1713)		X	X	X	X	X	X	X		X
8. Quadruple Alliance (1718–1720)			X							
9. Polish Succession (1733–1738)			X							
10. Jenkin's Ear/Austrian Succession (1739–1748)		X	X							X
11. Seven Years (1755–1763)		X	X							X
12. American Revolution (1778–1783)			X							
13. French Revolutionary/ Napoleonic (1792–1815)	X	X	X	X	X	X	X	X	X	X
14. Crimean (1854–1856)		X								
15. World War I (1914–1918)	X	X	X	X	X	X	X	X	X	X
16. World War II (1939–1945)		X	X			X	X	X	X	X

Note: This table represents a modification and extension of one found in Levy (1985).

are different, markedly similar periodicities are produced, and a fairly high level of agreement is obtained on the critical general/hegemonic/ global war punctuations in the systemic cycles. This is not meant to imply that table 5.3 is representative of the much broader historical-structural school (or schools) of thought. For a variety of reasons, it is not particularly representative. But if we survey the various identifications of systemic wars, as reflected in table 5.4, there is perhaps more agreement than is frequently thought.

Table 5.4 represents a modification of an analysis performed by Levy (1985). The candidates put forward by nine authors are arrayed in chronological succession. Although table 5.4 conceals some differences in how each event is dated, a very strong majority agree on the distinctive status of five of the sixteen candidates. Table 5.5 summa-

Table 5.5

Level of Agreement in Identifying Systemic Wars

Candidates	Citation Frequency	Percent
Strongest:		
League of Augsburg	8	80.0
Spanish Succession	8	80.0
French Revolutionary/Napoleonic	10	100.0
World War I	10	100.0
World War II	8	88.9
Disputed:		
Italian/Indian Ocean	3	30.0
Dutch Independence	3	30.0
Thirty Years	7	70.0
Dutch War	5	50.0
Jenkin's Ear/Austrian Succession	3	30.0
Seven Years	3	30.0
Weakest:		
Franco-Spanish	1	10.0
Quadruple Alliance	1	10.0
Polish Succession	1	10.0
American Revolution	1	10.0
Crimean	1	10.0

Note: The number of citations and proportions are based on 10 identifications arrayed in table 5.4. Only 9 of the 10 were published after 1939. Therefore, the potential number of citations for World War II is 1 less than the possible number for the other 15 wars.

rizes the level of agreement and disagreement indicated in table 5.4. Strong agreement is found on the League of Augsburg and Spanish Succession Wars (1688–1713), the French Revolutionary/Napoleonic Wars (1792–1815), and World Wars I and II (1914–1918/1939–1945). Another five wars are advanced only by Wright (1942/1965) as part of his general war set: the Franco-Spanish, Quadruple Alliance, Polish Succession, American Revolution, and Crimean Wars. These wars, it is suggested, can be safely regarded as unlikely candidates for special cyclical consideration.

In between the ten strongest and weakest candidates are another six candidates with varying degrees of support: the Italian/Indian Ocean, Dutch Independence, Thirty Years, Dutch, Jenkin's Ear/Austrian Succession, and Seven Year's Wars. Of these six, two—the Thirty Years' and the 1672–1678 Dutch War, which is often linked to the 1688–1713 war as an opening prelude—receive more support than the remaining four. But while we can appreciate the virtual absence of disagreement on the 1688–1713, 1792–1815, and 1914–1945 frays, it seems unlikely that the status of the disputed candidates can be resolved by a poll of the relevant literature.

How one goes about resolving the appropriate status of the disputed war candidates depends on what one thinks these wars are about. For instance, world-economy analysts take the position that the wars that are most important are those wars that usher in new eras of economic hegemony. Their task thus involves developing a longitudinal measure of hegemony that could be matched with the different war candidates. Although the balance of power concept is notoriously fuzzy, adherents to more classical approaches could focus on determining whether or to what extent each war really involved a similar type of balancing process—however defined.

Still another approach consists of resolving the dispute through the development of definitional prerequisites. Levy (1985:371) provides an example when he defines "general war" as a war

in which a decisive victory by at least one side is both a reasonable possibility and likely to result in the leadership or dominance by a single state over the system, or at least in the overthrow of an existing leadership or hegemony.

Levy goes on to require that each general war meet three additional criteria: (1) the participation of the system's leading power, (2) the participation of at least half of the system's other major powers, and (3) the attainment of a conflict intensity level, exceeding one thousand

battle deaths per one million European population. The main liability
of such an approach, of course, is that other analysts may not find all of
the specified prerequisites to be equally important. Definitional criteria
cannot be divorced from theoretical presuppositions. If the presuppositions do not enjoy consensus, the definitional criteria will also fail to
avoid dispute.

Long-cycle analysts have found a different way to seek validation for
the salience of the global wars identified in table 5.4. Global wars are
not defined in terms of geographical scope, number of participants,
length of duration, or number of casualties. They are apt to score
highly on these various criteria, but theoretical emphasis is placed primarily on the structural consequences. Global wars significantly reconcentrate capabilities of global reach. In essence, a prewar multipolar
system is transformed into a postwar unipolar system (see chapter 9).
Since the fluctuations in one principal type of global reach capability,
naval power, have been captured for a respectably lengthy period of
time, it should be possible to test whether the correct set of global wars
is identified by long-cycle theory. Is each global war associated with a
substantial transformation in the distribution of naval capabilities? How
exclusive are these associations? Are other, nonglobal wars also associated with capability reconcentration?

The Evidence on Capability Reconcentration

Thompson and Rasler (1988) have addressed these questions in an effort to model the impact of war on the leadership long cycle since
1494. Several substantive problems influenced the way in which the
war-impact modeling was executed. A number of the wars listed in
table 5.5 are sufficiently lengthy to encapsulate some amount of war-
time capability oscillation. In one year, one side may appear to be
ahead while in another year the other side clearly leads. Some wars
also need to be merged as one prolonged struggle. The brief pauses
between the intervals of combat in the League of Augsburg and Spanish
Succession Wars or the French Revolutionary and Napoleonic Wars are
not all that meaningful. In addition, World Wars I and II are viewed as
representing one extended global war period because a new world
power did not emerge in 1918–1919. Accordingly, we would have little
reason to expect the first phase of warfare to have much impact on the
concentration of naval power. It is the second phase that tends to be
decisive. These considerations encourage a focus on the immediate
postwar impact—as opposed to looking for structural shocks during
the wars.

Table 5.6

Impact of War on Naval Concentration

Global War Candidates	Impact Parameters
1580–1608	positive*
1618–1648	negative*
1672–1678	negative*
1688–1713	positive*
1739–1748	negative*
1755–1763	positive
1792–1815	positive*
1914–1945	positive*

Note: Asterisk denotes statistical significance at the .05 level. This table summarizes statistical analyses conducted on 5, 10, and 15 postwar year intervals. The specific findings sometimes vary according to the length of the postwar interval examined; but not in a way requiring significant qualification of the summary outcome. See also Thompson and Rasler (1988).

While the statistical technicalities of the test would require some amount of discussion, the basic structure of the test is quite simple. The four global wars of the long cycle (1580–1608, 1688–1713, 1792–1815, 1914–1945) are expected to transform the level of capability concentration.[1] The impacts of these wars should be both positive and statistically significant. The four other systemic war candidates [the Thirty Years' War (1618–1648), the Dutch War (1672–1678), Jenkin's Ear/Austrian Succession (1739–1748), and the Seven Years' War (1755–1763)] are not expected to transform the concentration series. Therefore, the impacts may be either weakly positive or they may be negative but they are not expected to be statistically significant.

Table 5.6 summarizes the statistical outcome of the Thompson-Rasler test. As predicted, all four of the impact parameter values for the long-cycle perspective's global war candidates are positive and statistically significant. For the other systemic war candidates, the results are mixed. At the same time, no positive, statistically significant impacts are registered. The three significant parameters that are reported (The Thirty Years' War, the preliminary Franco-Dutch fighting in the 1670s and the Jenkin's Ear/Austrian Succession combat of the mideighteenth century) are negatively signed. Negative parameter values indicate that deconcentration—as opposed to reconcentration—took place in the aftermath of these three wars.

Table 5.6's outcome is quite supportive of the long cycle argument. Some wars bring about significant structural reconcentration while oth-

ers do not. The wars identified as global wars in the long-cycle framework possess this key empirical attribute required of global wars. A
new system leader, commanding a disproportionate share of the system's pool of global reach capabilities, must emerge for the war to
qualify. If this does not occur, the war need hardly be dismissed as
trivial. It certainly is hard to argue, however, that a nonqualifying war
represents one of the watershed punctuations in the global system's
process of concentration and deconcentration.

CONCLUSION

Scholarship continues to disagree about the identity of the world system's elite, variously referred to as great powers, major powers, core
powers, or global powers. Since we do not have consensus on how best
to conceptualize military power, there are disagreements on which
states are leading at any given time. We do not fully agree on whether
the theoretical focus should be the balance of power, hegemony, or
power concentration and deconcentration. We do not even agree on
whether the number of battle deaths really matters from a definitional
perspective as long as other, more important, criteria are satisfied.

As long as we continue to disagree about such matters, it is unlikely
that we will be able to fully agree on a single set of critical systemic
wars. And if we cannot agree on a common set of critical systemic
wars, the debate over the timing of war and peace periodicities will
continue as well. But this debate, it is argued, is an improvement over
the types of questions addressed in the literature reviewed in the first
part of this chapter. The question is not whether some periodicity can
or cannot be coaxed from—let alone explain—the welter of statistical
information available on deadly quarrels. Rather, the historical-
structural question is which theoretical interpretation of the cycle of
war and peace is best supported by the evidence (assuming any are) and
which one provides the most rewarding theoretical insights on the functioning of the world system's key processes.

At the same time, Levy's (1985) call for more explicit definitions in
the identification of system transforming wars is well taken. The empirical challenge, however, is to distinguish between those wars that transformed the system in some theoretically significant way from those
wars in which the key players may have tried to transform the system
but failed.

An appreciation for the periodicity of war and peace is fundamental
to a better understanding of "system time." The underlying premise of

this concept is that important political, social, and economic processes proceed according to a clock (in the probabilistic sense) measured not in calendar time but in terms of structural change at the global level. To accurately model the process of system transformation, war, and peace, we need to be able to tell time according to the most appropriate clock that is available.

Deciding what is the most appropriate clock (or clocks) will require examinations of the system's basic processes and drives—the system's clockwork mechanisms. Chapter 6 will go directly to the heart of the system's drives and processes by underscoring the connections between leading economic sectors and the rise and decline of systemic leadership.

6

Toward a Partial Explanation of the Roots of Global War: Leading Sectors and Systemic Leadership

Why do global wars occur? For historical-structural analysts of world politics, the answer to this question is inextricably connected to the phenomenon of structural change. Global wars are brought about by the repetitive processes of concentration, deconcentration, and reconcentration in the system. More specifically, deconcentration leads to global war, the outcome of which ushers in a new period of concentration. But how are we to account for the repetition of concentration and deconcentration processes? To seek the roots of this systemic process (or, more appropriately, processes), it is necessary to shift our analytical attention away from the systemic whole to the jostling and vying for power among the system's major state actors. At this level, systemic concentration-deconcentration is translated into the rise and decline of systemic leaders. As one state becomes more powerful than its rivals, the systemic distribution of power becomes more concentrated. As the system leader's relative power advantages ebb, the system becomes less concentrated.

Thus to explain why global wars take place, we must seek to account for the rise and fall of system leaders and the consequent struggle for leadership—a principle *raison d'etre* for global war. While it is certainly tempting to isolate *the* key factor in rise and fall dynamics, this chapter will refrain explicitly from doing so. Instead, the focus here will be on *one* of the key factors in rise and fall dynamics, namely the emergence and decline of leading sectors and their significance for the "economic" dimension of systemic leadership.

Two related questions or sets of questions will also be pursued. First, to what extent do historical-structural analysts, despite the proliferation of alternative interpretative schema, converge on this dimension of systemic leadership? Are system leaders identified utilizing similar crite-

112

ria? Do the explanations for leadership decline overlap to a significant extent as well?

A second cluster of questions concerns leading sectors specifically. If, as hinted at above, leading sectors constitute an important common denominator across various schools of thought, is it possible to clarify the discussion of systemic leadership by explicitly operationalizing the positions of the major actors at various points in time? The answer developed in this chapter is an affirmative one which will facilitate the pursuit of several important empirical questions in chapter 7.

HEGEMONY, LEAD ECONOMIES, AND
SYSTEM LEADERSHIP

To examine the extent to which historical-structural analysts converge or diverge on "the root" of systemic leadership's economic dimension, two types of literature need to be examined. One type encompasses conceptual definitions of economic leadership—"hegemony" for structural realists and world-economy analysts, "lead economy" for long-cycle students. Three pertinent definitions (Keohane, 1984; Wallerstein, 1984; and Modelski, 1981, 1982) will be reviewed here—one each for each of the principal schools of thought. A second type involves the literature attempting to model the decline (and sometimes the rise) of systemic leadership. Four fairly explicit models (Bousquet, 1980; Chase-Dunn, 1982; Goldfrank, 1983; and Gilpin, 1981) will be scrutinized. However, this time, the examples are tilted toward the world-economy school—in large part because world-economy analysts have simply demonstrated more interest in this topic than have other approaches.

Hegemony

There must be something intrinsic to the topic of hegemony that mysteriously inhibits its analysts from engaging in specificity about what the concept means. Either that or many analysts must hold the belief that the concept's meaning is self-evident. But if that is the case why then do we quarrel about which states, if any, have played this role in the past? However one wishes to resolve this conundrum, explicit definitions of hegemony remain rare. The typical approach is to keep the conceptual explication to a minimum as in Gilpin's (1981:116) footnote equation of the term *hegemony* with the "leadership of one state over other states in the system." The most obvious liability of such approaches, other than the sheer parsimony of communication, is that leadership itself is hardly a restrictive concept in its own right. What does it mean to be a leader? Is a state a leader if it leads only in the development of material resources? Must a leader have followers?[1]

Nor does leadership connote a necessarily mutually exclusive role. One country may lead in economic power, another in the military sphere, and still others in other sectors such as culture, ideology, humanitarian aid, or sports. Alternatively, one country may lead in Africa while another is supreme in some sense in Latin America. The seemingly innocent phrase "over other states" also fails to tell us how many other states must be involved. This observation is not intended to imply that there is some numerical threshold for the number of states that must fall within the leader's sphere of influence. Rather, it asks whether we need to differentiate between regional and global hegemony? It also raises the question of whether hegemony can mean the same thing in systems where there are multiple hegemons scattered around the globe as opposed to systems where there is only one leader at a time.

To be fair, it is easy to concede that such imprecision is not really what most commentators who choose to employ the hegemonic term seem to have in mind. The usual implication, aside perhaps from the Gramscian mode (Cox, 1987), seems to be one of economic dominance or preponderance at the core of the world system with a corollary implication that the other types of dominance (e.g., military, cultural, and so forth) are likely to be aligned with the spatio-temporal concentration of economic power. Two very representative examples are available to support this statement. The first example is taken from the structural realist school while the second is quite visibly associated with the world-economy school.

Keohane (1984:32) stipulates that:

> The theory of hegemonic stability, as applied to the world
> political economy, defines hegemony as preponderance of
> material resources. Four sets of resources are equally important.
> Hegemonic powers must have control over raw materials, control
> over sources of capital, control over markets, and competitive
> advantages in the production of highly valued goods.

The hegemonic status is equated quite clearly with economic preponderance in Keohane's definition. At a later point, although, Keohane (1984:39) does add the following observation:

> A hegemonic state must possess enough military power to be
> able to protect the international political economy that it
> dominates from incursions by hostile adversaries.

This military power caveat notwithstanding, it is evident that Keohane's definitional emphasis is concerned principally with the sources of economic influence. Adequate access to crucial raw materials and capital decreases the costs of a state's ability to assist its allies and punish its enemies. SImilarly, the ability to open or close a large domestic market to outsiders is another important resource in a state's arsenal of threats and rewards. Finally, Keohane (1984:33) stresses the preponderant economy's need to possess a productive edge in certain types of commodities:

> Competitive advantage does not mean that the leading economy
> exports everything but that it produces and exports the most
> profitable products, and those that will provide the basis for
> producing even more advanced goods and services in the future.
> In general, this ability will be based on the technological
> superiority of the leading country . . .

Keohane's definition of hegemonic power is a welcome exception to the peculiar reluctance to provide concrete definitions within the structural realism perspective. Yet while it is certainly possible to extract the principal components of the definition—raw materials, capital, domestic market size, technological superiority, and military power—it is another thing entirely to know precisely what to do with some of these items.[2]

The first three definitional components appear to be the most dubious elements of the set of five. Keohane himself doubts that any state prior to the rise of the United States' leadership era qualified as the system's hegemonic power. Yet this very conclusion is very much a reflection of the definitional elements emphasized by Keohane. In this respect, the first three components identify phenomena whose significance vis-à-vis systemic leadership have varied historically. Some states have always enjoyed better resource bases than others. Similarly, some states have been more dependent on foreign sources of crucial raw materials than others.

However, at least three things have changed. First, industrialization and the concomitant decline of agricultural self-sufficiency have increased external dependencies for various types of resources. Second, the ability to deny other states access to external resource supplies has improved as well. In the sixteenth century, it was possible to interfere with the flow of silver from South America to Spain. Yet no one was able to stop the flow completely. By the twentieth century, much more effective tools had been developed, and applied, to interrupt external supply lines. Third, the minimum size of the competitive nation-state has escalated to the point where near-continent-scale state organizations are likely to be the most competitive. Seemingly gone are the days when small and relatively vulnerable island states can rise to the ultimate position of systemic prominence.[3]

All three of these factors impinge on the significance of the access to raw materials element. Various political-economic processes of change have enhanced the importance of, and the difficulty of maintaining, access to resources. Yet should we handicap our definitional focus by concentrating only on more recent developments? In this context, one is reminded of Mahan's (1890) older argument that states with limited resource bases are more likely to seek to improve their position and, in doing so, to become system leaders, than are states with ample resources at home and, therefore, little incentive to search for supplies, colonies, and markets abroad. The observation has some utility for explaining why the Dutch and the English became maritime powers in the sixteenth and seventeenth centuries and why the French were less motivated to do so. But the usefulness of this observation is also dated. Nor would most of us be eager to incorporate resource shortages as a necessary prerequisite to contemporary economic leadership.

Access to capital has also become an increasingly important factor as the costs of nation-state operations have escalated over the past five centuries. Yet the utility of this factor as a way of distinguishing between winners and losers in the world system's struggle for leadership has actually diminished since the nineteenth century. The Dutch and the English developed fiscal techniques, such as the public debt, to more than compensate for their relatively small populations and limited wealth bases (Rasler and Thompson, 1983). Their opponents initially were unable to match the Anglo-Dutch success at financing war-making operations. Eventually, however, this innovation spread throughout the system. In this particular sense, the definitional significance of capital access as a distinguishing criterion would seem to have declined over time.

Discussing these definitional elements is rendered more awkward by their nonoperational nature. When one is considering the matter of access, whether it be to raw materials or to capital, the question of how much access is enough to qualify as hegemonic is difficult to avoid. It is also difficult to answer until or unless a potential hegemon's politico-economic activities grind to a half due to acute resource shortages. This comment would also seem to apply to the large import market criterion. Not only is it a dimension that seems inextricably intertwined with the relatively recent emergence of the American marketplace's consumption power, how many consumers or import purchases are necessary to qualify on this criterion? Alternatively, how significant is a large import market if system leaders also tend to have more open economies than their competitors and, at the same time, have a history of being only moderately successful in persuading their competitors to be less protective of their own economies?

In sum, there is no denying the importance of possessing a wealthy economy capable of digesting large amounts of imports. Historically, however, it remains to be demonstrated just how essential this dimension has been in developing and exercising economic leadership. It may be, moreover, that this element is more critical to the relative decline of economic leadership than to its rise—a subject to which we will return later.

Keohane's (1984:40) military component, too, can only be regarded as rather vague:

> The military conditions for economic hegemony are met if the economically preponderant country has sufficient military capabilities to prevent incursions by others that would deny it access to major areas of its economic activity.

The term *incursions* presumably refers to some form of armed attack (as opposed to economic competition). Analytically, then, we find ourselves in something of a dichotomous box again. If there are no significant incursions, the hegemon presumably will receive credit for possessing sufficient capabilities to militarily deter the opposition. Alternatively, only when the incursions are ultimately successful can we be fully confident that the military conditions for economic hegemony are no longer being met.

A final problem with the Keohane hegemony definition concerns the repeatedly invoked question: how much is enough to be hegemonic? Keohane's general answer is that the hegemonic power must be stronger on the raw material, capital, import market, and competitive advantage dimensions, taken as a whole, than any other country. This rule of thumb hardly seems to relate to the earlier stress on preponderance. If we were to operationalize the four criteria, calculate the shares of each factor held by various states, and then average the four factor scores, a hegemonic power score would result. Imagine a three-contender situation where states A and B each possess 33 percent of proportional shares. State C has a 34 percent score. Although only marginally stronger than states A and B, state C would seem to satisfy the definitional threshold for hegemonic power status. Being stronger, on the whole, than any other country, is simply not sufficiently restrictive for us to recognize hegemonic power when we encounter it.

Perhaps the most well-known definition of hegemonic power is the one supplied by Wallerstein (1984:38–39):

> Hegemony in the interstate system refers to that situation in which the ongoing rivalry between the so-called "great powers" is so unbalanced that one power is truly *primus inter pares;* that is, one power can largely impose its rules and its wishes (at the very least by effective veto power) in the economic, political,

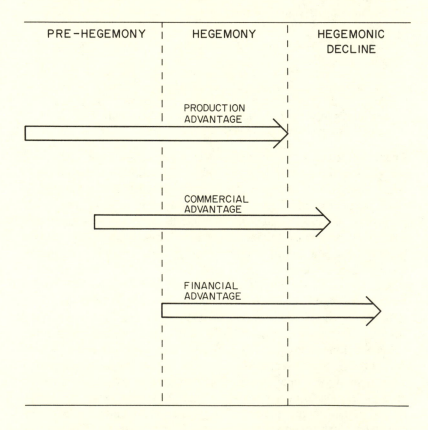

Figure 6.1   Hegemony and Simultaneous Efficiency Edges in Three Major Economic Spheres
Source: Based on Wallerstein (1984:40)

military, diplomatic, and even cultural arenas. The material base of such power lies in the activity of enterprises domiciled in that power to operate more efficiently in all three major economic arenas—agro-industrial production, commerce, and finance. The edge in efficiency of which we are speaking is one so great that these enterprises can not only out bid enterprises domiciled in other great powers in the world market in general, but quite specifically in very many instances within the home markets of the rival powers themselves.

Figure 6.1 helps to illustrate some of the implications of Wallerstein's definition. A state first develops its competitive advantage in agro-industrial production. The hegemonic status is not conferred, however, until similar advantages are developed in the commercial and financial spheres. Since these edges are thought to be lost in the same order (production, commercial, and financial) that they are gained, a state loses its hegemonic status when it no longer possesses a competitive advantage in agro-industrial production.

In discussing his own definition, Keohane (1984:33) notes that Wallerstein fails to differentiate between productive advantages in "established products and those using very complex or new techniques." Whether this is an act of commission or one of omission on Wallerstein's part, the point is well taken. There seems to be little point in expecting a hegemonic power to possess a competitive edge in producing all commodities. Ricardo's idea of comparative advantage still retains some value. It should also be stressed that the order of attaining competitive edges (and of course their loss) in the three spheres of economic activity remains to be demonstrated empirically.

For that matter, it is not self-evident that the major historical candidates for the hegemonic status have achieved or possessed their respective competitive edges simultaneously, to the same extent, or that, theoretically, it is absolutely necessary that they have done so. For example, it could be argued that the Dutch strong suit was associated primarily with the commercial sphere. While there is no need to downplay the Dutch productivity edge (documented in Maddison, 1982), it was not necessarily the exclusive root of the Dutch success in monopolizing much of Europe's carrying trade for some portion of the seventeenth century. However, to the extent that the Dutch commercial role was predicated on its shipbuilding innovations, one type of production edge, productivity and commercial advantages were not entirely separate phenomenon either.

Nevertheless, the contrast to be made is with the nineteenth century's

Table 6.1

Proportional Distribution of Trade and Industrial Production: Great Britain and the United States, 1720–1983

Year	Great Britain		United States	
	Trade	Industrial Production	Trade	Industrial Production
1720	13			
1750	13			
1780	12		2	
1800	33		5	
1820	27	24	6	4
1830	24		5	
1840	25	21	7	5
1850	22		7	
1860	25	21	9	14
1870	31	32	8	23
1880	27		10	
1881–85	22	27	10	29
1889	22		9	
1891–95	19		10.5	
1896–1900	20	20	11	30
1901–5	19		11	
1906–10	18	15	11	35
1913	16	14	11	36
1919	21		19	
1926–29	11	9	11	42
1928	11		14	
1936–38	19	9		32
1938	19		10	
1946	15		25	
1948	15		20	
1958	10		16	
1963	8.5	5	13.5	32
1968		5		34
1971	7	4	13	33
1975	5		12	
1980	5		11	
1983	5		12	

Sources: Rostow (1978:52–53, 70–72); Banks (1971); Reagan (1984).

much closer connection, implied in table 6.1, between production advantages, exports, and commercial power in the British case. And yet, in the twentieth century, has the connection between these phenomena become less close once again? When these processes eventually are given the close empirical scrutiny they deserve, it is conceivable that we will learn that the development of financial centrality in the world economy has been less than linear and perhaps less synchronized with the other spheres as well.

In the absence of the appropriate evidence, it is too soon to dismiss or accept what amounts to a hypothesis about the development of economic preponderance. But this means that we need to be cautious about adopting a definition of hegemony that essentially hinges on the accuracy of the hypothesis. Even so, Wallerstein (1984:39) does emphasize one facet of economic leadership that tends to be left obscure by structural realists.

> It is not enough for one power's enterprises simply to have a
> larger share of the world market than any other . . . I mean
> hegemony only to refer to situations in which the edge is so
> significant that allied major powers are de facto client states and
> opposed major powers feel relatively frustrated and highly
> defensive vis-à-vis the hegemon.

That Wallerstein insists on genuine economic preponderance, as opposed to permitting marginal advantages, for bestowing the hegemonic label is clear. What is left unclear is the threshold for significant edges that will subordinate allies and frustrate the opposition.

Lead Economy

Modelski's (1981, 1982, 1983) conceptualization of a lead economy is based in part on Perroux's (1979) interpretation of how economies are composed:

> [An] economy is understood as a heterogeneous entity made up
> of parts (zones or sectors) which are more or less dominant and
> more or less dominated and capable of actions that do not result
> in reactions of equal force.

Perroux had hoped to break away from the tendency in classical economic theory, a tendency that also applies to much of classical international relations theory as well, to portray or treat actors as roughly equal in their relative influence (if not their comparative advantage). Any real economy is an aggregation of zones or sectors that can be described as relatively active or passive. Relatively active zones or sectors, in turn, are more likely to exert asymmetrical influences, whether intentionally or unintentionally, over more passive sectors. The greater the asymmetry of sector A's influence over sector B, the more dominant A is over B. Moreover, these observations hold at all levels of economic interaction (i.e., local, national, and international).

At the international level, the national economies of states are unequal in terms of size, bargaining power, and the nature of the economic activities in which they engage. Modelski focuses in particular on one of the more extreme variants of these inequalities—one in which a single state constitutes the world system's most active zone. As such, this singular state, the world power, occupies central place in the world economy because it is the predominant source of innovation, growth, development, credit, investment, and exchange. It is this multi-faceted, quasi-monopolistic position that enables the world power to dominate the world economy in terms of its highly asymmetrical influence and in terms of the rest of the world's dependence on the economic services it provides. Nonetheless, the extent of the world power's influence still falls short of a ruling role in the traditional imperial connotation.

To divorce the lead economy concept from the notion of political centrality is merely a matter of expositional convenience. As much as the world power is the predominant source of economic innovation, it is also the principal source of political innovation, order, and leadership, all of which are buttressed by its predominance in naval capabilities. The concentration of economic influence is thus conjoined with the concentration of political and military (of the global reach variety in any event) influence for at least several decades.

And rather than the chicken and egg question of which comes first— economic or political activity and predominance—Modelski is content to say that economic and political centrality are mutually reinforcing. The political role requires a material base for financial support. The economic role requires politico-military leadership to create and maintain the ground rules for economic transactions.

> A lead economy requires the political stability and international
> protection afforded by the services of the quality and the
> dimensions afforded by the world power. Each world power has
> been, in its time, the area of the greatest security of rights and
> entitlements, and of lowest transaction costs and superior global
> information, services, and therefore also most frequently the
> economy of refuge. On the other hand, world power is also costly
> and cannot be maintained without the support of an active and

growing economy. Operations of global reach and global wars in particular cannot be conducted on the cheap. Hence a lead economy built upon a global flow of activities becomes a *sine qua non* of world power (Modelski, 1982:104).

Although the question of measuring naval capability distributions has been a major preoccupation of long-cycle analysis until recently (Modelski and Thompson, 1988), Modelski (1982:104) does provide an operational or at least part of an operational definition that can be contrasted with the two earlier definitions advanced by Keohane and Wallerstein.

> To operationalize the concept of "lead economy" we emphasize not size (as it might be indexed by area, population, or GNP) but those indicators that bear on status as "active zone": the creation of leading sectors and the relative size of the industrial economy, and participation in world trade, both qualitatively (in goods of the leading sectors) and quantitatively (in shares of world trade or of foreign investment). We also note that each lead economy has been engaged in forms of advanced agriculture . . . all have led in the organization of intensive food production . . . Each lead economy has also been linked to basic innovations in global services relating to transportation and communication as well as information.

While Modelski's emphasis on food production and innovations in transportation, communication, and information may appear to represent something of a departure from what the other authors are stressing, the degree of overlap is otherwise quite impressive. "Lead" economies are not "hegemonic" but Modelski's operational advice parallels some of the emphases of Keohane and Wallerstein's definitional efforts. Modelski stresses industrialization (after the mid-eighteenth century) and leading sectors—definitional elements with overt association with Keohane's high value added comparative advantages and Wallerstein's productive efficiency edges. Modelski mentions shares of world trade, which relates to Wallerstein's stress on the commercial sphere. All three definitions share an interest in financial leadership as well. In sum, it does not seem unfair to suggest that while lead economies may not always be hegemonic, economic hegemons are likely to be lead economies.

Where the three definitions can really be said to conflict is on the quantity versus quality dimension. Hegemonic definitions tend to stress material preponderance. Leadership definitions are more likely to stress more subtle, innovational advantages. Even so, the quantity-quality dichotomy is less than pure. An edge in leading sector production implies both qualitative and quantitative dimensions. An economy that retains a lead in innovating leading sectors but that has lost its initial lead in producing the leading sector commodities also has lost an important part of its claim to represent the world economy's most active zone. Much the same can be said, albeit in reverse, of comparative advantages in productive efficiency. Efficiencies in producing relatively less important or more common commodities may yield a comparative advantage of sorts, but it is not necessarily one that is particularly conducive, as Keohane observes, to developing a *primus inter pares* preponderance in certain material resources.

MODELS OF SYSTEMIC LEADERSHIP DECLINE

Leading sectors have roles to play in the three definitions of economic leadership. At the same time, each of the authors reviewed is prone to introducing additional elements that work toward obscuring the leading sector common denominator. The same generalization is much less applicable to models of systemic leadership decline. In all four of the models to be inspected, the role of leading sectors is far too prominent to be obscured easily.[4]

The Bousquet Model

Within the world-economy school, Nicole Bousquet (1980) has put together one of the most specific models of the rise and decline of systemic leadership. For Bousquet, the concentration and deconcentration of economic power reflect the irregularity of development in time and its unevenness in space. Less descriptively, international disparities in productive efficiency characterize two opposing trends in the world economy: one of differentiation in which one state attains productive supremacy and hegemony versus one of indifferentiation in which non-hegemonic core states regain the full ability to compete.

The trend toward differentiation depends on the coming together of several factors including unusually scarce and expensive labor, the adoption of capital intensive techniques, and sufficiently favorable market demand circumstances. The interaction of these factors improve the probability that major innovations will be created and applied throughout the pertinent economy. If, in addition, radical innovations in the methods of production in one or more key sectors take place, the multiplying effects of the productive breakthrough throughout the economy can transform the status of an economy from one of productive superiority to one of supremacy in the system.

> Thanks to these major innovations, the entity wherein they occur first finds itself in a position of production supremacy within the world-economy, and eventually obtains other dimensions characteristic of authentic hegemony, namely commercial and financial supremacy, and political leadership coupled with military supremacy (Bousquet, 1980:79).

To account for the trend toward indifferentiation, Bousquet points out that it is a function of processes taking place within the hegemon as well as within competitors and challengers. The most central process within the leader is the tendency for innovation to become less important or at least for innovative energies to be placed increasingly on improving established products as opposed to developing new ones. Four possible reasons are given for the deemphasis on innovation. First, economies may be subject to aging processes that are accompanied by the development of biases against change. Presumably related, there may also be a tendency to overspecialize in the sectors that initially were responsible for the attainment of production supremacy.

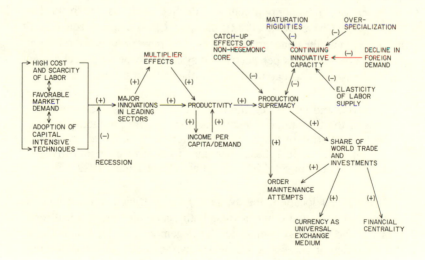

Figure 6.2   Bousquet's Model of Hegemonic Rise and Decline
Source: Based on the discussion in Bousquet (1980)

New sectors of production are further deterred by this inclination to concentrate on expanding established sectors.

A third possibility is that the set of factors that were responsible for bringing about the innovations in the first place may be altered substantially. For example, labor might become less scarce and/or less expensive due to substantial immigration. Still another explanation is suggested by the decline of foreign demand for the leader's exports either due to a phase of recession and/or increasing protectionist barriers.

Of the four explanations for hegemonic decline (with the hegemon) depicted in figure 6.2, Bousquet finds the one emphasizing overspecialization the most attractive. In this sense, productive success breeds the foundation for its own downfall. Yet, as Bousquet acknowledges, there is hardly enough evidence at this time to be in a position to pick one explanation at the expense of the others. Moreover, for the gap between the hegemon and the rest of the core to narrow, significant catch-up efforts on the part of the rest of the core are also necessary. Catching up, ultimately, is dependent not only on the diffusion and importation of the leader's technology, but also on the challengers' differential mixes of demand and production factor circumstances.

The Chase-Dunn Model

A second world-economy ascent and decline model is put forward by Christopher Chase-Dunn (1982). Despite Chase-Dunn's equation of hegemony with the concentration of military power *and* economic competitive advantage, his perspective on systemic leadership decline, not unlike Bousquet's, is captured well in the following statement:

> The rise and fall of hegemonic core states can be understood in terms of the formation of leading sectors of core production and the concentration of these sectors, temporarily, in the territory of [a] single state, which hence becomes [the] most economically and politically powerful of core states (Chase-Dunn, 1982:80).

Geographical location, the availability of sufficient human and investment capital, and other factors, both economic and political, contribute to the rise of system leaders or hegemons but, for Chase-Dunn, the dynamics of ascension are nearly synonymous with the development of the ability to create leading sectors.

If the temporary concentration of leading sectors is thought to be a crucial hallmark of hegemony, it is not surprising that the most important explanation for decline, among those outlined in figure 6.3, is the

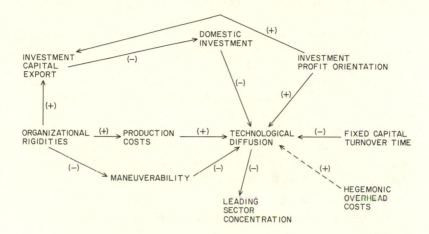

Figure 6.3   Chase-Dunn's Model of Hegemonic Decline
Source: Based on the discussion in Chase-Dunn (1982)

diffusion of technology and capital from the area of concentration and to the hegemon's economic competition. The diffusion is facilitated, in turn, by a variety of additional factors. One is the latecomer's advantage in developing leading sectors. The leader must pioneer new techniques that are subject to fixed capital turnover times. The latecomer can evade some of the initial trial and error associated with an industry's start-up. It can also begin with the most recently developed technology at its disposal while the pioneer struggles to compete with its outdated productive infrastructure. Some form of economic nationalism and reindustrialization policies might be expected to counter this growing gap in the ability to remain competitive. Yet these tendencies are defeated by what Chase-Dunn terms the "purely profit-oriented logic of investment." Tariff barriers aside, there is little incentive for investors to back domestic efforts that try to compete with the foreign products that can be produced more cheaply abroad.

The way in which the socioeconomic system comes to be organized eventually results in social rigidities that constrain the ability of an economy to continue to lead in productivity. For instance, the formation of unions facilitated labor's political articulation, increased costs of production through improvements in wages and benefits, and, in general, decreased the maneuverability of capital and capitalists. As these rigidities become more binding, investors have increasing incentive to seek more profitable risks away from the domestic economy. Capital is exported increasingly making new investments at home less probable and less possible.

Finally, Chase-Dunn points tentatively to the overhead burdens of centrality in the system. Since he emphasizes the need to suppress deviance from the rules of the system, one gathers Chase-Dunn primarily has military costs in mind. Yet Chase-Dunn prefers not to stress this explanatory factor because, as he contends, the costs of leadership only begin to outweigh the benefits after once closely allied core states begin to challenge the hegemon in economic competition. The timing could suggest that the cost dimension is at least secondary to the diffusion of economic competitiveness and may, in the end analysis, be more of a symptom than a genuine cause of decline.

The Goldfrank Model

A third world-economy interpretation, Goldfrank's (1983) model of hegemonic decline, is less a full-fledged model with interconnected components than it is a list of similarities between British and American hegemonies. The model does overlap to some extent with the Chase-Dunn model, but the emphases are different and for this reason it is worth considering. In Goldfrank's model, the loss of leading sector competitiveness is also attributed to a large degree to other states simply catching up through importing and imitating capital and technology (diffusion). Yet the loss of productive superiority is accelerated by

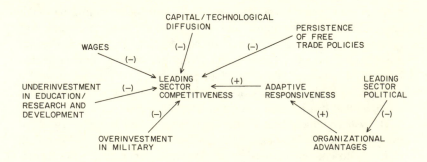

Figure 6.4　Goldfrank's Model of Hegemonic Decline
Source: Based on the discussion in Goldfrank (1983)

other factors as well. Wage increases are interpreted as a negotiated price for workers participation in the "hegemonial project" that, ultimately, undercut international competitiveness. Underinvestment in education and research and development is also thought to characterize hegemonic behavior. At the same time, hegemons tend to overinvest in the military sector.

One factor in figure 6.4 that receives more stress from Goldfrank than is customary in world-economy analyses, although it definitely is related to the rigidity factors remarked upon by Bousquet and Chase-Dunn, is the political power of earlier leading sector industries (however, see Bergesen, 1981, 1982 and, of course, the nonworld-economy analysis of Kurth, 1979). As new waves of industrial production appear, the key products and the nature of the organizations (e.g., small businesses to large corporations to state/corporation partnerships) that produce them tend to change or evolve. Powerful interest groups associated with older, now declining, industries hinder the ability of the hegemonic economy to adapt to the changes, especially in the new way in which things are being done. Seemingly related, as are many of the other explanatory arguments (although the link is not made specific by Goldfrank) is the observation that the ideology of free trade and kindred policies persist despite increasing protectionism in other parts of the world. While free trade may serve specific interests such as banking, Goldfrank views this persistence as another form of maladaptive response that makes the loss of competitiveness more probable.

The Gilpin Model

Gilpin's (1981) model of hegemonic decline is presented in such a fashion that it is open to varying interpretations. However, the model does stress quite emphatically the pivotal role of leadership overhead costs:

> The governance of an international system involves a fundamental economic problem. Although control over an international system provides economic benefits (revenues) to the dominant power . . . domination also involves costs in manpower and material resources. In order to maintain its dominant position, a state must expend its resources on military forces, the financing of allies, foreign aid, and the costs associated with maintaining the international economy. These protection and related costs are not productive investments; they constitute an economic drain on the economy of the dominant state (Gilpin, 1981:156–157).

Yet the problem, for Gilpin, is much more complicated (see figure

6.5) than merely the drag of defense burdens. Protection costs are influenced by external competition and to some extent compete with other forms of consumption. In turn, the various types of societal consumption are dependent upon the creation and continued maintenance of the most advanced, most efficient, and most productive economic foundation.

This economic foundation is in part a product of technological innovation. Unfortunately, the edge in technological innovation has not proven to be either a constant or any society's monopoly for long.

> . . . every innovation is subject to . . . the tendency for the
> growth impulse of any innovation to come to an end. Moreover,
> economic and technological innovations tend to cluster in time
> and space, favoring this society, then that society. In the absence
> of new spurts of innovation or a borrowing of technology from
> abroad, the growth of the wealth and power of a society begins
> to slow, describing an S-shaped curve. . . . the consequences are
> a reduced or negative rate of growth and a reduction in the
> economic surplus available for consumption, protection and
> investment (Gilpin, 1981:159–160).

The S-shaped rate of growth is affected not only by the tempo of innovative impulses but also by international diffusion and maturation tendencies. In the short run, the world market tends to favor and to concentrate wealth in the more advanced and efficient economy. In the long run, wealth and economic activities (trade, foreign investment, and the transfer of technology) tend to diffuse to new centers of eco-

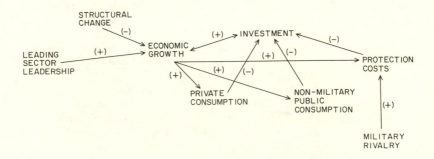

Figure 6.5   Gilpin's Model of Hegemonic Decline
Source: Based on the discussion in Gilpin (1981)

nomic growth from the old centers. As the technological advantages of the dominant power are diffused to other states, the costs of domination are therefore increased. The diffusion process, furthermore, is apt to be accelerated to the extent that a goodly proportion of the leader's labor force has made the transition from agricultural, through manufacturing, to what are thought to be less productive. service-oriented activities.

Operating in conjunction with these broader economic tendencies are another set of historical tendencies that alter or affect the allocation of national income. Dividing national income into three broad sectors—protection, consumption, and investment—Gilpin asserts that protection and consumption shares tend to rise over time at the expense of the investment share and subsequent economic growth. Protection costs, of course, are likely to be influenced by the number and strength of military rivals. The effects of external competition are compounded further by two internal tendencies: (a) the most efficient military techniques tend to rise in cost over time and (b) the costs of military power in affluent societies tend to rise at disproportionately rapid rates due to competition from other sectors for scarce manpower and resources.

But private and public consumption are both driven upward with time as well. If two of the three components of national income are increasing, presumably it must come at the expense of the third component (investment)—at least in relative terms. Specifically, Gilpin contends that increasing affluence increases the demand for consumer goods and services that spreads downward through the social hierarchy in a form of trickle-down effect. The consumption (private and nonmilitary public) share of national income also tends to increase as a society ages.

> [If protection shares increase as well] This, in turn, means that
> the share of gross national product reinvested in the economy
> must of necessity decrease . . . As a consequence, the efficiency
> and productivity of the productive sector of the economy on
> which all else rests will decline. If the productive base of the
> economy erodes, it becomes more difficult to meet the rising
> demands of protection and consumption, without further cutbacks
> in productive investment, thus further weakening the future health
> of the society (Gilpin, 1981:158).

A Brief Comparison of the Four Models

There are a number of observations one could make about these models. There are also a number of hypotheses that deserve further empirical inquiry. In both cases, many of the observations and much of the hypothesis testing must await other forums. For the purposes of this chapter, a few general statements about the models taken as a group should suffice. If we were to lay figures 6.2 through 6.5 on top of one another, some thirteen distinguishable components would emerge. As identified in table 6.2, these components range from leading sectors through various sorts of rigidities to nonmilitary public consumption. Since the sample admittedly is biased toward one perspective, there is little point in evaluating the plausibility of each and every component. Given the nature of the model pool and the state of our empirical information on the subject of decline processes, it would be rather difficult to argue that a component found in three models was likely to be more significant, or more valid, than, say, a component found in only one model. Bousquet's overspecialization factor with only one "vote," for instance, could prove to be more telling than labor factors (supply and wages) in spite of their appearance in three models.

Yet while one might not wish to use table 6.2 to weight the significance of the factors thought to have explanatory utility, it is interesting

Table 6.2

**Components Stressed in Four Models of
Systemic Leadership Decline**

Model Components	Models			
	Bousquet (1980)	Chase-Dunn (1982)	Goldfrank (1983)	Gilpin (1981)
1. Leading sectors	X	X	X	X
2. Diffusion/catch-up	X	X	X	X
3. Underinvestment		X	X	X
4. Rigidities	X	X	X	
5. Overhead/protection costs		X	X	X
6. Labor factors	X	X	X	
7. Foreign demand	X			
8. Overspecialization	X			
9. Capital flight		X		
10. Military rivalry				X
11. Private consumption				X
12. Structural change				X
13. Nonmilitary public consumption				X

that only two components are central to all four models—leading sector innovation/concentration and diffusion. Nor can there be any doubt about the significance of these components for the four models. In each model, with the partial exception of Gilpin, who pairs it with economic growth, leading sectors and their diffusion are either the phenomena to be explained or the phenomena through which, or upon which, most of the other variables operate.

To paraphrase Gilpin, the leading sector concept is synonymous with the productive base of the economy on which all else rests. Once the system leader begins to lose its edge in the leading sectors of its time, a number of other factors—innovation, investment, consumption, protections costs, productivity, trade—become more difficult to maintain. The process of catching up on the other hand becomes correspondingly less difficult as the leader's motor runs down.

Whether or not "all else rests" on this fragile leading sector foundation is not really at stake here. Nor do we need to dwell long on whether all or most or even some of these ideas are on target. All are at least associated with reasonably plausible arguments subject, of course, to differing interpretations. What is of primary importance here is the pervasiveness of the leading sector concept across three different definitions and four separate models. The triangulation of three distinctive perspectives suggests that we have at least found, if not the blind men's elephant, one of the larger beasts to be identified in the world-system herd.

It almost goes without saying that we will continue to argue over the identity and nature of the beast's body parts. Yet one of the ways in which social scientists customarily attempt to resolve some of their verbal arguments is through measurement. Measurement alone, of course, is unlikely to resolve anything. However, measurement applied to specific theoretical and empirical questions, within the context of a shared conceptual base, should prove to be helpful.

MEASURING LEADING SECTORS

Analysts have long experienced some degree of difficulty in measuring the rate of technological innovation (see Mensch, 1979; van Duijn, 1983). The problem seems to be due largely to the uncertainties encountered in weighting the relative significance of various inventions. Taking into account the variable length of time between conception to genuine application also poses problems. Some investigators have sought to avoid these problems by relying on productivity measures such as output per man hour (Bousquet, 1980; Maddison, 1982; Lake, 1984) or proportional shares of world manufacturing output produced or exported (Rupert and Rapkin, 1985). Unfortunately, there are restrictions on how far back in time one can construct these indicators. In addition, there are clear problems of aggregation from a leading sector point of view. Neither output per man hour nor shares of total manufacturing output exported discriminate among the various types of commodities that are produced. Improvements in the service sector presumably can boost output. Similarly, items involving high or low technology/value added may be manufactured and exported.

What is needed, it is argued, is a more direct way of capturing the concept of leading sector production. The basic premise is that a growing economy is characterized by different rates of growth in various sectors of output. Some sectors may be stagnating while others are expanding at a moderate pace. A few sectors, however, are able to introduce the major technological breakthroughs that lead to the consequent increases in efficiency, rapid sectoral growth, and a number of secondary, stimulative implications for the rest of the economy. Among the conceivable implications that must be considered are reductions in prices and transportation costs, population relocations, employment and export increases, and spin-off demands for related sectors.

In this regard, Rostow's (1978:365–560) study of leading sectors in the economic history of a number of states is particularly useful. He first identifies what he refers to as the classical sequence of leading sectors since the late eighteenth century (see also Landes, 1969; Gilpin, 1975:67): cotton textiles, iron, railroads, steel, chemicals, electricity, and motor vehicles. Specific output indicators are suggested for each sector and analyzed in terms of their rates of growth.

While this approach is appropriate for Rostow's (1978) purposes some modifications are necessary to adapt his indicators to the current purpose. Since Rostow analyzes each country separately, the outcome expressed in national sectoral data will not necessarily pinpoint who leads and who follows. A very small producer, especially one just beginning to produce a particular commodity, might have a much faster rate of growth than a more established producer. National rates of growth per se, therefore, are less than helpful for establishing leading sector leadership. There is also the problem of assessing which sectors should be regarded as leading in any given year. Rostow views this question from a national lens. Yet what may be a leading sector in a latecomer's economy may be relatively passé in the larger world economy. Pre-World War II Japan offers a good illustration of this problem. Last but not least, Rostow's list of leading sectors seems dated. The most recent sector, plastics, is dated as beginning in the mid-1950s. While it is wise to exercise some caution in designating contemporary leading sectors, it is also difficult to overlook some of the most recent candidates for leading sector status.

To internationalize Rostow's indicator system, one can simply aggregate, for the most important actors (here taken to include Great Britain, Russia/the Soviet Union, France, Germany, the United States, and Japan), the national sectoral outputs per year. The corresponding proportional values for each of the six states are then calculated. To arrive at a relative leading sector or leadership score for each state, one need only average the proportional country shares for each sector. Table 6.3 lists the leading sector indicators suggested by Rostow (1978), augmented by two additional indicators intended to represent the electronics and aerospace industries.[5] Also identified are the periods of time the various sectors can be regarded as leading for the world economy (as opposed to the respective national economies as identified in table 6.4).

The problem is one of avoiding phasing new and old leading sectors in or out either too early or too late—thereby unwittingly biasing the indicator system. The economic history literature is not very helpful in specifying this dimension, at least not at the world level, which is still not a familiar level of analysis. Some experimentation, nonetheless, suggests that the threat of bias may not be all that critical. Moving the introduction and demise of a leading sector back and forth in time can alter the average proportional scores, but only in a marginal fashion. The direction of the national trajectories remain very similar. In any event, the dates of sectoral leadership assigned in table 6.3, and based to a large extent on the information reported in table 6.4, are most likely to err on the sectoral demise end. That is, the initiation of a sector's salience is reasonably conspicuous. However, the loss of status is much more problematic. For this reason, the lengths of sectoral tenure in table 6.3 are overly generous. To make them shorter would presume more information than is available currently.

One possible exception to this need for more information is suggested by table 6.5. Some twenty-eight product classes are rank-ordered according to their research intensity ratio as a measure of its "high tech" character. The ratio is measured by dividing total sales by the amount of research and development funds allocated to each product class. The rank order listed in table 6.5 is dated now (it was com-

Table 6.3

A Leading Sector Measurement of Economic Leadership in the World Economy

Sector	Indicators	Systemic Tenure as Leading Sector
Cotton textiles	Raw cotton consumption (thousand metric tons)	1780–1913
Iron	Pig iron output (thousand metric tons)	1780–1913
Railroads*	a. Railroad track open (thousand kilometers) b. Railway track open/ square kilometer	1830–1913
Steel	Crude steel output (thousand metric tons)	1870–
Chemicals*	a. Sulphuric acid output (thousand metric tons)	1870–1945
	b. Nitrogen fertilizer output (thousand metric tons)	1945–
	c. Plastics/resins output (thousand metric tons)	1947–
	d. Synthetic fiber output (thousand metric tons)	1950–
Electricity	Electrical energy production (gigawatts)	1910–
Motor vehicles	Motor vehicle production (thousand units)	1910–
Electronics	Semiconductor production (monetary value in current U.S. dollars)	1954–
Aerospace	Civilian jet airframe production (units)	1958–

*Proportional shares in sectors (multiple indicators) averaged annually within the sector, producing one sector score. The second railroads indicator is not found in Rostow's (1978) treatment; it has been inserted here to correct for problems involved in comparing large countries with relatively small countries on the basis of the first railroads indicator.

Table 6.4

Rostow's Beginning and Ending Dates for National Leading Sectors

Sectors	Great Britain	United States	France	Germany	Japan	Russia/Soviet Union
Cotton textiles	1780s–1860s	1820s–1870s	* –1880s	* –1890s	1880s–1900s	* –1880s
Pig iron	1780s–1880s	1840s–1910s	1830s–1950s	1850s–1950s	1880s–1900s	1890s–1950s
Railroads	1830s–1870s	1830s–1890s	1840s–1880s	1840s–1880s	1900s–	1890s–
Steel	1870s–1920s	1870s–1920s	1870s–1950s	1870s–1950s	1900s–	1890s–1950s
Electricity	1900s–	1900s–	1900s–1960s	1900s–1960s	1920s–1950s	1920s–1950s
Motor vehicles	1920s–1960s	1910s–1950s	1920s–	1920s–1960s	1930s–	1950s–
Sulphuric acid	*	* –1920s	* –1950s	* –1930s	* –	* –
Nitrogen	* –	* –	* –	* –	* –	* –
Plastics/resins	* –	* –	* –	* –	* –	* –
Synthetic fibers	* –	* –	* –	* –	* –	* –

Source: Rostow (1978:379–435).

Note: Absence of date indicates sector continues to lead. Asterisk indicates sector not considered a leading sector by itself. Source does not clarify how a leading sector can be judged as "ceasing to lead" after failing to become a leading sector.

piled in 1968–1970), but a similar effort attempted in 1984 (*The Economist,* 1986) lists the same top ten product classes but places them in different rank positions.

High tech and leading sectors are not equivalent concepts. Nevertheless, the perception that current and future leading sectors are and will continue to be high tech in nature is widespread. In this respect, table 6.5 helps to justify the addition of aircraft frames and semiconductors to Rostow's list. After guided missiles, aircraft and their parts had the highest high tech tanking in the late 1960s/early 1970s. Semiconductors are synonymous with the number-three-ranked electronics class and critical as well to the second-ranked office machines category.

A second implication of table 6.5 is that several sectors are being retained too long in table 6.3's tenure schedule. The three chemical indicators (nitrogen fertilizer, plastics, and synthetic fibers) are supported by the highly ranked positions of product classes six and eight. Electrical energy production is not a form of manufacturing and thus has no representation in table 6.5. Steel and motor vehicles, however, rank low on the list—numbers fourteen and twenty-six. Both are also "below average" (as determined by the research intensity ratio for total manufacturing) on the high tech scale. Nonetheless, it still seems a bit premature to jettison two sectors that have been so critical to growth and economic performance in the twentieth century. As noted, it is preferable to err on the liberal side when deciding exactly when it is appropriate to abandon a given sector as passé.

Following the procedures outlined above facilitates the creation of a data base that enables us to place each of the six major actors, between 1780 and 1980, in terms of their combined leading sector production shares. Table 6.6 provides representative scores at ten-year intervals for the 201-year period. It should be immediately apparent that the measurement system is not without its liabilities. For example, the early Russian lead in pig iron production inflates its proportional share unduly for several decades in the late eighteenth and early nineteenth centuries.[6]

Naturally, it would also be helpful to have an equally long series on the extent to which the system's leading sector export markets are shared by the six states. This information is more difficult to obtain, but it would add a commercial indicator to the present focus on production. Similarly, some indicator for financial centrality would also be highly useful. However, the commercial or export indicator specifically would assist in resolving some of the limitations of depending solely on the production indicator. For instance, is the Soviet Union's relatively

Table 6.5

Product Classes Rank Ordered According to High-Tech Character

Product Class	Research Intensity Ratio
1. Aircraft and parts	12.41
2. Office machines	11.61
3. Electronics	11.01
4. Optical and medical instruments	9.44
5. Drugs and medicines	6.94
6. Plastic materials and synthetics	5.62
7. Engines and turbines	4.76
8. Agricultural chemicals	4.63
9. Ordnance (except guided missiles)	3.64
10. Professional/scientific instruments	3.17
11. Industrial chemicals	2.78
12. Radio/television	2.57
13. Farm machinery/equipment	2.34
14. Motor vehicles/equipment	2.15
15. Other electrical equipment—construction/mining machinery	1.90
16. Other chemicals	1.76
17. Fabricated metal products	1.48
18. Rubber and other plastic products	1.20
19. Metalworking machinery/equipment	1.17
20. Other transportation equipment	1.14
21. Petroleum and coal products	1.11
22. Other nonelectrical machinery	1.06
23. Other manufactures	1.02
24. Stone, clay, and glass products	0.90
25. Nonferrous metals and products	0.52
26. Ferrous metals and products	0.42
27. Textile mill products	0.28
28. Food and kindred products	0.21
Total manufacturing	2.36

Source: Kelly (1977) as reported in Scott (1985b:75–76). First ranked product class (guided missiles and space craft) excluded. However, its intensity ratio is described as almost 7 times as high as the ratio associated with aircraft. (Research intensity is measured as the ratio of applied research and development funds by industry to shipments by product class.)

Table 6.6

Proportional Shares in Leading Sectors, 1780–1980

Year	Great Britain	France	Russia/ USSR	United States	Germany	Japan
1780	.292	.311	.256	.103		
1790	.455	.163	.230	.105		
1800	.534	.160	.175	.092		
1810	.603	.128	.134	.097		
1820	.549	.192	.095	.110		
1830	.643	.182	.025	.101		
1840	.583	.123	.034	.200		
1850	.546	.110	.037	.205		
1860	.500	.138	.036	.216		
1870	.519	.129	.031	.175	.135	
1880	.430	.112	.048	.261	.149	
1890	.333	.109	.041	.347	.176	.005
1900	.245	.106	.072	.363	.194	.021
1910	.146	.093	.053	.504	.182	.022
1920	.100	.077	.003	.687	.108	.026
1930	.082	.094	.039	.620	.121	.045
1940	.075	.042	.106	.566	.129	.082
1950	.093	.048	.103	.642	.066	.040
1960	.087	.081	.095	.575	.091	.072
1970	.070	.056	.114	.521	.089	.158
1980	.039	.059	.142	.485	.083	.187

Note: Values for 1960–1980 period do not always sum to 1.00 because of Japan's nonparticipation in airframe production to date and lack of data on Soviet airframe and semiconductor production. Although scores could be adjusted to treat this absense of production/information neutrally, Soviet and Japanese shares are computed with zero entries for these sectors—thereby penalizing their leading sector share scores.

high leading-sector production rank really appropriate when so little of its production is competitive in world markets?[8]

Imperfections aside, the leading-sector measurement strategy does appear to capture reasonably well an important dimension of the qualitative economic leads enjoyed by the successive system leaders, Great Britain and the United States. Britain emerged from the Napoleonic Wars with a greater than 50 percent share that peaked around 1830. Decline began to accelerate dramatically after 1870—an index change that corresponds closely with many treatments of British economic history and the erosion of its nineteenth-century economic leadership. As

demonstrated in figure 6.6, the United States crossed the British downward trajectory in the 1880–1890 interval, reaching its own peak share
at the end of World War I. Interestingly, the direction of movement in
the American share turns upward briefly around the time of World War
II. It then resumes its downward movement almost as if there had been
no global war from 1939 to 1945.

Readers should keep in mind that the leading-sector scores are aggregations. As such they disguise the unevenness of sectoral growth patterns. In general, however, one can discern a wave pattern in the
development of leading sectors and in the leadership positions carved
out by the primary producers. Tables 6.7 and 6.8 provide a more clear
illustration of this feature. The "Industrial Revolution" wave, the first
one that is reflected in the sectoral data encompassed cotton textiles,
iron, and later, railroads. Britain's lead clearly was highly dependent
upon this first wave. Innovations in steel and chemicals ushered in a
second wave in the last third of the nineteenth century. Great Britain led
in both sectors but only very briefly. Hence, one way to describe the

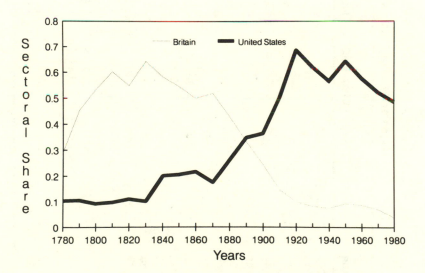

**Figure 6.6   Rise and Decline of Britain's and the United States'
Leading Sector Positions**
Data Sources: See footnote 5, Chapter 6

Table 6.7

Rise and Fall of Britain's Leading-Sector Position

Year	Cotton	Pig Iron	Railroads	Steel	Chemicals	Electricity	Motor Vehicles	Electronics	Aerospace	Leading-Sector Share
1780	.375	.209								.292
1790	.690	.219								.455
1800	.694	.374								.534
1810	.787	.419								.603
1820	.590	.507								.549
1830	.671	.491	.766							.643
1840	.635	.590	.525							.583
1850	.545	.628	.464							.546
1860	.540	.612	.348							.500
1870	.499	.585	.312	.524	.677					.519
1880	.484	.493	.248	.331	.593					.430
1890	.512	.345	.203	.325	.381					.333
1900	.320	.250	.182	.195	.280					.245
1910	.249	.177	.168	.123	.184	.062	.056			.146
1920				.142	.140	.094	.023			.100
1930				.094	.086	.087	.060			.082
1940				.105	.092	.075	.027			.075
1950				.105	.094	.094	.090			.093
1960				.098	.090	.082	.136	.040	.078	.087
1970				.067	.068	.069	.083	.060	.071	.070
1980				.026	.050	.055	.044	.030	.031	.039

Table 6.8

Rise and Decline of the United States' Leading-Sector Position

Year	Cotton	Pig Iron	Railroads	Steel	Chemicals	Electricity	Motor Vehicles	Electronics	Aerospace	Leading Sector Share
1780	.125	.080								.103
1790	.113	.097								.105
1800	.104	.079								.092
1810	.101	.093								.097
1820	.196	.024								.110
1830	.114	.106	.082							.101
1840	.156	.107	.337							.200
1850	.241	.139	.235							.205
1860	.209	.116	.322							.216
1870	.210	.145	.312	.119	.089					.175
1880	.265	.216	.331	.320	.174					.261
1890	.309	.355	.382	.389	.299					.347
1900	.337	.385	.378	.405	.308					.363
1910	.363	.471	.397	.502	.380	.676	.742			.504
1920				.659	.507	.630	.950			.687
1930				.525	.531	.569	.855			.620
1940				.486	.398	.483	.896			.566
1950				.494	.673	.586	.814			.642
1960				.353	.488	.538	.504	.800	.769	.575
1970				.279	.432	.489	.403	.630	.895	.521
1980				.231	.427	.457	.269	.630	.894	.485

productive dimension of Britain's decline is that while the British economy dominated the first wave, it failed to catch the second one.

As shown in table 6.8, the United States gradually mastered this part of the second wave around the time of the First World War (and the first wave as well). At the same time, the initial American dominance in the extension of the second wave (electricity and motor vehicles) was even stronger than the British position after the Napoleonic wars. While positional erosion is quite evident in the older sectors (e.g., steel and motor vehicles), the latest round of innovations after World War II has also been dominated by the United States. In this respect, the current system leader has been somewhat more successful than its immediate predecessor in absorbing the technological shocks associated with each new wave of innovations. Any comparison must also note that Britain benefitted from fewer competitors and somewhat longer intervals between waves as well. But it is also this U.S. success in adapting to technological change that muddies the waters on the extent of its economic decline. Based on the aggregate scores in table 6.8, one could argue that the American relative economic position has been decaying since the 1920s. Even so, the relative decay has been quite mild—not unlike the slow phase of the British slide in the midnineteenth century (1830–1880). Whether the decay will accelerate as in the British case or simply continue to slide moderately remains to be seen.

CONCLUSION

There is an unusually strong consensus that leading sectors are one of the keys to deciphering structural change in the world system. An economy at the forefront of technological change can develop such an impressive lead in efficiency and productivity that it dominates all other economies. Its domination is not so much a question of outright rule. To paraphrase Tylecote (1982), it is more a question of trading up and down the technological gradient. The system's lead economy is at the top of the gradient, at least for awhile, and the rest of the world must trade up the gradient to it. Eventually things change for a variety of reasons that deserve further investigation. But what is clear is that some economies slide up and down the gradient. Once relatively passive zones of the world economy become more active zones and vice versa. A new lead economy emerges as the system's most active zone. The former leader becomes less active.

After 1780 and the late eighteenth-century Industrial Revolution, data on the distribution of leading sector production are readily available to capture movements up and down the technological gradient. Leading-sector concentration is not the only way to empirically capture this phenomenon, but it does offer easily accessible and disaggregated information for a long period of time. With its aid, it is possible to follow the economic fortunes of the system's major powers somewhat more precisely. It is also possible to examine the interactions of leading-sector production with global war and military power distributions—a topic pursued in the next chapter.

7

Leading Sectors, Naval Power, and Global War

The measurement of leading sectors in chapter 6 hardly tells us all that we might wish to know about the economic foundations of systemic leadership. For instance, information on the extent to which leading-sector goods are exported could be quite useful. The system leader's centrality to the world economy's financial subsystem is also very much of interest. Yet the data created in chapter 6 are sufficient to initiate the pursuit of several empirical questions pertaining to the leader's economic resources.

One such empirical question has to do with the occasionally heard comment that assessing the current leadership position of the United States is rendered difficult by the outcome of World War II (see, for example, Russett, 1985). In the aftermath of the war, the U.S. economic lead is said to have been enhanced abnormally by the temporary, war-induced setbacks suffered by the competition (among both winners and losers). The return to a more competitive (should we read less abnormal?) situation, accordingly stimulates talk of leadership decline that tends to be exaggerated.

As Pollard and Wells (1984:333–334) point out, there is no doubt that the United States' position in the system was enhanced during World War II:

> America emerged from the Second World War as the preeminent economic power in the world. Unlike virtually every other industrialized country, the United States escaped the conflict with its productive capacity unscathed. Indeed, the war fueled an unprecedented boom in American industrial production while the economies of all other powers lay shattered or damaged. . . . Steel production grew by more than one-half. By 1947, the American share of world trade had climbed to

one-third, compared to one-seventh in 1938, and by 1948, the United States produced 41 percent of the world's goods and services. Since it controlled so much of the world's industrial and financial assets, any action or inaction by the United States in the economic sphere had a profound impact on the postwar world order. . . .

The evidence reported in chapter 6 indicates that it is equally true that the United States no longer enjoys such a commanding lead. The real question is whether the temporary, postwar positional edge held by the system leader is normal or abnormal. For most historical-structural analysts of world politics, the relative decline of a system leader after a postglobal war positional peak not only is normal, it also is precisely what the fundamental process of concentration and deconcentration is all about. How unusual then were the effects of World War II? More importantly, does this case illustrate a general propensity, namely, is it possible that global wars are important and regular facilitators of politico-economic power concentration? And, if the facilitation is only temporary, then can it also be said that systemic wars foster decline as well?

A second empirical question pertains to the occasional schism over the variable significance of different types of resources and their equally variable utility as indicators of systemic leadership, decline, and the movement toward a renewed struggle for leadership. Some schools of thought tend to subordinate military position to economic position. Others, such as the long cycle of global leadership camp, prefer to treat both types of systemic position equally, at least in theory. But it is also fair to say that long-cycle analysts have consistently stressed the utility of indicators capturing the distribution of naval power as excellent measures of global reach. What one stresses obviously makes some difference to how the world is assessed and how one tells system time. But just how divergent are indicators of economic and naval preeminence in the world system? Since both types of capabilities may be construed as indicators of global reach, to what extent do they rise and fall in unison? Should we find a fair degree of synchronization, it should serve to bolster the argued utility of sea power measures. It may also suggest once again that we have less to quarrel about than so frequently appears to be the case.

LEADING SECTORS AND GLOBAL WAR

It would not be too great an exaggeration to suggest that all studies of war's economic impact tend to fall between two extreme positions. On the one hand is Sombert's (1913) contention that war stimulates innovation and industrial technology. At the other extreme, represented by Nef (1950), is the argument that war stimulates very little of positive benefit.[1] In any event it destroys far more than it produces. Empirical analyses of this dispute are not particularly numerous (see Kuznets, 1964, 1971; Barbera, 1973; Wheeler, 1980; Organski and Kugler, 1980; Rasler and Thompson, 1985b). Even so, the general tendency is to examine the effects of war on highly aggregated measures of economic performance. As a consequence, the finding that global wars exert temporary economic impacts (both positive and negative) on national products may not tell us much about what happens to specific leading sectors.

Interest in this question is sparked to some extent by the renewed interest in the close link between war, the needs of the armed forces, the industrial change (McNeill, 1982; Smith, 1985; Roland, 1985; Macksey, 1986). One need not embrace Sombart's extreme stance to appreciate the historical connections between military and industrial change. But there is also a more concrete stimulus located within the historical-structural literature. Although the emphasis varies considerably, all three of the main perspectives accord a special role for systemic warfare as an agent of structural change. All three schools agree, for instance, that the best opportunity for creating a new power hierarchy and new rules of the game for the system's operations is associated with the aftermath of systemic warfare.

Wallerstein (1984:44) goes a bit further and suggests that world wars are necessary to solidify the hegemonic power's newly dominant status. Of particular interest, however, is Modelski's "alternating innovations" model. We have already described how Modelski views the global political system and world economy as mutually reinforcing spheres of action. The growth or expansion of both are also propelled by streams of different types of innovations. Both also consume resources from the same resource pool. The question Modelski raises is thus whether there is a systematic pattern to the expansion of the two subsystems. His answer is yes and, given a choice between joint or alternating growth phases, Modelski (1981, 1982) opts for the latter.

The alternating innovations model predicts an alternation between phases in which either political problems or economic problems and their solutions are most salient. When political problems command the lion's share of attention, new political institutions are created. When economic problems are most salient, new leading sectors tend to emerge. Coordinating these alternating phases are Kondratieff fluctuations in resource scarcities and prices (rising prices in phases of political salience and stable/declining prices in phases of economic salience). Finally, every second phase of political salience constitutes an extra strong upbeat in the system's circulatory system. Global war leads to a major overhaul of the political system by setting the stage for the emergence of a new world power and a new world order.

A portion of Modelski's test of the alternating innovations model is determining whether the maximum rate of expansion for leading sectors since 1763 is located in periods of stable/declining prices and therefore periods of economic salience. With the exception of plastics, this prediction is borne out by Rostow's (1978) data (see chapter 8 and table 8.9). What this means is that leading sectors tend to be introduced in the Kondratieff downturns. The prediction says nothing about the concentration of leading-sector production, which is as important, if it is not more important, to our understanding of structural change (capability concentration/deconcentration) than is the phase of sector conception that usually overlaps with its maximum rate of expansion.

A Mixed, Alternating, and Joint Expansion Model for Leading Sectors

Given the picture of the growth of the leading-sector concentration/ deconcentration that has emerged in tables 6.6, 6.7, and 6.8 and figure 6.6, it seems quite likely that an ad hoc case for a mixture of alternating and joint expansion of the political and economic spheres needs to be considered. Expressed most simply, global war works to enhance the lead economy's relative productive position in the leading sectors of its time for at least two reasons: (1) global war-induced demand is more beneficial for the system's lead economy than it is for other economies in terms of increasing demands and expanding infrastructure, and (2) global war ultimately is far less beneficial to the war's losers, who experience serious setbacks (usually temporary but not always) in their ability to compete in the world economy.[2]

Thus, in respect to capability concentration, the upswing phasing is more synchronized than it is alternating. Historically, naval capabilities (and naval power of global reach) have been most likely to be expanded during periods of global war. Consequently, new system leaders emerge from a global war at the peak of their relative naval power. They also tend to first match or exceed a partially arbitrary 50 percent threshold of major-power naval capabilities during or immediately after a global war (chapter 3 and Modelski and Thompson, 1988). These findings do not mean that global wars work, as in alchemy, to transmute instantaneously otherwise ordinary states into world powers. The changes in relative power have been ongoing for some time prior to the outbreak of war. Global wars, however, do put an aspiring system leader "over the top" and bring the radical structural changes to fruition.

It is hypothesized here that something similar happens with respect to leading-sector production concentration. A lead economy's peak concentration may not necessarily coincide with periods of global war due to the episodic (and alternating) introduction of new sectors. Yet it does appear that the same 50 percent threshold (the equivalent of all others) for leading-sector concentration is first crossed during periods of global war. The second phase of political saliency (global war), therefore, also constitutes an extra strong upbeat from an "economic" perspective as well. Expressed in a different way, the platforms for military and economic leadership, or at least their culmination, are established conjointly—reflecting again the mutual reinforcement of the world system's political and economic subsystems.

Evidence for the Mixed Model

Some evidence in support of this hypothesis has already been presented. The information reported in table 6.6 demonstrated that Britain and the United States achieved and surpassed the 50 percent leading-sector threshold in the Napoleonic Wars and World War I eras respectively. Figures 7.1 to 7.3 provide sectoral evidence that speaks to the same subject even if not every leading sector behaves precisely the same way. Figure 7.1, for instance, charts the rise of Britain's cotton textiles and pig iron sectors in the 1780–1820 period. The peak of this series, 1809–1811, is very much associated with years of global war. In contrast, Britain's relative standing in the iron sector climbs steadily throughout the war and finally exceeds the .5 threshold shortly after the end of the war (1818–1819). What this reflects in absolute terms is very uneven growth rates across the major producers. Russian and American output changed very little between 1791 and 1816. German output doubled, and French pig iron production tripled. But the growth of British output—approximately a 500 percent increase—was the most impressive.

Figure 7.2 shows a similar picture for the United States. Strong leadership positions in steel and motor vehicles predate the advent of

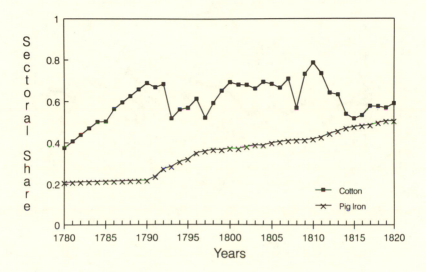

Figure 7.1   Global War and Britain's Leading Sectors, 1780–1820
Data Sources: See footnote 5, Chapter 6

World War I. In both cases, the peaks of the series are located in or immediately after World War I (steel, 1920; vehicles, 1917; and 1919). The chemistry sector series exceeds the .5 mark in 1918 and peaks (prior to the introduction of new chemical products after World War II) in the following year. Departing from the British pattern, all three series, plotted in figure 7.3, declined in the years between the twentieth century's two global wars. In each case, the positional decay trend is reversed in 1939–1940. And, again in each of the three cases, the highest points of the post-1930 series are located in World War II.

Sectors that are introduced between or after global wars are, of course, much less likely to be directly influenced by a global war. As a consequence, we would not expect to find the same pattern in the British railroad sector that is associated with, say, the pig iron industry. However, for most sectors, global wars increase the amount of sectoral concentration linked to the primary winner's lead economy. The extent of the leader's economic lead is thus shaped in a significant fashion by

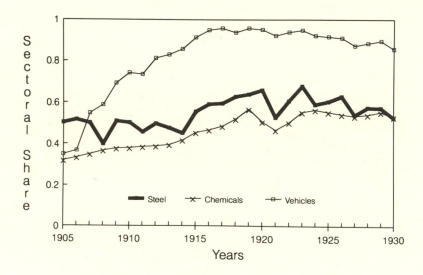

Figure 7.2 Global War and the United States' Leading Sectors, 1905–1930

Data Sources: See footnote 5, Chapter 6

a global war. And even though this generalization is based on the examination of post-1780 data, its applicability can be pushed back in time fairly easily.

In the earlier, more trade-oriented era, the Portuguese were facilitated considerably in their attempt to develop an alternative avenue to the spice trade by the war-time preoccupation of the Ottomans, the Venetians, and other Europeans. Temporarily at least, the ability of the traditional Middle Eastern land routes for delivering spice to the Mediterranean market was reduced severely. A century later, the Dutch might have been much slower to enter the Mediterranean and Asian trade circuits if their link to the Spanish economy had not been severed officially by the war with Spain. Opening up new trade routes and markets is not exactly the same thing as producing new leading industrial sectors. Yet in a system in which the base for economic leadership has gradually shifted from the engine of trade to industrial production, the innovation of new trade routes may be something like a functional equivalent to more current preoccupations. In both examples, as well,

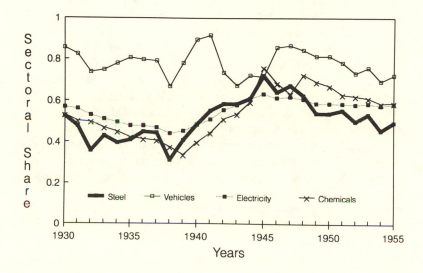

Figure 7.3   Global War and the United States' Leading Sectors, 1930–1955
Data Sources: See footnote 5, Chapter 6

shipbuilding was a highly significant leading sector that could not have gone unaffected by the associated increase in demand for ships.

GLOBAL WAR AND NAVAL POWER CONCENTRATION

Global war's impact on naval power concentration is similar but much stronger. It is conceivable that the leading-sector threshold might have been crossed at or about the same point in time if the global wars had not occurred when they did. The same generalization would be far more difficult to apply to the concentration of naval power. Ostensibly, major changes in military inventories require a clear perception of threat in order to override the numerous types of resistance to spending money on world-class navies.

The development of naval preponderance is an unusually expensive proposition. Once achieved, it is still expensive to maintain, but the magnitude of expense is not of the same order. Preponderance requires (increasingly so) the mobilization of a large proportion of national resources—so large a proportion is required that the resources are only likely to be made available in the midst of a national emergency situation such as is encountered in global war. Preponderance is also facilitated greatly if one's rivals' navies are reduced or decimated. This outcome is also most likely to be associated with global warfare, and perhaps only global war.

True, most of the states that have sought naval predominance even during global war have been unsuccessful. This only suggests that other factors (such as a lead economy and a global orientation) are important for success. It does not detract from the observation—based on the data discussed in chapter 4—that global war appears to be a necessary, if not sufficient, context for achieving high levels of naval power concentration. It logically follows that the decay of preponderance is highly probable once the global war is over. The ultimate winner will no longer be willing to devote all of its resources to military ends. Eventually, rivals will also be in a position to build or rebuild their own naval capabilities.

Rates of Decay

The probability of immediate decay is a testable proposition. If we were to examine the longitudinal record of the building of capital warships, we would expect some level of concentration of inventory growth in times of global warfare and much less growth in nonglobal war periods. Table 7.1 lists the 1494–1983 net growth in the capital warship fleets of three types of power contenders (the world power, the primary challenger, and the successor to the world power) by decade. The decades during which global war takes place are indicated by asterisks.

As is to be expected, events in every century do not duplicate exactly those of other centuries. Rather than dwell on the exceptions, the general pattern may be best illustrated by aggregating across the 490-year record. The average decennial net change for the world-power column is .56. However, the average net change in the decades of global war is 5.04 ships. Figures 7.4 through 7.8, which plot the decennial net changes for each successive world power, provide a visual demonstration of this phenomenon. Periods of global war tend to be the exceptional periods of naval capability expansion. Decades of nonglobal warfare, with some exceptions, tend to be periods of little growth or decay. The reader should keep in mind as well that the decennial calculations tend to understate the growth in global war periods for two reasons. First, some decades mix years of warfare with years of non-warfare and, in some cases, immediate postwar decay or demobiliza-

Table 7.1

Net Changes in Capital Warships by Decade

Decade	World Power	Primary Challenger	Successor World Power
	Portugal	Spain	Netherlands
*1494–1503	21	6	
*1504–1513	79	24	
*1514–1523	–43	–12	
1524–1533	–16	– 6	
1534–1543	1	0	
1544–1553	2	4	
1554–1563	–16	– 5	
1564–1573	10	5	
*1574–1583	–20	22	34
*1584–1593		31	4
*1594–1603		–37	5
*1604–1613		–14	14
	Netherlands	France	England
*1580–1589	15	– 2	5
*1590–1599	– 3	0	3
*1600–1609	14	0	– 5
1610–1619	23	4	3
1620–1629	50	35	14
1630–1639	7	0	– 1
1640–1649	–75	– 4	27
1650–1659	13	– 5	22
1660–1669	15	46	–15
1670–1679	–40	7	0
*1680–1689	17	13	– 6
*1690–1699	10	22	43
*1700–1709	1	–22	7
*1710–1719	–23	–83	– 3
	Great Britain	France	
*1688–1697	29	27	
*1698–1707	7	–11	
*1708–1717	8	–65	
1718–1727	– 6	6	

Table 7.1 (*continued*)

Decade	World Power	Primary Challenger	Successor World Power
1728–1737	5	3	
1738–1747	–10	– 4	
1748–1757	–27	35	
1758–1767	23	– 1	
1768–1777	–12	5	
1778–1787	20	6	
*1788–1797	7	– 2	
*1798–1807	9	–10	
*1808–1817	–24	–24	

	Great Britain	Germany	United States
*1792–1801	– 2		
*1802–1811	17		
*1812–1821	–34		
1822–1831	–29		
1832–1841	– 8		
1842–1851	– 6		
1852–1861	–69		
1862–1871	36	0	
1872–1881	–30	– 5	
1882–1891	14	3	
1892–1901	4	4	9
1902–1911	–12	2	– 3
*1912–1921	23	– 9	14
*1922–1931	–22	0	– 5
*1932–1941	– 2	5	0
*1942–1951	1	– 5	5

	United** States
*1914–1923	1
*1924–1933	2
*1934–1943	16
*1944–1953	9
1954–1963	–14
1964–1973	2
1974–1983	– 1

*Asterisk indicates decade encompasses years of global war.

**Aircraft carriers only.

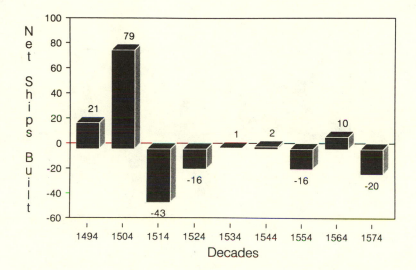

Figure 7.4   Global War and Naval Capability Expansion,
1494–1613
Data Source: Modelski and Thompson (1988:62–64)

tion. Second, no attempt is being made to differentiate global wars in which a rising world power is triumphant from those in which an exhausted former world is replaced by its successor. Hence, the 5.05:–.56 ratio understates the dynamics of the naval power deconcentration process.

As noted, preponderance is greatly facilitated by the reduction and destruction of rival navies. Table 7.1 also illustrates this dimension of the naval-power concentration process. Focusing only on the primary challenger column, it is instructive to note what happens to the fleet of the primary loser toward the end of each global war, but especially in the 1580–1608, 1688–1713, and 1792–1815 bouts. Dramatic fleet decreases are the rule due to exhausted treasuries, combat losses, or reparations and scuttling. Consequently, the winner emerges from global war with an unusually large navy and faces little, at least initially, in the way of naval competition.

This absence of naval competition works for and against the success-

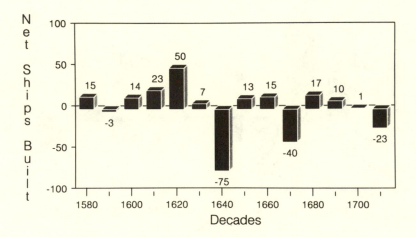

Figure 7.5   Global War and Naval Capability Expansion,
1580–1719
Data Source: Modelski and Thompson (1988:63–65,67–69

ful system leader. Its initial naval leadership is exaggerated by default. At the same time, the lack of opposition at sea probably hastens the system leader's own demobilization efforts. But the postwar shrinking of the leader's absolute capabilities is not reflected in the relative rankings thanks to the poor naval shape of nearly everyone else. The real losses in relative naval position come only after new rivals emerge or old rivals are prepared to make come-back bids.

Thus the long cycle of naval power concentration differs from leading-sector processes in terms of its much closer dependence on global war, the postwar reduction in absolute capabilities, and the role of political decision making. Unlike the less coordinated activity of economic innovation, MITI notwithstanding, political decision makers much choose to develop their state's naval capabilities, either to improve their competitive position, to challenge the leader, or to react to the challenges of rivals. These decisions can be made in less prosperous times. Similarly, decisions not to develop naval capabilities can be

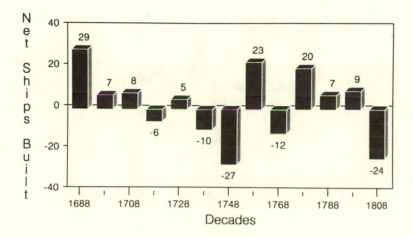

**Figure 7.6   Global War and Naval Capability Expansion,
1688–1817**
Data Source: Modelski and Thompson (1988:68–71)

made at various points in time and for reasons which may not be
strictly or entirely a matter of cost or resource scarcity. Two examples
are the perennially intermittent French naval reform efforts in the seventeenth and eighteenth centuries and the American reluctance to challenge British sea power in most of the nineteenth century.

LEADING SECTORS AND THE DISTRIBUTION OF
NAVAL POWER

If naval and economic capabilities tend to become concentrated at the
same juncture in time, should we also expect the relative proportional
scores to decline at the same rate? Alternatively put, does the deconcentration process unravel simultaneously in all spheres and in the
same way? The answer is probably no. Nor should we expect identi-
cally paced deconcentration processes. The concentration of leading-
sector production seems more likely to decay quickest. The diffusion of

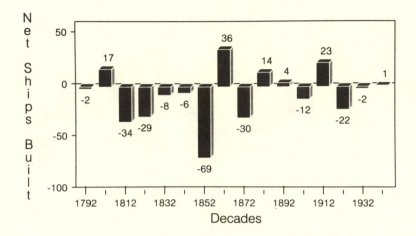

Figure 7.7   Global War and Naval Capability Expansion,
1792–1951
Data Source: Modelski and Thompson (1988:70–72, 75–76, 78, 331)

technology and innovation is extremely difficult, it not impossible, to stop or even to seriously hinder. Moreover, the models on systemic leadership decline reviewed in chapter 6 suggest a number of reasons why leaders are apt to undercut the bases of their own economic success. We have no strong reasons as yet to isolate one or more decline factors as the primary culprit (e.g., protection costs, overspecialization, capital flight, and so forth), but the general image of leaders who, wittingly or unwittingly, gradually retard their own forward economic momentum is quite pervasive in the literature.

One way to describe the general situation, then, is to treat the urge to compete economically as a near constant—regardless of Kondratieff fluctuations. For periods of time, some states are more successful in this competition than are others. It is the ability to be successful that shifts over time. The most successful are unable to maintain their leads. Old and new challengers are made bolder as the leader's dominance erodes. Increased military rivalries and competition therefore become more likely. By this time, the challengers are more economi-

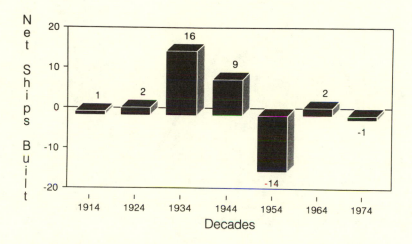

**Figure 7.8   Global War and Naval Capability Expansion,
1914–1983**
Data Source: Modelski and Thompson (1988:78, 331–332)

cally capable of expressing their political rivalries in military terms—or
they may come to think that they are more ready to do so. As a consequence, we might expect leading-sector production concentration to
decay more quickly than military-power concentration. One type of
decay encourages the decay of the other. The more quickly the economic lead unravels, moreover, we should expect reverberations in the
hierarchy of military power. Whether or not the system leader is able to
draw on its economic reserves—something that is as much a political
question as it is an economic one—will have a strong influence on its
ability to stay competitive in the military race. And staying in the competition may be as much as a former system leader can hope for as the
number of competitors and the costs of the competition escalate—short
of a renewal of the economic basis for its claim to leadership.

Comparative Rates of Decline
As before, the available data are restricted to the past two hundred
years. Figures 7.9 and 7.10 chart the relative decline of two consecu-

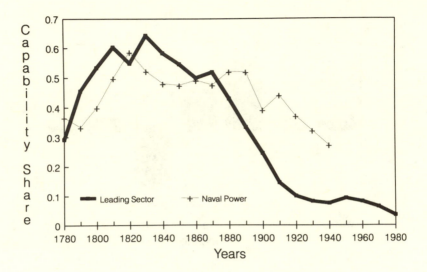

**Figure 7.9   Rise and Decline of Britain's Naval Power and
Leading-Sector Positions**

Data Sources: Leading sector, see footnote 5, Chapter 6; naval power,
Modelski and Thompson, 1988:120–124)

tive system leaders, Britain and the United States. Two types of capability are depicted as well. One is the by now familiar concentration of
leading-sector output. The other indicator measures the distribution of
naval power as reflected in the leader's proportional share of: (a) the
number of ships of the line prior to 1816, (b) the average of naval
expenditures and front-line battleships (the criteria for which are subject to change as naval technology evolves) between 1816 and 1945,
and (c) the average of the number of heavy aircraft carriers, nuclear
attack submarines, and the quality (CMP) and the quantity (EMT) of
its ballistic missile force at sea. A more extensive discussion of the
admittedly complex character of this series can be found in Modelski
and Thompson (1988).

As predicted, the plots of leading-sector and naval-power distribution
data in figures 7.9 and 7.10 are reasonably congruent. The British lead
in both areas is strong throughout the first two-thirds of the nineteenth
century. The leading sector positional decline, after the 1870s, is more
abrupt than the decay in the naval position. British decision makers

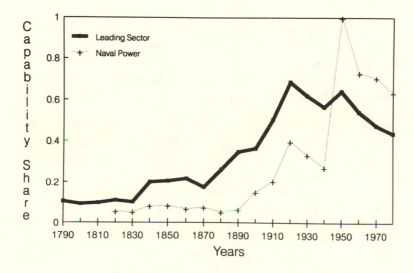

Figure 7.10   Rise and Decline of the United States' Naval Power and Leading-Sector Positions

Data Sources: Leading sector, see footnote 5, Chapter 6; naval power,
Modelski and Thompson, 1988:92, 121–124)

were determined to maintain some semblance of their former naval leadership despite their faltering industrial position. Vis-à-vis the German challenge, the British were ultimately successful, at least at sea. The American challenge was a different matter entirely.

Figure 7.10 depicts the American emergence from World War I as the undisputed leader in leading-sector production. The United States might also have emerged from that war as the world's predominant naval power. If the war had lasted longer and/or if the 1916 naval construction plans had gone forward, rather than being diverted to building destroyers for Atlantic convoy duty, the U.S. navy might have become, as Wilson wished, second to none. Signifying their unwillingness to assume the full responsibilities of the world power role and, in particular, its related expenses, United States decision makers attempted to freeze the postwar naval power status quo. However, naval expansion resumed in the 1930s as a prelude to the global war in which the United States finally emerged as the political and economic system leader.

The discrepancy between the two leadership dimensions after 1945 is more apparent that real. The very strong U.S. naval position in the late 1940s and 1950s that is indicated does not seem all that misleading. But it should be kept in mind that what is being utilized as an index is the possession of heavy aircraft carriers. Moreover, the postwar military competition eliminated all but the Soviet Union as a potential military rival. Since the Soviet Union is not expected to launch its first large carrier before the early 1990s, if then, figure 7.10 is merely capturing the American carrier monopoly prior to the introduction of nuclear submarines. In contrast to the bipolar nature of the military competition, economic competition has retained a multipolar flavor— even if three of the players (France, Germany but especially Britain) have become less central than the other three.

These nonparallel structural changes render comparison a bit more awkward. Relative positions based on a 2-actor world do not mean quite the same thing as relative positions based on a global power subset of 6 states. If we control for this difference, the post-World War II movement of the two indicator systems corresponds roughly to the British nineteenth century case with two major exceptions. Both of the series in figure 7.10 register relative positional decline after World War II. In this case, however, it is the relative naval position that seems to decline the more precipitously of the two. Yet much of this apparent departure from the "norm" must be attributed to the nature of the naval-power index and the two-power military structure.

The other exception is that the global war that ushered in the American world order, World War II, was responsible for only a brief respite in the longer-term relative decline in leading-sector production dating from the end of World War I. Thus, analysts who argue that the apparent U.S. decline since World War II is dependent on misperceptions of the war-induced, "abnormal" inflation of the United States' relative position are partially correct—even if for the wrong reasons. The fact that these two dimensions of leadership seem out of step with one another, nonetheless, raises an interesting speculation. Should we clock the U.S. relative decline from World War I, despite its reluctance to assume the leadership, or from World War II, when it was prepared to assume the politico-military role? In other words, has the interwar period thrown system time, or our ability to tell system time, out of kilter?

Putting aside the two exceptions, the major similarity between the British and U.S. cases lies in the fact that economic leadership tends to erode more quickly than military power. While the 1980 U.S. relative economic position remains quite respectable and considerably ahead of its closest rivals, relative economic positions can change very rapidly. Should the United States fail to retain its lead in the newest leading sectors, just as the British failed to do in the 1870s, the American leading-sector position could plummet in the future as quickly as the British position did between 1870 and 1910 (.519 to .146). At the same time, the military standoff between the United States and the Soviet Union presumably will continue. New military contenders are not inconceivable, but their possible development seems much less imminent than does the possibility of continued relative economic decline on the part of the United States. If the theoretical scenario developed earlier is correct, it will require continued decline in the American relative economic position—a possibility that one hastens to add is by no means foreordained or inevitable—to motivate the development of new military challengers.

CONCLUSION

As argued here, global war puts lead economies "over the top" in terms of both relative economic and naval positions. As most competitors are set back at least temporarily, the rising leader profits and is able to cross an arbitrary threshold of technological superiority (.5 on the leading-sector and naval-power concentration scales). One difference, however, is that the concentration of leading-sector technology is less dependent on the impact of global war than is naval power. Changes in leading-sector technology historically have been subject to less coordination and, therefore, tend to be more gradual and cumulative. The development of naval power, again historically, instead has been subject to growth spurts greatly aided by perceptions of direct threat.

Global wars thus demarcate a period in time when economic and military power concentrations come together to provide a systemic leader with the underpinnings for altering the rules of the system and promoting a new world order. Decades later, the relative decline in economic power will begin to slip first. As the leader's economic position slides down the technological gradient, competitors, allies, and would-be successors alike are encouraged to augment their own military positions. Relative economic decline therefore facilitates relative politico-military decline. The incumbent system leader may be able to maintain a fairly strong military position in the face of increased competition, but unless it can reverse its slide down the technological gradient, it will not have the resources to do much more than remain competitive. Ultimately, a new global war may need to be fought to resolve the question of leadership in the system.

This chapter has argued that the positional slides up and down the technological gradient, the outbreak of systemic war, and the emergence of political-economic capability concentration are all interconnected. Some historical-structural analysts are prepared to take this argument one step further by suggesting that the interconnections are governed by long-term fluctuations in the world economy that have come to be known as Kondratieff long waves. It is to this possible approach to monitoring system time (and explaining the outbreaks of global wars) that we will turn in chapter 8.

Long Economic Waves and Global War

There are two general historical-structural approaches to assessing the relationship between long, wave-like economic fluctuations, frequently referred to as Kondratieffs, and global warfare. One approach prefers to link the long waves directly to hypothesized changes in the hegemonic power cycle. Economic upswings and downturns thereby develop additional significance as settings for conflicts between ascending and declining powers. the second approach has tended to be more empirical. The central question from this angle is the interaction between periodic major wars and changes in the behavior of price and production indexes. Do wars generate the long-term swings in prices and production? Is it the other way around? Or is not some amount of reciprocal causation the most likely connection?[1]

The answers to these different types of questions remain disputed. Demonstrating historical-structural patterns of causality is rarely a simple, straight-forward matter of assembling the evidence that pertains to some set of rival hypotheses. As often as not, much of the historical evidence is more than a bit murky. Nor is it unusual for the evidence to be interpretable in several different ways. Before exploring some of these linkages between expectations and data, however, we need to first consider the initial source of many of the controversies relating war to long-term economic fluctuations. After introducing the ambiguous foundation advanced by Kondratieff (1935/1979), we can then proceed to a discussion of more contemporary analyses.

KONDRATIEFF'S LONG WAVE

In the first quarter of the twentieth century, several economists in Holland and the Soviet Union produced evidence for the existence of long economic waves. The most widely known of these analyses, those published by N. D. Kondratieff in the 1920s, focused on British, French, German, and American price, production, and consumption series. Whether long waves could be discerned and precisely what shape they assumed depended on which series were examined. The most systematic evidence was associated with price series that suggested the three long waves outlined in table 8.1. Kondratieff also believed that a number of generalizations (also in table 8.1) could be made about behavior within the up- and downswings of the long wave.[2]

Table 8.1

Kondratieff's Long Wave

Long Wave	Upswing	Downturn
Chronology		
First	late 1780s–1810/17	1810/17–1844/51
Second	1844/51–1870/75	1870/75–1890/96
Third	1890/96–1914/20	1914/20–
Regularities		
	1. Years of business prosperity are relatively more frequent.	Years of business depression dominate.
	2.	Agriculture experiences a pronounced and long depression.
	3.	An unusually large number of technological discoveries and inventions are made but not applied until the beginning of the next upswing.
	4. At the beginning, gold production increases and the world market is expanded by the assimilation of new territories.	
	5. The most disastrous and extensive wars and revolutions occur.	

Source: Based on discussion in Kondratieff (1935/1979).

Kondratieff insisted repeatedly that these behavioral regularities—prosperity and depression, agricultural productivity, the rate of invention and innovation, gold production, market expansion, and the most deadly wars—were the effects and not the causes of the long waves. Yet prior to his deportation to Siberia in 1930, Kondratieff failed to develop a theory to explain the empirical regularities that he thought he had uncovered. The only clue that he advanced for the war-upswing, for example, was to suggest that the rising phases of the long wave tended to be characterized by high tension. High tension, in turn, increased the likelihood of extensive wars and revolutions.

Despite the reluctance of many conventional economists, especially in the United States, to work with the idea of a 40- to 60-year cycle, a moderately large literature on the Kondratieff long wave has emerged. A useful if very brief and increasingly dated overview of much of this literature may be found in Barr (1979). Of the 172 studies reviewed by Barr, at least a third appear to advance some form of causal explanation for the long wave. Table 8.2 constitutes an attempt to summarize the types of variables employed in these explanations.

Table 8.2

Explanatory Variables in the Kondratieff Literature

Explanatory Variable	Frequency
1. Gold Supply	16
2. War	14
3. Capital depreciation/investment	6
3. Crises of capital accumulation	6
5. Technological change	5
6. Psychological factors	4
7. Innovation	3
7. Territorial expansion	3
9. Overproduction	2
9. Raw material shortages	2
9. Productivity changes	2
9. Arms production	2
9. Production cost changes	2
10. Agricultural output growth rates	1
10. Population change	1
10. Meterological factors	1
10. Accident	1

Source: extracted from the synopses supplied by Barr (1979).

Table 8.2 indicates the relative frequency of certain types of explanations by counting the number of times they appear in the literature reviewed by Barr. However, Barr's bibliographic annotations were not meant to be exhaustive summaries of the examined materials. There is little doubt that some variables or factors are understated. Moreover, the fact that gold supply and war appear to be the most popular explanations should not be interpreted as implying that there is only one way in which gold supply or war may be employed to account for long waves in economic activity. Finally, it should be noted that while there are 55 studies which appear to offer explanations, only 17 types of explanations emerge. Obviously then, the 17 cannot represent mutually exclusive explanatory factors.

It does not seem coincidental, for instance, that gold becomes more scarce during periods of major warfare. Similarly, it is somewhat arbitrary to separate a more general emphasis on technological change (number 5) from the somewhat more specific innovation explanatory factor (number 7). Suffice it to say that many of the 55 studies promote more than one of the listed causal factors. Nor should this be particularly surprising since a number of the explanations preceded the discovery of the long wave. A case in point is Jean Bodin's 1568 explanation of sixteenth-century European inflation as including the influx of gold and silver, war and the consequent reduction of supplies, coinage debasement, the luxuries of kings and princes, and the actions of monopolies (see Miskimin, 1977:36).

In any event, table 8.2 is intended to serve at least two purposes. First, it suggests, rather inelegantly, that the ultimate explanation of the long waves is likely to be complex and multicausal. Comprehensive testing of these ideas, no doubt, will require the consideration of a number of variables. Even if we narrow the field to Goldstein's (1985:412) four major competing theories of the long wave—capital investment (Forrester, 1978); innovation (Schumpeter, 1939; Mensch, 1979); Freeman et al., 1982; capitalist crisis (Gordon, 1980; Mandel, 1980); and war (Wagemann, 1930; (Dickenson, 1940; Rose, 1941)—the operationalization and analysis of the various models would still constitute an ambitious undertaking. Such a project will not be pursued in this chapter in preference for a more modest concentration on one of the key factors emphasized in both table 8.2 and Goldstein's theoretical quartet. Indeed, the second purpose of table 8.2 is to underscore the very prevalence of the war explanation. It is in fact one of the two most popular explanations in Barr's literature. Approximately one-fourth of the analyses surveyed delineate war as a significant causal force in generating long waves.

A quick examination of the war evidence for much of the period with which Kondratieff worked also helps to underscore the apparent accuracy of Kondratieff's generalization placing "the most disastrous and extensive" wars in the upswing phase. Table 8.3 rank-orders the Correlates of War project's (Singer and Small, 1972:134) 1816–1914 list of interstate wars according to their severity or number of battle deaths. If we accord Kondratieff a slight benefit of the doubt by counting wars which begin during the years (1810–17, 1870–75, 1890–96, and 1914–20) which overlap the upswing and downswing of the long wave as occurring during the rising segment of the wave, it is abundantly clear that not only the most severe wars but also most of the interstate wars of the 1816–1914 period were initiated during the long wave's upswing. Of thirty-five wars, as many as twenty-eight (80 percent) began during the upswing. The upswings also encompass twelve of the fourteen most bloody wars. If a war list that matched Kondratieff's late 1780s beginning point had been generated, the support would appear to be even stronger. The French Revolutionary/Napoleonic, and 1812 Anglo-American wars could be added to the upswing side of the ledger without altering the number of wars allocated to the downswing column. Hence, Kondratieff's war generalization is readily substantiated, at least as a descriptive statement for the era between the Napoleonic Wars and World War I. Yet while the degree of association is quite striking, what table 8.3 cannot answer are the questions of whether economic long waves help to bring about wars or whether wars contribute to the generation of economic long waves.

These questions could be pursued empirically and, for that matter, have been. But before moving to a discussion of the findings on the war-Kondratieff relationship, some theoretical guidance should be useful. What relationship between war, structural change, and long-term economic fluctuations should we expect based on a reading of historical-structural analyses of international relations?

ECONOMIC HEGEMONY AND THE
KONDRATIEFF LONG WAVE

Table 8.4 summarizes one interpretation of the links between, and the periodicities of, economic hegemony and the Kondratieff long wave. For the Research Working Group on Cyclical Rhythms and Secular Trends, headed by Terence K. Hopkins and Immanuel Wallerstein, hegemony refers, as has been discussed in chapters 3 and 6, to an exceptional period "in which one core power exceeds all others in the efficiency of its productive, commercial and financial activities, and in

Table 8.3

War Severity and the Kondratieff, 1816–1914

Rank Order	Kondratieff Upswing	Kondratieff Downswing
1	World War I (1914)*	
2		Russo-Turkish (1877)
3	Crimean (1853)	
4	Franco-Prussian (1870)	
5		Russo-Turkish (1828)
5	Russo-Japanese (1904)	
7	First Balkan (1912)	
8	Second Balkan (1913)	
9	Seven Weeks (1866)	
10	Italian Unification (1859)	
11	Franco-Mexican (1862)	
11	Italo-Turkish (1911)	
13	Mexican-American (1846)*	
14	Sino-Japanese (1894)*	
15		Pacific (1879)
16		Sino-French (1884)
17	Spanish-Moroccan (1859)	
17	Spanish-American (1898)	
17	Spanish-Moroccan (1909)	
20	Austro-Sardinian (1848)*	
21	1st Schleswig-Holstein (1848)*	
22	2nd Schleswig-Holstein (1864)	
23		Navarino Bay (1827)
24	Roman Republic (1849)*	
25	Anglo-Persian (1856)	
25	Greco-Turkish (1897)	
27	La Plata (1851)*	
28		Franco-Spanish (1823)
28	Italo-Roman (1860)	
28	Italo-Sicilian (1860)	
28	Ecuadorian-Columbian (1863)	
28	Spanish-Chilean (1865)	
28		Central American (1885)
28	Central American (1906)	
28	Central American (1907)	

Data Source: For war severity rank order, Singer and Small (1972:134).

Note: Kondratieff upswing periods are late 1780s–1810/17, 1844/51–1870/75, and 1890/96–1914/20. Kondratieff downswing periods are 1810/17–1844/51, 1870/75–1890/96, and 1914/20–unspecified. Wars initiated during overlapping turning points denoted by an asterisk after the initial year.

Table 8.4

World-Economy Dating of the Kondratieff

Hegemonic Phases	A Phase	B Phase
Ascending hegemony	1450– ?	
Hegemonic victory		?
Hegemonic maturity	? –1559	
Declining hegemony		1559–1575
Ascending hegemony	1575–1590	
Hegemonic victory		1590–1620
Hegemonic maturity	1620–1650	
Declining hegemony		1650–1672
	1672–1700*	
		1700–1733/50*
	1733/50–1770*	
		1770–1798*
Ascending hegemony	1798–1815	
Hegemonic victory		1815–1850
Hegemonic maturity	1850–1873	
Declining hegemony		1873–1897
Ascending hegemony	1897–1913/20	
Hegemonic victory		1913/20–1945
Hegemonic maturity	1945–1967	
Declining hegemony		1967– ?

Source: Based on Research Working Group on Cyclical Rhythms and Secular Trends (1979:499).

*1672–1798 period excluded from hegemonic rivalry cycle.

military strength" (1979:497). Full hegemony or "hegemonic maturity" constitutes only the peak phase in this hegemonic cycle. Immediately preceding formal hegemony is a phase labeled "hegemonic victory." Characterized as a transitional period, it encompasses the era during which the position of the rising hegemon passes that of the declining hegemonic power. Prior to this transitional phase is a period of "ascending hegemony" in which rival core powers compete with one another for succession to the hegemonic power position. This phase, in due cyclical turn, is preceded (or the "hegemonic maturity" phase is followed) by another conflictual interval—"declining hegemony"—which pits a descending hegemon against aspiring successors.

The link between economic hegemony and the Kondratieff is quite direct. The system is said to experience two Kondratieff long waves for every four phases of the hegemonic cycle. That is, each phase of the hegemonic cycle is associated with either a Kondratieff upswing or downturn. "Ascending hegemony" and "hegemonic maturity" are linked to upswings while the other two phases encompass periods of downturn. Essentially, the Kondratieff long wave is viewed as an alternating sequence of expansion (upswing) and stagnation/contraction (downturn). In the hegemonic maturity phase, the competitive superiority of the hegemonic power leads it to espouse free trade policies that facilitate a growth spurt and expansion until supply exceeds market demand. Contraction inescapably sets in along with the decline of the hegemonic power (although decline per se is viewed as a function of the probabilities of inflationary pressures within the hegemon and technological emulation by rivals). Contraction, in turn, creates the necessary conditions for another expansion and movement toward the imposition of another hegemonic power ("ascending hegemony"). But another phase of contraction intervenes before a new hegemon becomes fully established.

The Bousquet Variant

Putting aside the ambiguous treatment of the Habsburg case and the awkward gap between 1672 and 1798 (mentioned previously in chapter 4), the Research Working Group seems to be aware that their asserted linkages appear a bit too neat. They are also less comfortable with the hegemonic phase-Kondratieff pairing the further back in time they extend their hypothesized framework. One member of the working group, Nicole Bousquet, evidently was made sufficiently uncomfortable by the nature of the assertions that she chose to advance a different and more intriguing version (or versions). Bousquet (1979) not only puts forward a different dating scheme for the hegemonic cycles, she also argues that the linkages between the hegemonic and Kondratieff phases are much less regular than those imagined by the Research Working Group. A better sense of the differences can be gained by considering the Bousquet (1979:509) timetable reported in table 8.5.

Although the basis for dating the hegemonic phases is not clear (Bousquet's definition of hegemony is the same as the Research Working Group's), the revised version shows much more independence between the hegemonic cycle and the Kondratieff long waves. For instance, the first "ascending hegemony" phase (1540–1590) overlaps with two upswings and one downswing while the second "ascending hegemony" phase (1700–1783) is associated with two downturns and one upswing. Alternatively, the Dutch period of "hegemonic maturity"

Table 8.5

Bousquet's Pairing of the Hegemonic Cycle and Kondratieff Phases

Hegemonic Cycle		Kondratieff Phases	
Phase	Date	Upswing	Downswing
Ascending hegemony	1540–1590	1540–1555	1555–1566
		1566–1586	
Hegemonic victory	1590–1620		1586–1620
Hegemonic maturity	1620–1650	1620–1650	
Declining hegemony	1650–1700		1650–1688
		1688–1710	
Ascending hegemony	1700–1783		1710–1735
		1735–1755	1755–1786
Hegemonic victory	1783–1814	1786–1815	
Hegemonic maturity	1814–1873		1815–1844
		1844–1873	
Declining hegemony	1873–1897		1873–1897
Ascending hegemony	1897–1945	1897–1913/20	1913/20–1939
Hegemonic victory	1945–1960	1939–1967	
Hegemonic maturity	1960–		1967–

Source: Based on Bousquet (1979:509).

(1620–1650) is considered to be a time of upswing while the corresponding British phase (1814–1873) is half downturn and half upswing. Yet the American full hegemony era is predominately a period of downturn after a few years of upswing. To further complicate the contrast between the two schemes, where the Research Working Group portrays the transitional "hegemonic victory" phase as a period of downturn, Bousquet envisions the British and American manifestations as upswings (the Dutch case is viewed as an exception to the rule).

In her 1979 article, Bousquet argues that the Kondratieffs should be viewed as shorter term oscillations around even longer term price trends: rising in 1540–1600/50, 1735–1815, and 1895–on and falling in 1650–1735 and 1815–1895. From this perspective, hegemonic victories occur in the A or rising price phases and are traceable to the development of leading sectors that are directly responsible for establishing the status of hegemonic power. In a 1980 article, however, Bousquet modifies her approach by dropping the pre-1814 Kondratieffs and merging the pre-1814 price (now price and growth movements) trends with the post-1814 Kondratieffs. Nevertheless, her conclusions remain similar: hegemons rise to power in A/upswing phases and lose their productive superiority and hegemonic status in B/downturn phases. Yet Bousquet regards this relationship as a relatively loose one. As indicated in table 8.6, every A phase does not usher in a new hegemonic power. Nor does every B phase return the system to a situation of competition among aspiring rivals for succession.

For Bousquet (1980), the general looseness of the overlap between the hegemonic power cycle and the Kondratieffs suggests that the fluctuations of the Kondratieff cycle cannot be relied upon to account for the ascent and decline of hegemons. Instead, she advances the Schumpeterian contention mentioned in chapter 6 that hegemonic powers are created when one core economy, confronted with the appropriate mix of production and demand factors, adopts innovative and capital-intensive techniques in one or more leading sectors. If the technological changes are sufficiently radical and pioneering for their times, the resulting gains in efficiency and production superior-

Table 8.6

A/B Phases and Hegemonic Power Status

Period	Phase Type	Hegemonic Power Status
Early 16th century to 1620/50	A	Dutch hegemony attained near end of period
1620/50–1720/50	B	Dutch hegemony lost toward end of period
1720/50–1814	A	British hegemony attained near end of period
1814–1849	B	
1849–1873	A	
1873–1896	B	British hegemony lost in latter 19th or early 20th centuries
1896–1929	A	
1929–1938/45	B	
1938/45–1970	A	American hegemony attained
1970–	B	American hegemony faltering

Source: Based on Bousquet (1980:48)

ity can lead, through multiplying effects, to production supremacy and hegemony.

Yet as old and still profitable leading sectors continue to monopolize investment capital and make new innovation less likely, the permanence of the hegemonic status becomes unlikely. In particular, the lull in the pace of technological change assists the catch-up efforts of rivals.

It is at this point that Bousquet reintroduces the Kondratieff cycle as an accelerator or retarder of hegemonic decline. Prosperous A phases accelerate the catching up process engaged in by economic competitors. Periods of contraction slow the efforts of other core powers to bridge the productivity gap. At the same time, however, these downswings may also discourage innovations within the economic hegemon.

The Research Working Group's (1979) merger of their hegemonic power cycle and the Kondratieff fluctuations has implications for the conflict propensities of core actors. But these implications have already been explored and found to be less than successful as war predictions go in chapter 3. The phases designated as periods of ascending and declining hegemony, viewed collectively, are not much more war-prone than would be expected given the distribution of years among the various categories (see table 4.8). Interweaving the long waves with the structural phases does not alter this outcome.

While Bousquet's arguments may seem more plausible in the sense that less of a lock-step relationship is seen linking the structural changes and economic fluctuations, the implications of her interpretation for patterns of warfare are not made explicit. Her version of the hegemonic-cycle dating scheme is different from the one presented by the Research Working Group. But her ascending and declining phases also capture only about as many war years (62.6%) as expected based on the categorical distribution of years (57.8%). It is also not clear whether war is supposed to be more or less probable during an upswing or downturn within any of the four hegemonic phases. The pattern of warfare is simply not a very salient topic of concern for Bousquet.

The Vayrynen Variant

In contrast, the outbreak of major-power warfare is very important to Raimo Vayrynen's (1983) eclectic analysis. Vayrynen believes that political-economic contextual change—both structural and cyclical—provides the necessary, although not the sufficient, conditions for outbreaks of major wars. While he acknowledges that economic dominance and political leadership are analytically distinct processes, his argument ultimately concentrates on the four-phased hegemonic power cycle/paired Kondratieffs of the Research Working Group. His dating scheme, however, follows Schumpeter's (1939) four-phased long wave (prosperity, recession, depression, recovery) and therefore departs somewhat from those advanced by the world-economy analysts. Vayrynen also focuses explicitly on economic growth phases while the earlier dating schemes were based on a mixture of price and growth periodizations. Nevertheless, when Vayrynen turns his attention to the probability of major-power warfare, it appears to be the world-economy perspective's hegemonic power cycle that is most crucial for generating a set of warfare predictions.

Keying on the assumption that predominance discourages challenges, Vayrynen argues that the hegemonic maturity phase should be the most peaceful. The least peaceful period should be the ascending hegemony one in which major-power rivalry and competition is the most intense. Although Vayrynen recognizes that the leading power may be particularly vulnerable to military challenges in the decline phase, the hegemonic victory phase is still expected to be more war-prone. Why this should be the case is not stated explicitly. It also marks a departure from the Working Research Group (1979) expectation of the most acute conflict being associated with ascending hegemony and hegemonic decline phases (see chapter 4). Given the rationales for the other predictions, it is conceivable that Vayrynen anticipates that the hegemon will need to continue fighting, especially in a decelerated growth phase, in order to seal its victory.[3]

Table 8.7 provides several pieces of information pertinent to the Vayrynen thesis. Within the framework established by the hegemonic-growth cycles, the four phases are identified historically using Schumpeter's dating scheme. Each phase is rank-ordered according to its predicted proneness to major-power warfare. Finally, the nine post-1825 major-power wars which meet Vayrynen's criteria for major-power participant status and minimal battle deaths are linked to their respective categorical phases.

Table 8.8 summarizes the warfare outcome by phase and indicates that the outcome varies—with the exception of the hegemonic decline phase—according to which measure is utilized to tap the war-proneness concept. Since all major power wars are hardly equal in significance, the frequency of warfare is the least interesting of the three indicators examined. Although the discriminating power of the nation-months of war indicator is burdened by the inclusion of the multiple participant Korean War, the "magnitude" (nation-months) and "severity" (battle deaths) indicators do at least produce the same rank orders: (1) hege-

Table 8.7

Vayrynen's Major-Power Warfare by Hegemonic/Kondratieff Phase

Hegemonic Cycle	Accelerated Growth	Decelerated Growth
Ascending hegemony (1892–1929)	Most war-prone Russo-Japanese (1904–5) World War I (1914–19) Russian Civil War (1917–21)	
Hegemonic victory (1825–1845) (1929–1948)		Second most war-prone Soviet-Japanese (1939) World War II (1939–45)
Hegemonic maturity (1845–1872) (1948–1973)	Least war-prone Crimean (1853–56) Austro-Prussian (1866) Franco-Prussian (1870–71) Korean (1951–53)	
Hegemonic decline (1872–1892) (1973–)		Third most war-prone
	No major-power warfare	

Source: Based on Vayrynen (1983:409, 411).

monic victory, (2) ascending hegemony, (3) hegemonic maturity, and (4) hegemonic decline.[4] Unfortunately, this outcome does not exactly match the predictions. The rank order of each category is off by one position. Put another way, the phase predicted to be the most war-prone

Table 8.8

Vayrynen's Findings on Major-Power Warfare

Phase	Expected War Proneness Rank Order	Number of Wars	Nation-months of War	Million Battle Deaths
Ascending hegemony	1	3	685.8	9.18
Hegemonic victory	2	2	900.5	15.03
Hegemonic decline	3	0	0.0	0.0
Hegemonic maturity	4	4	672.1	2.47

Source: Based on Vayrynen (1983:411).

was actually the second most war-prone. The predicted second place phase was the observed first and so on down the rank order.

What went wrong? Vayrynen is not very helpful on this score. Conceivably, one might quibble about the identification of major powers and their warfare. Were Austria and Prussia really major powers before 1871? Was China a major power in the early 1950s? Should the major-power intervention in the Russian civil war be considered a major-power war? Yet, however these questions are answered, their significance remains rather moot. The outcome recorded in table 8.8 is entirely dependent on the placement of the twentieth century's first world war in one phase and the second one in another phase. This facet of the outcome raises an interesting question that does not seem to have been considered by analysts employing the hegemonic-Kondratieff cycles framework. Assuming the phases are appropriately identified—a matter not subject to a great amount of consensus—would there have been a hegemonic victory phase after World War I if that succession struggle had been more conclusive? If the United States had emerged as the system's politico-economic leader in 1918–19, could the system have moved directly from an ascending hegemony phase to hegemonic maturity? If the answer is possibly yes, something important is missing from the framework. Is it, therefore, also conceivable that some wars have consequences for the likelihood of predominance and growth prospects that other wars do not?

This last observation underscores a major weakness of analyses on the intertwining of hegemony and the Kondratieff. The concept of hegemony may or may not be defined, but it is never operationalized. Of course, the reluctance (aversion?) to pursuing some form of operationalization is more understandable prior to the late nineteenth-century period for which comparative economic indicators are scarce. It is less understandable in the twentieth-century transition from Great Britain to the United States. Falling back on Kondratieff dating schemes, of course, not only evades the question of how closely aligned these cyclical movements really are, it also makes empirical analysis more vulnerable to the continuing disputes about whether the Kondratieff long wave exists, what it represents, and how best to measure or date it.

WAR AND PRICES; PRICES AND WAR

The hegemonic power cycle approach to looking at Kondratieffs and conflict is not monopolized by world-economy analysts. However, to adopt this approach does seem to necessitate adopting as well some of the central assumptions and propositions of the world-economy perspective. The second approach to the Kondratieff-war nexus is somewhat more open-ended. But even a more open-ended approach may also assume more inductive and deductive versions. The more inductive slant, which may be found in various works such as Wright (1942/1965), Toynbee (1954), and Goldstein (1985, 1986), begins with the observation that years of prosperity and depression tend to cluster. So too do years of warfare. Could there be a connection? The problem then becomes one of attempting to align the two types of clusters—both empirically and conceptually.

The second more deductive version is represented by Modelski's (1981, 1982) alternating innovation model described in chapters 3 and 7. Since the relative autonomous structures of politics and economics draw upon the same resource base, Modelski proposes that an increase in the demand for political innovation will increase general resource scarcity and the general price level. Global war and the resolution of the system's struggle over leadership is regarded as a critical political innovation taking place within the context of a Kondratieff upswing. Economic priorities take precedence in the downturn that is characterized as the locus for leading sectors to undergo maximum expansion, as demonstrated in table 8.9. But the emphasis continues to be placed on global wars as the system's major pulse that takes an extra strong upbeat (by overhauling the political system) every other Kondratieff upswing.

Hence, not completely unlike the world-economy arguments, the long-cycle interpretation of Kondratieffs also ties the economic fluctuations to structural concentration/deconcentration. Even so, this connection is limited to the extra strong upbeat every other upswing. The

Table 8.9

Long-Cycle Phases and the Kondratieff Wave

Long-Cycle Phases	Price Trends	Leading-Sector Maximum Rate of Expansion
1763–1792 Deconcentration	Stable	Cotton textiles Britain (1780s)
1792–1815 Global war	Up	
1815–1848 World power	Down	Railroads Britain (1830s)
1848–1873 Delegitimation	Up	
1873–1913 Deconcentration	Down	Steel Britain, France, Germany, U.S. (1870s) Sulphuric acid Britain, Germany, U.S. (1870s) Electricity U.S. (1890s) Motor vehicles Britain, France, Germany, U.S. (1900s)
1914–1946 Global war	Up	Plastics U.S. (1940s)
1946–1973 World Power	Stable	Synthetics U.S. (1950s) Electronics, aerospace U.S. (1960s)
1973– Delegitimation	Up	

Source: Based on Modelski (1982:111).

more general political analogue of the Kondratieff is found in a model of phased oscillations in the supply of, and demand for, resources and world order (Modelski and Thompson, 1981/1987).

In Modelski's model the behavior of prices is viewed as an index of systemic values that coordinate and synchronize the movements of politics and economics.

> The value system monitors, reflects, and adjusts the social priorities, and the price system reflects not just the state of particular markets but also the value demand for political goods and services (e.g., guns) and for particular political innovations rises, the scarcity of resources (including food and inter alia, butter) will rise, and the general price level is likely to rise too. As the demand for guns goes down we would expect the demand of basic resources, hence also the general price level, largely to move in the same way as the demand for political goods and services of world order.

The implications of this interpretation for warfare per se are reasonably clear. As explored in chapter 4, the upswing phases of delegitimation and especially global war, the time of the extra strong upbeat, are expected to be the most conflict-prone periods. These periods are unusually conflict prone not merely because they are upswing phases. Nor is it accurate to say that they are upswing phases because they are conflict prone. The causation is reciprocal with global politics and world economics "listening to the same drummer" and reflecting changes in systemic priorities.

The Impact of Global War since the Late Eighteenth Century

Thompson and Zuk (1982) can be viewed as providing some further empirical support for Modelski's alternating innovations model—especially in terms of the extra strong upbeat occasioned by global war. Nonetheless, their initial intention was to examine the direction of causation in the war—long-term price fluctuations relationship. They begin by acknowledging that it is difficult to move empirically much beyond Kondratieff's stopping point as long as one asserts that upswings, for whatever reasons, make major war more probable. One, can count the number and types of warfare associated with each type of phase. The largely nineteenth-century outcome, as Kondratieff claimed, is highly supportive of the generalization linking upswings and war. Demonstrating a causal link form upswing to war is an entirely different matter. In fact, it is both easier and more feasible to pursue the reverse question: to what extent do major wars disrupt normal economic processes? After all, wars reduce supplies. Demand also tends to increase. The combination leads to higher prices. After a war is over, supply and demand, in general, will become more equilibrated. Prices should fall. In hypothesis form, this interpretation can be expressed in the following way:

H1: The initiation of major warfare inaugurates the upswing of the Kondratieff long wave.

H2: The termination of major warfare inaugurates the downturn of the Kondratieff long wave.

Hypotheses one and two are clearly extreme versions of the "war produces long waves" interpretation. A more moderate position suggests simply that

H3: Major wars significantly reinforce the upswing of the Kondratieff long wave.

To test these hypotheses, Thompson and Zuk choose to focus on the price histories of the two most recent system leaders—Great Britain and the United States. As table 8.3 suggests, it is not all that difficult to collect information on the system's amount of warfare. A single price index for the world economy as a whole, though, does not exist for any respectable length of time. To avoid a level of analysis fallacy, it seemed more prudent to match the lead economy's price fluctuations with its own warfare—as opposed to including everyone else's as well.[5] In addition, a fourth hypothesis is also developed. If, as suggested in Modelski's (1981/1982) alternating innovation model, global wars function as the world system's major pulse and principal transmitter of structural instability, there is no reason to assume that all wars will have an equal impact on price fluctuations. Global wars, for example, should be much more likely to have a significant impact on the long wave than other types of warfare.

Hypotheses one and two proved to be easy to test. No major war immediately preceded the beginning peaks (1789/90, 1849, 1896) of Kondratieff's upswings. Therefore, upswings must have preceded major wars in contrast to the first hypothesis/ prediction. Yet almost all of the long wave's upper turning points (1814, 1866/1873, 1920)—the beginnings of the downturns—did coincide with the termination of major wars. The Napoleonic Wars and World War I are easily associated with 1814 and 1920. The American turning point of 1866 obviously follows the American Civil War. The one exception is Britain's 1873 shift. Given this exception, it would seem then that major wars are not necessary, even though they may be sufficient, causes of price downturns.

The third hypothesis sidesteps in part the causality question by stressing the possibility of reinforcement. This hypothesis is clearly supported by the calculations reported in table 8.10. Thompson and Zuk compared the annual price changes in each upswing period with the annual changes in the same period prior to the advent of a war. The problem with such a comparison is that at least one upswing (1789–1814) is composed almost exclusively of years of warfare. A cleaner approach, utilized in table 8.10, involves contrasting annual increases in the upswing phases with the annual rate of change for nonwar years.

Support for the reinforcement interpretation is quite evident in table 8.10. The rate of upswing varies from wave to wave, but in every case the average amount of increase presumably would have been considerably less if certain wars had not occurred when they did. Note that in three of the five upswings examined, the average increase might have been less than 1 percent a year in the absence of the years of war identified in the column to the far right. The third upswing (1896–1920) average increase without World War I could also be reduced even further if a more liberal approach were taken to identifying the impact of the first world war.[6]

Thompson and Zuk proceed to test their fourth hypothesis by contrasting the impacts of global wars versus those of interstate wars on wholesale prices for Britain (1750–1938) and the United States (1816–1977). In both series, the impacts of the global wars (the French

Table 8.10

Major Wars and Wholesale Price Index Proportional Changes during Kondratieff Upswings

Kondratieff Upswing	Annual Percentage Increase	Annual Percentage Increase Minus Selected War Years	Selected War Years
Great Britain			
1789–1814	2.67	0.50	1793–1814
1849–1873	1.17	0.85	1854–1856
1896–1920	6.78	3.80	1914–1918
United States			
1849–1866	5.12	0.82	1861–1865
1896–1920	5.10	3.39	1917–1918

Source: Based in part on Thompson and Zuk (1982:635).

Revolutionary/Napoleonic Wars, World Wars I and II) were statistically significant. In comparison, the interstate wars were associated with relatively insignificant impacts. Global wars, therefore, are an important influence in shaping long-term price fluctuations, at least in the post-1750 world. As expressed in the Thompson and Zuk (1982:634) study:

> Overall, one gets the impression that, were it not for wars (especially global ones), Kondratieff's long waves might well have more closely resembled ripples on the national, if not the world, price pond . . . Not only do major wars reinforce the Kondratieff upswing; they appear to be largely responsible for the fundamental shape of the Kondratieff wave phenomenon. In particular, the height and timing of the crests are directly attributable to major wars in most of the pre-1920 U.S. and British cases.

Another way of looking at this same question involves inspecting a few plots of these price fluctuations. Figure 8.1 depicts the fluctuations in British prices between 1750 and 1938. The peak influences of 1792–

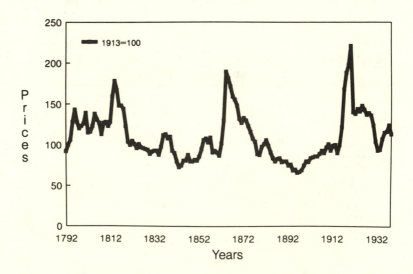

Figure 8.1   British Wholesale Prices
Data Source: Mitchell (1980)

1815 and 1914–1918 global wars are difficult to overlook. Equally apparent is the absence of a midnineteenth-century global war impact which might add some greater symmetry to the shape of the upswings. The absence of a midcentury bulge is even more apparent in the French and German prices charted in figure 8.2.

It takes the American Civil War to provide some of the impact symmetry that is missing in the British, French, and German graphs. Figure 8.3 displays the shape of the U.S. series between 1792 and 1938. Much of the symmetry that is apparent would be lost or swamped if the post-Second World War period was plotted in the same figure.[7] Unlike the earlier global wars, the end of World War II did not initiate a downturn in prices. Instead prices remained high and continued to climb. From a Kondratieff point of view, the question is thus not so much whether prices go up or down but one of how quickly they climb. After World War II, some analysts equate downturns with relative stability or slow growth in price increases. Stability is, of course, a fairly subjective state of affairs. But it is worth pointing out that it required the passage of some 26 years (1945–1970) of the U.S. wholesale price

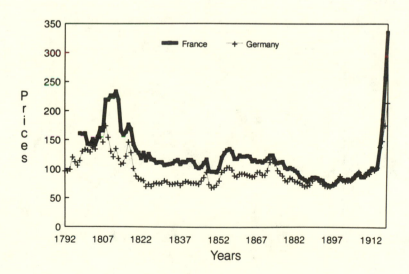

Figure 8.2   French and German Wholesale Prices
Data Source: Mitchell (1980)

index to double in nonwar years. Prices doubled again between 1970 and 1978/79—a considerable acceleration possibly indicating the return to an upswing phase.[8]

Tracking the relationship between the Kondratieff and various wars definitely becomes more difficult after World War II. Fortunately, major wars have been scarce since 1945. Unfortunately, the change in the scale of the price increases renders serial analysis somewhat more difficult. But what about the period prior to Kondratieff's 1789/90 commencement point? If it is accepted that a modern era in world politics and economics began around 1494, did it require three hundred years for the Kondratieff phases to emerge? Or, is there support for the various arguments tracing long waves back to the sixteenth century and, therefore, for a longer history of interaction between war and long-term economic fluctuations? To date, there has been only one empirical attempt to investigate this subject.

War, Expansion, and Contraction in the Long Term

While Thompson and Zuk were content to remain within the chronological parameters (late eighteenth century on) established by Kondrati-

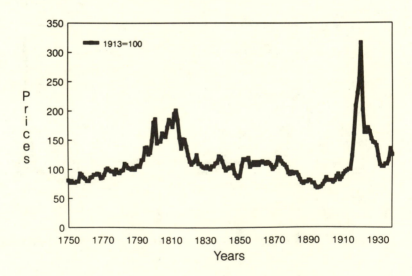

Figure 8.3　United States Wholesale Prices
Data Source: U.S. Department of Commerce (1975)

eff, Joshua Goldstein (1985) has sought to examine a much more ambitious slice of time—1495 to 1975. Goldstein argues that Kondratieff long waves can be traced back at least to the late fifteenth century. To support this assertion, Goldstein inspected the pattern of upswings and downswings in some 31 price and production series that encompassed various portions of the 1495–1975 era. However, rather than examine these series completely inductively, a schedule of expansions and contractions was constructed more or less following the phase delineations advanced by four different scholars: 1494–1650, Braudel (1972); 1670–1790, Frank (1978); 1790–1920, Kondratieff (1935/1979); 1920–1975 Mandel (1980). The 1651–1669 gap evidently is filled by Goldstein.

This particular approach to dating some 481 years of economic fluctuations, in conjunction with the 31 time series, no doubt represents one of the weakest components in Goldstein's analysis. For one thing, the four authors consulted have very different frames of reference. Braudel's (1972) classical analysis is clearly centered on prices in the Mediterranean region. Frank's (1978:104) discussion is focused on production fluctuations in Britain for which no sources are offered. Kondratieff's (1935/1979) dates are based primarily on British-American prices. Finally, Mandel (1980) returns the focus to indexes of productive growth.

These shifts in geographical and economic references are compounded further by the 31 economic time series to which the phase delineations are applied. While they are predominately price series (26 of 31), more than one-third (12) are associated with one country (England/Britain). The remaining 19 series are distributed among 8 states or, in some cases, cities in 8 states or regions (France, Germany, Netherlands, Spain, Sweden, Belgium, Italy, and the United States). The rules that governed the selection of these series are simply not made explicit. One must imagine, however, that convenience in the sense that they were readily available had some role to play in the selection process.

These criticisms do not negate Goldstein's findings on war behavior. Rather, they are meant to underscore the debatable long economic-wave foundation upon which they are based. Goldstein does strengthen his case by subjecting his 1495–1975 phase schedule to statistical tests. Tests for a systematic pattern of alternating upswings and downturns (based on slope directions) proved statistically significant in terms of the price, if not the production, series. Even so, the differences in ups and downs are sharper after 1790 than before.

Based on this evidence for a long-wave pattern of alternating phases, Goldstein proceeded to examine the distribution of great-power battle fatalities across the economic phases. On the average, the expectation was that fatalities would be higher during upswings as opposed to the downswing periods. Almost without exception, the hypothesized relationship is readily observable in Levy's (1983a) fatality data. Only the 1575–1594 period deviates in the pattern displayed in figure 8.4 and table 8.11.

One could raise questions about whether the number of fatalities tells us as much as we need to know about the significance of the various bouts of warfare. There are also reasons to be skeptical about the wisdom of averaging a long war's total number of battle deaths on an annual basis. Even so, Goldstein's evidence seems quite formidable. Yet the evidence remains very much dependent on the phase assignments.

Some concerns have already been raised about the nature of the phase-delineation sources and the multiple series inspected. An even closer look at the technique used to legitimize the alternating phase

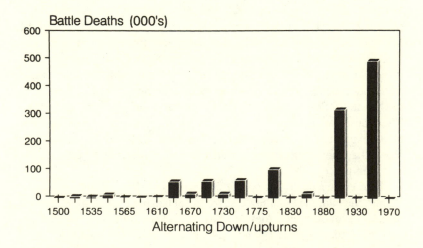

Figure 8.4   Goldstein's Long-War Wave
Data Source: Goldstein (1985:423)

Table 8.11

Goldstein's Great-Power Warfare and Kondratieff Phases

Phase	Average Annual Fatalities Mainly in Period (000s)		Number of Wars	
	Downturn	Upswing	Downturn	Upswing
1495–1508	1.9		2	
1509–1528		8.0		6
1529–1538	6.0		2	
1539–1558		13.8		7
1559–1574	3.8		4	
1575–1594		2.3		1
1595–1620	4.3		3	
1621–1649		60.9		3
1650–1688	17.1		9	
1689–1719		63.1		4
1720–1746	17.1		3	
1747–1761		66.1		1
1762–1789	1.2		2	
1790–1813		105.5		2
1814–1847	0.0		0	
1848–1871		18.8		4
1872–1892	0.0		0	
1893–1916		322.2		1
1917–1939	0.9		2	
1940–1967		496.5		2
1968–1975	0.0		0	
1495–1975	5.9	126.6	27	31

Source: Based on Goldstein (1985:423).

sequence suggests the need for caution in accepting the match between wars and economic phases.

Comparing slopes or trends within phase periods, the procedure Goldstein relied upon to validate the long-wave phase schedule, can be a tricky proposition. Table 8.12 provides one illustration. Rather than examining a number of different price series from various parts of Europe, a long-cyclist would prefer to focus on the world economy's lead economy. The system's most active zone should be the best single site to search for long-term economic fluctuations. Accordingly, table 8.12 lists Dutch grain prices (Posthumus, 1946), one of Goldstein's 31 series and the only one applicable to the Netherlands, in four columns matching the Goldstein upswing/downturn delineations from the seventeenth century.

The problem that table 8.12 is intended to illustrate is that a comparison of phase slopes assumes that there are meaningful linear slopes (trends) to compare. That is not always the case, especially in many of the older price series and particularly for twenty to thirty segments of prenineteenth-century price fluctuations. Table 8.12 demonstrates this characteristic of older price series and some other interesting facets as well. Note that both of the downturn phases begin in the midst of wartime (1595) or immediately after a long period of war (1650). Both downturns also end (1620 and 1688) immediately before the next bout of warfare begins or before it has had much of an opportunity to make an economic impact. What is true for the end of the downswings is of course also true for the beginning of the upturns. However, the end of upturns are not far removed from the ending points of long wars.

As far as these observations go, they would seem to provide nothing less than additional support for the asserted relationship between economic phases and warfare. Unfortunately there is a catch. In order to calculate a slope, one seeks to draw a best-fitting line through the array of data observations across time. The positive or negative tilt of the best-fitting line is apt to be influenced strongly by the first and last points in each phase. If the first few points are high scores and the last few points are low scores, the slope or trend will be downward or negative. A low to high progression, on the other hand, will yield a positive slope.[9]

As indicated in table 8.12, the seventeenth-century downturns begin high and end low. The upswings begin low and end high. The question one must ask, however, is whether the positive or negative signed slopes accurately capture the behavior of prices within each phase? The direction of price movement in the 1595–1620 downswing is downwards and one could say that the direction of movement in the 1621–1649 upturn is more or less upwards or at least consistently higher than in the decade preceding the upswing. The mean for the 1595–1620 period is 116 while the 1621–1649 mean is 158. Yet the fragmentary evidence that is available on grain prices in the 1570s and 1580s suggests that the 1595–1620 period (or some portion of it) could also be described as an upswing era with prices returning to the prewar level during the 1609–1620 break in fighting between the Dutch and the Spanish.

Table 8.12

Prussian Rye Prices at Amsterdam, 1597–1719

Downturn (1595–1620)		Upswing (1621–1649)		Downturn (1650–1688)		Upswing (1689–1719)	
1597	*174*	1621	*87*	1650	228	1689	*100*
1598	*175*	1622	*127*	1651	246	1690	*105*
1599	*162*	1623	*170*	1652	*240*	1691	*113*
1600	*140*	1624	*190*	1653	*182*	1692	*128*
1601	*125*	1625	*169*	1654	*125*	1693	*196*
1602	*114*	1626	*153*	1655	113	1694	*183*
1603	*127*	1627	*157*	1656	149	1695	*154*
1604	*104*	1628	*169*	1657	149	1696	*150*
1605	*81*	1629	*230*	1658	155	1697	*182*
1606	*71*	1630	*284*	1659	168	1698	244
1607	*81*	1631	*263*	1660	182	1699	306
1608	*122*	1632	*151*	1661	222	1700	178
1609	125	1633	*125*	1662	301	1701	*137*
1610	110	1634	*147*	1663	*215*	1702	*114*
1611	112	1635	*146*	1664	*146*	1703	*110*
1612	130	1636	*126*	1665	*163*	1704	*122*
1613	118	1637	*146*	1666	*140*	1705	*107*
1614	102	1638	*155*	1667	*134*	1706	*105*
1615	91	1639	*139*	1668	103	1707	*99*
1616	111	1640	*158*	1669	*82*	1708	*119*
1617	128	1641	*137*	1670	84	1709	*279*
1618	111	1642	*118*	1671	96	1710	*225*
1619	89	1643	*136*	1672	*131*	1711	*161*
1620	84	1644	*158*	1673	*134*	1712	*129*
		1645	*132*	1674	*158*	1713	*141*
		1646	*107*	1675	*217*	1714	165
		1647	*128*	1676	*188*	1715	152
		1648	*163*	1677	*154*	1716	138
		1649	205	1678	*123*	1717	123
				1679	96	1718	131
				1680	85	1719	*123*
				1681	99		
				1682	98		
				1683	101		
				1684	121		
				1685	121		
				1686	108		
				1687	88		
				1688	*84*		

Source: Posthumus (1946:573–575) for grain prices.

Note: Prices for years of global-power warfare for the Netherlands are in *italics*.

The behavior of Dutch prices in the second half of the century is more difficult to characterize in terms of upswing and downturn. In the long 1650–1688 downswing, prices peak in 1651, fall for a few years, peak again in 1662, decline again through 1669–1671, rise again to a third, more moderate peak in 1675 before falling and remaining reasonably low in the last decade of the phase. The sawtooth motion characterizes the upswing as well. There are successive, short-term peaks in 1693, 1699, and 1709. While the low points in this upswing are not as low as those reached in the preceding downturn, the means for the two phases (147 for the downturn and 152 for the upswing) are not all that different.

The general conclusion one reaches in contemplating the series displayed in table 8.12 and figure 8.5 is that the generic phases taken from Braudel's interest in the Mediterranean and Frank's interest in English development do not fit the Dutch seventeenth-century price experience all that well. Alternatively, if a group of people were presented with the Dutch data and asked to partition it into upswings and downswings, it

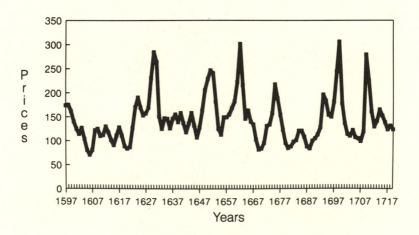

Figure 8.5   Seventeenth-Century Prussian Grain Prices
Data Source: Posthumus (1946)

is doubtful that an overwhelming amount of consensus would emerge from the group.[10]

Of course, the problem could be our heavy dependence on grain prices, which are apt to be sensitive not only to crop failures, which are not of direct interest, but also to destructive land wars such as the Thirty Years' War, which may or may not be of much direct interest depending on one's theoretical perspective. A more comprehensive index, such as the wholesale price indexes that have been constructed for more recent periods, might present a different, less erratic picture of price fluctuations at the center of the seventeenth-century world economy.

CONCLUSION

The question of whether prenineteenth-century Kondratieff waves existed is apt to remain both open and controversial. Their existence will certainly remain an open-ended question as long as we assume that they existed and can thus be merged theoretically with changes in structure. Much less controversial is the generalization that wars have inflationary consequences. Just how much they are responsible for Kondratieff fluctuations in price series will probably remain open as well. Nevertheless, the evidence made available to date suggests that wars, especially global wars, have played a major historical role in at least shaping upswings and downturns in prices. How far back in time this process can be traced is debatable. but the impact of war, and especially global wars, on prices certainly becomes easily discernible between the late eighteenth and the midnineteenth centuries—the period with which Kondratieff was most concerned.

Overall, the empirical evidence on the relationships between Kondratieffs and major-power warfare suggests the advisability of remaining agnostic about the historical existence of Kondratieff's long waves and their hypothesized effects on conflict. By "agnostic" I merely mean to suggest that we should leave the question open to further theoretical and empirical inquiry.

There are other systemic processes with somewhat better established claims to explaining warfare patterns with which we have yet to deal. Indeed, one of the more truly classical topics in the study of international relations is the hotly disputed relationship between changes in polarity and war. Generating one historical-structural answer to this perennial but still central question will constitute the principal focus in chapter 9.

9

Polarity and Global Power Warfare

Among the many potential explanatory factors involved in global dynamics, including those reviewed in earlier chapters, the distribution of power must be acknowledged as one of the more significant keys to deciphering systemic behavior. As testimony to this assertion, a very large group of analysts have explored, and continue to explore, this route to explaining international political behavior.[1] For a while, it may even have seemed as if this area of research had exhausted its potential. Analytical assumptions often differed, historical interpretations conflicted with systemic abstractions, conceptual terminology only occasionally overlapped, and the empirical results were often discouraging. Yet the perceived importance of this explanatory path seems to be making something of a comeback through its centrality for historical-structural modes of analysis. Needless to say, the introduction of a bevy of new models has not eliminated the problems with assumptions, historical interpretations, conceptual terminology, and empirical results. But because uncertainty surrounds debate on the potency of this factor does not mean that we can safely ignore it. On the contrary, polarity must command central attention in accounts of systemic war. It is to this subject, accordingly, that attention now turns.

The purpose of this chapter is twofold. First, despite clear intermodel differences, far too many observers fail to appreciate the fundamental differences associated with various applications or utilizations of the power-distribution variable. Despite some common denominators, conflicting findings are to be expected given the extant differences in basic assumptions. Frequently, even the common denominators turn out to be far less than common when scrutinized more closely. Any hope of eventually sorting out, and perhaps even resolving, these analytical disagreements hinges upon first recognizing them explicitly. Consequently, it is our goal here to illuminate them.

Second, once the differences in approach are exposed, it is essential that we confront them with empirical evidence. In this spirit, the present examination will compare and contrast two approaches to the relationship between a system's distribution of power or polarity and the system's conflict behavior. It is unlikely that the work of any one scholar can be expected to embody perfectly the thrust of prehistorical-structural analyses of polarity, but Kenneth Waltz's (1964, 1967, 1979) highly influential studies are representative in many respects. The second approach to be examined is the long cycle, which has been discussed in earlier chapters.[2] After first delineating the distinctive divergences in perspective, an empirical examination of the 1494–1983 relationship between the global political system's capability distribution and global-power warfare will be undertaken.

WALTZ'S APPROACH TO POLARITY AND SYSTEM STABILITY

Waltz's theoretical departure point is the ideal type dichotomy which played such a formative role in the development of the social sciences. Two pure types of political systems, described in table 9.1, are advanced as the embodiments of the political system continuum's end points. On the one hand, there is the domestic political system type. Functionally differentiated units that perform specific functions are knit together in a centralized and authoritative relationship of super- and subordination. A political order augmented by formal organizations is institutionalized on a systemwide basis just as governmental agents are established to restrain nonpublic uses of force.

In marked contrast, the international political system type's distinguishing characteristics represent everything that domestic systems are not. International political systems are anarchic, decentralized, and informally organized. Nearly anything goes as relatively autonomous units seek to perform functionally similar tasks—in which the ability to perform is distinguished primarily by greater or lesser amounts of unit strength. In the absence of institutionalized order, formal organizations (other than international organizations), and legitimized authority patterns, self-sufficiency and self-help operate as the principal guidelines for actor behavior.

Waltz would no doubt be among the first to acknowledge that these conceptual types are, in many respects, idealized portrayals of real

Table 9.1

Ideal Characteristics of Domestic and International Political Systems

Domestic	International
Hierarchic	Anarchic
Centralized order and formal organization	Lack of order and formal organization
Constrained	Nearly anything goes
Highly articulated division of labor	Slight division of labor
Authority, administration and law	Power, struggle and accommodation
Units move toward integration	Units move toward anarchy
Public agents organized to prevent/counter private uses of force	Self help
Agents with systemwide authority	Authority an expression of relative strength
Governmental institutions and offices	International organizations

Source: Based on the discussion in Waltz (1979)

world political systems. Domestic political systems are never quite as hierarchically integrated as the conceptual imagery suggests nor are international systems always the orderless Hobbesian jungles conveyed by the notion of an "anarchic" system. Yet while all real political systems are apt to be located somewhere on the continuum *between* the conceptual poles, rather than *at* the poles, the theoretical point is established that political systems tend to approximate one or the other type. Moreover, the distinguishing characteristics associated with each type are regarded as important clues to discerning the relationship(s) between system structure and expected behavior.

The theoretical key to understanding international political systems for Waltz is that, as anarchic type systems, a functional division of labor is largely absent. An anarchic system's units are functionally undifferentiated. Each unit more or less seeks to accomplish what the other units are striving to achieve. A unit's ability to be successful, therefore, depends on its relative capabilities. Stronger states are thus apt to be more successful; weaker states tend to be less so. Since systemic structure is defined by the arrangement of its parts, it is the system's distribution of capabilities—and particularly those of the system's major actors—as well as changes in the distribution to which we must be especially attentive in attempting to decipher international politics.

> The structure of a system changes with changes in the distribution of capabilities across a system's units and changes in structure change expectations about how the units of the system will behave and about the outcomes their interactions will produce (Waltz, 1979:97).

Waltz further assumes, somewhat inexplicably, that the capability distribution's range of variation is bounded between bipolarity and multipolarity or between two and three or more powers. If given a choice, Waltz argues, bipolarity is vastly preferable to multipolarity in terms of structural simplicity, stability, and durability. The reason—or, more accurately, the reasons—for this preference are predicated on an impressively large number of propositions relating an increase in the number of actors to a variety of consequent, and destabilizing, behaviors. Indeed, it is possible to extract at the very least the following twelve hypotheses about the consequences of multipolarity from his discussion:

1. The relative size of actors declines, which decreases the probability of actor survival.
2. The relative size of actors declines, which lowers the entry barriers to further competition.
3. The costs of bargaining increase.
4. The incentives to bear the costs of bargaining decline.
5. The size of actors' stakes in the system decline along with the incentives to maintain the system.
6. The expected costs of enforcing agreements and of collecting gains increase disproportionately.
7. The diversity of the group is likely to increase, which also increases the difficulty of reaching agreements.
8. The problems associated with monitoring the effects of agreements and the desirability of maintaining or amending them increase disproportionately.
9. The economic and military interdependence of the actors is likely to increase, and if interdependence grows at a pace that exceeds the development of some form of regulation or central control, the probability of war will increase [because interdependent states whose relations remain unregulated must experience conflict and, occasionally, violence].
10. The correction of imbalances of power becomes more complicated—with two parties, imbalances can only be corrected by internal efforts; with three or more parties, shifts in alignment become an additional, more

flexible, yet less reliable and precise means of adjustment [Internal balancing is more reliable and precise because actors are less likely to misjudge relative strengths than they are to misjudge the strength and reliability of opposing coalitions]. An increase in the flexibility of alignment and defection possibilities thus increases uncertainty.

11. The ability to monitor and interpret other actor's behavior with any degree of certainty declines, which further increases the chances for miscalculations and the probability of destabilizing wars [Miscalculation is more likely to permit the unfolding of a series of events that finally threatens a change in the balance and brings the powers to war as opposed to the overreaction associated with bipolar systems, which costs only money and the fighting of limited wars].

12. The confusion associated with selecting appropriate responses to the actions of other actors increases because dangers are diffused, responsibilities are unclear, and the definition of vital interests are easily obscured.

Viewed as an isolated set, the twelve propositions summarized in figure 9.1 represents an interesting mixture of deductive logic and, contrary to Waltz's own rules for theory building, historical observation. Moreover, the historical observations are strongly flavored by an important assumption about the nature of modern international political history.

> Until 1945, the nation-state system was multipolar and always with 5 or more powers. In all of modern history the structure of international politics has changed but once. We have only two systems to observe (Waltz, 1979:163).

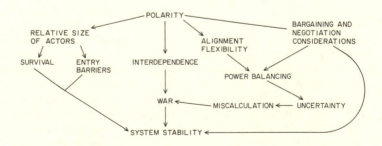

Figure 9.1   Waltz's Polarity-Stability Model
Source: Based on the discussion in Waltz (1979)

With but one historical benchmark in 1945, the appropriate systemic comparison is the pre-1945 period with the post-1945 era. This assumption is useful in evaluating such propositions as numbers 2 and 9. Contemporary entry barriers to international competition at the highest level are extremely formidable. But whether the high entry barriers are due to a bipolar structure or due instead to such factors as historical trends toward larger-scale nation-states with richer resource endowments or the astronomical increases in the costs of strategic weapon systems remains highly debatable. Similarly, the variation in economic and military interdependence may also be a product of the upward shifts in organizational scale. In these contexts, bipolarity may be more an effect than a cause.

Nevertheless, there are more interesting topics to pursue than quibbling over the ad hoc nature of some of Waltz's theoretical observations. It suffices to say that Waltz's argument brands multipolarity, in contrast to bipolarity, as the more complicated and downright messier world for decision makers to survive or somehow muddle through. This conclusion does not imply that the frequency of warfare covaries with polarity. The frequency of warfare is not really a matter of theoretical concern for Waltz. What is of concern is system destabilizing warfare.

> To say that an international political system is stable means two things: first, that it remains anarchic; second, that no consequential variation [changes that would lead to different expectations about the effect of structure on unit behavior] takes place in the number of principal parties that constitute the system (Waltz, 1979:161–162)

In sum then, Waltz's argument may be simplified, for our immediate purposes, as saying that warfare leading to a structural change and transformation is far more likely in a multipolar system than in a bipolar system.

WALTZ'S APPROACH AND THE LONG CYCLE

In what respects does the long-cycle perspective on polarity differ from a number of earlier realpolitik approaches to capability distributions and, in particular, the argument advanced by Waltz? There appear to be five or six major differences.

Global System versus Regional Subsystem

Unlike its predecessors, the long-cycle perspective emphasizes a distinction between the European regional subsystem and the global political system. The conventional approach frequently treats the European regional subsystem as if it were coterminous with the international system through some point in the late nineteenth/early twentieth century. The emergence of non-European great powers such as the United States and Japan finally globalized what had been an entirely European-dominated arena. Contrary to this view, long-cycle analysts argue that a global political system began to emerge in the sixteenth century when some Europeans discovered how to move from the confines of Europe to other parts of the world by sail and began to specialize in these activities as opposed to the more traditional, territorial pulling and hauling of intra-European interactions. To be sure the global political system was long dominated by states located in Europe that were also active in the affairs of the European regional subsystem. Yet some European great powers were only marginally involved in the core affairs of the global political system. As a consequence, the identities of the global powers, the major actors of the global political system, are not necessarily the same set of actors conventionally identified as European great powers.

Table 9.2 illustrates this point by matching the long cycle's global powers with Waltz's great-power list derived from Wright (1942/1965). Thirteen states are listed in all. All of the global powers, with the exception of Portugal, appear at some point in the great-power list. The converse does not hold. Turkey, Sweden, Austria (Austria-Hungary), Prussia, and Italy never qualified (in terms of meeting specific thresholds of global capability and activity) as global powers. The table also illustrates different statuses vis-à-vis longevity as major actors for Spain, the Netherlands, Russia, the United States, and Japan. The only solid convergence that emerges in the table is the exclusive preeminence of the United States and the Soviet Union after World War II.

Major Actors and Their Identifying Attributes

A second difference underlies the identification of the major actors. Waltz (1979:131) states that

> . . . rank depends on how they score on all the following items: size of population and territory, resource endowment, economic capability, military strength, political stability, and competence.

From the long-cycle perspective, none of these attributes need be dismissed as insignificant. Nonetheless, it is rather difficult to view all of them as possessing equal significance. Long-cycle theory stresses

Table 9.2

Global Powers and Great Powers

State	Global Powers					Great Powers					
	1494–1608	1609–1713	1714–1815	1816–1945	1946–	1700	1800	1875	1910	1935	1945
1. Portugal	X[a]										
2. Spain	X	X	X			X					
3. France	X	X	X	X		X	X	X	X	X	
4. England (Great Britain)	X	X	X	X		X	X	X	X	X	
5. Netherlands	X[b]	X	X			X					
6. Turkey						X					
7. Sweden						X					
8. Austria (Austria-Hungary)						X	X	X	X		
9. Russia (USSR)			X	X	X		X	X	X	X	X
10. Prussia (Germany)				X[c]			X	X	X	X	
11. United States				X	X				X	X	X
12. Japan				X[d]					X	X	
13. Italy								X	X	X	

Source: For the great powers, Waltz (1979:162).

[a]To 1580
[b]To 1579
[c]From 1871
[d]From 1872

the role of capabilities for global reach as a primary index of status in the global political system. Modelski and Thompson (1988) present a detailed exposition of the argument for measuring global reach capabilities in terms of selected indices of ocean-going naval strength. But a preference for naval indicators does not imply that other types of capability do not contribute to rank and status.

For instance, some level of economic capability is certainly implicit to this emphasis and increasingly so as the fixed costs of building and operating navies has escalated over the centuries. Alternatively, the population, territory, and resource endowment variables have not always held the same significance they have now. In earlier eras, small populations, territory (depending on where it was located), and even resource endowments were positive incentives in developing global reach capabilities. The disagreement in this case is not so much one of whether systemic elite status is the outcome of multiple factors but, rather, whether everything that may contribute is of equal importance and for all periods of modern systemic history, as well as whether one needs to explicitly measure all of the considerations of conceivable significance.

Inequalities among the Major Actors

The divergence in approaches to identifying major actors leads to a third difference. By focusing on oceanic naval capabilities, it is possible to measure the relative capability positions of the major actors with some degree of accuracy and over the entire 1494-to-present period of interest (at least to long-cycle theory). Waltz does not appear to be particularly interested in such an undertaking and, perhaps in part due to this disinterest, he adopts a much different approach to the question of counting the number of poles in the system.

Not only are all of the capability attributes of seemingly equal weight but so too are all major actors. As a consequence, the five or more great powers in action prior to 1945 are translated as signifying constant pre-1945 multipolarity.[3] Yet to make such a translation, one has to assume either that inequalities of power among the major actors do not matter or that the power inequalities that did exist were negligible. The first assumption seems most unlikely. If changes in structure are thought to influence actor behavior and if arguments can be advanced for anticipating different behavior in systems with two, three, four, or five actors as Waltz does, power inequalities should be expected to make some difference. For example, if we assume structure can influence behavior, is it plausible to entertain precisely the same behavioral expectations for a five-power system in which two of the five actors control 80 percent of the capabilities and for a five-power system in which each actor controls exactly 20 percent of the capabilities? Each system has five actors, but that would be about the full extent of the similarity. Capabilities are much more concentrated in the former system than in the latter, and if the two strongest actors in the more concentrated system each controlled roughly half of the 80 percent (leaving 20 percent to be divided among the other three actors), it is unlikely that most observers would be willing to label both systems as multipolar. Indeed, the highly concentrated system has a distinctly bipolar flavor about it.

The second possible assumption—that the five or more powers were roughly equal in power—is equally unlikely. The relative capability of Waltz's 1700–1945 great powers and Waltz's particular set of capability attributes (population size through competence) have yet to be operationalized. Various efforts to measure great-power capabilities after 1815 (Singer, Bremer, and Stukey, 1972; Organski and Kugler, 1980; Doran and Parsons, 1980) however are available. The Singer et al. capability index encompasses several variables for each of three dimensions (demographic, industrial, and military), which is not exactly what long-cycle analysts have in mind (see Thompson, 1983), but it does have the virtue of at least overlapping with facets of Waltz's suggested index. Table 9.3 enumerates the great-power capability distribu-

Table 9.3

COW Relative Capability Scores for Major Powers
1816, 1913, 1946

State	Percentage Share		
	1816	1913	1946
England	42.0	14.0	15.2
Russia (USSR)	25.5	16.7	26.3
France	16.4	10.3	6.2
Austria-Hungary	12.0	6.3	
Prussia (Germany)	4.5	18.0	
United States		24.8	52.7
Italy		5.0	
Japan		4.5	

Source: Correlates of War (COW) relative capability data reported in Hopkins and Mansbach (1973:111).

tions that result when the Singer et al. (1972) index is applied to three selected years: 1816, 1913, and 1946.

The information reported in table 9.3 is not displayed for the purpose of extensive analysis. It is intended instead to demonstrate that data (of nonlong-cycle origin) exist that suggest that capability distributions among major actors change from time to time and that years regarded as multipolar based on the number of major actors (three or more) may overlook vastly different capability distributions. In table 9.3 the years 1816 and 1913 are viewed as equally multipolar by Waltz; 1946 is labeled a bipolar year. However, in terms of capability concentration, the distribution in 1816 has far more in common with the one in 1946 than it does with the one in 1913.

The general point to be made here is that it serves little purpose to count the number of major actors without also taking into consideration the extent to which capabilities are concentrated within the elite group. Some abstract and empirical reasons for this generalization have been presented in preceding paragraphs. Put even more simply, it is virtually impossible to count the number of major actors without an implicit or, more preferably, an explicit minimal threshold for major power status. Once this step has been taken, it becomes far more difficult to overlook the fact that some major actors exceed the minimum only marginally (if at all) while other major actors' capability positions may double or triple the minimum expectation. Or, as indicated in table 9.3, the leading major actor may control 9.3 times as many capabilities as the weakest (compare the relative capability scores for England and Prussia in 1816). Presumably such inequality will have some impact on the behavior of the affected states as well as on the impact of the overall capability distribution.

Structural Change and Global Power Warfare

Table 9.2 revealed some disagreements about which actors to count, but both perspectives identify a sufficient number of actors to qualify the pre-1945/46 system (the regional and the global) as multipolar if the emphasis is to be placed on the number of major actors alone. Yet counting the slowly changing number of actors in a group while ignoring dynamic shifts in concentration patterns is problematic in another sense. The static-number approach is likely to overlook the essence of the long-cycle process—namely, that the regular dynamic of global structural change is punctuated by periodic global wars fought over leadership in the system. With the emergence of a new leader during or immediately after the war, the capabilities that count most in the global system tend to be highly concentrated. So highly concentrated, in fact, that neither of Waltz's bipolar or multipolar possibilities are appropriate in describing systemic structure. Only unipolarity or something close to it will fit. High concentration, nevertheless, is not a permanent condition. Gradually, it erodes into a state of dispersed capabilities that it is appropriate to describe as multipolar. Hence, where Waltz sees little fundamental change in system structure—only once in 1945— long-cycle analysts perceive continuous structural change as the distribution of capabilities cycles from high concentration to low and back to high and so on.

High concentration is ushered in by global warfare—still another difference of theoretical opinion with Waltz's approach. Waltz (1979:112) states that

> Wars among states cannot settle questions of authority and right; they can only determine the allocation of gains and losses among contenders and settle for a time the question of who is the stronger.

For many wars this may be an accurate evaluation. For a select few wars, the periodic global wars that bring about major structural transformations, the above observation is not quite on the mark. Questions of authority and even right have been resolved by global wars, not so much because they settle for a time the question of who is the strongest in the system. A system leader emerges with some amount of authority and with some ability to declare what is right and what is wrong by establishing or modifying the rules of the system. The process is not particularly well institutionalized as in many domestic political systems nor did it spring fully into being in the sixteenth century. Instead, the process has evolved with each successive system leader (Portugal, the Netherlands, Britain, and the United States) being somewhat stronger and more authoritative than its predecessor.

Eventually, the complications do accelerate but not simply because of the ever larger number and variety of coalitions that can be made. The real source of trouble can be traced to the erosion of the system leader's relative capability and the improvements in the relative capabilities of the challengers. The crux of the problem is the systemic deconcentration process because it recreates a situation that, so far, has been perceived to be resolvable only by force of arms in a global war. Thus, one way of viewing a fundamental difference between Waltz's approach and the long-cycle approach is that Waltz from the very beginning, dichotomizes the two types of political systems (hierarchical and anarchic) and freezes the variations that can take place around the opposing conceptual poles. Structural change in international politics is thereby restricted to different variations on the anarchic theme. A long-cycle analysis, in contrast, is predicated on long-term movements back and forth between forms of "anarchy" (low concentration—unipolarity). Both approaches agree that multipolarity is the least stable arrangement. But where Waltz expresses a preference for his one structural alternative of bipolarity, long-cycle analysts regard unipolarity as the most stable arrangement even though it is inherently unlikely to persist. In this respect, long-cycle analysts view the entire concentration/deconcentration process as fundamentally unstable while Waltz focuses on the comparative stability and durability of phases of the more general process.

There are, of course, important areas of overlap between the two approaches. Agreement exists, for example, on the importance of systemic structural influences, the inadvisability of confusing polarity with polarization tendencies, and the structural transformation dangers of multipolarity.[4] Yet from a long-cycle perspective, Waltz's conclusions about multipolarity may be right but for the wrong, or at least some of the wrong, reasons. What is obviously needed is an empirical test. Such a test may not be able to validate or invalidate the differences in fundamental assumptions about how the world works, but it should be able to give us some significant clues about which approach best captures the history of interactions between system structure and major-power behavior.

Measuring Polarity and Warfare

It needs to be stated at the outset that it is patently impossible to be entirely neutral in testing the two approaches to theorizing about polarity's behavioral consequences. Waltz's emphasis on counting the number of actors drastically reduces structural variance to one long period of multipolarity and one rather short period of bipolarity that is still unfolding. If this interpretation were to be adopted in an empirical test, there would be little doubt about the outcome. But such an approach would not begin to address long-cycle concerns. Nor does one have to choose sides in accepting the criticism that merely counting the number of major actors overlooks conceivably significant variations in capability concentration. Consequently, it will be necessary to measure polarity variations in terms of concentration patterns.

Polarity

Polarity will be operationalized, subject to certain modifications and always less than ideally, according to the following schedule formulated by Modelski (1974) and Rapkin, Thompson with Christopherson (1979):

1. in a unipolar system, one state controls 50 percent or more of the relative capabilities that matter;
2. in a bipolar system, two states control at least 50 percent of the relative capabilities and each of the two leading actors possess at least 25 percent with no other state controlling as much as 25 percent;
3. in a multipolar system, three or more states each control at least 5 percent of the relative capabilities but no single state controls as much as 50 percent and no two states have as much as 25 percent apiece.

In applying these rules to the relative capability data yet to be discussed, two areas of ambiguity emerge. The more obvious one involves a system with only two actors, as developed after World War II. If one actor controls 50 percent thereby satisfying the unipolarity condition, how does one interpret the position of the other actor, who must also control 50 percent? Clearly, the two states are equal in relative capabilities. Therefore, rule number 1 can only apply to systems with three or more actors. To modify the unipolar rule for two-actor systems, it is necessary to adjust the 50 percent threshold, which is based on one actor controlling as many capabilities as all other actors combined. If the system is reduced to only two major actors, one solution is to fall back on the 25 percent threshold used in rule 2 as a criterion for bipolarity. The 75/25 distribution exposed in rule 1b may seem much too asymmetrical to function as the boundary between unipolarity (76/24) and bipolarity. But it should be kept in mind that one of the reasons that the system has been reduced to two major actors is the enormous expenditure associated with the development of nuclear weapons. The great destructiveness of nuclear weapons, in turn, suggests the advisability of a more flexible accounting scheme in comparing capability positions. Many analysts, for example, would hesitate to say that a state with 1,000 nuclear missiles, other things being equal, was twice as powerful as a state with 500 missiles.

1b. in a two actor unipolar system, one state controls 76 percent or more of the relative capabilities that matter.

A second gray area that requires some attention because it turns out to be more common than anticipated is a situation that is multipolar according to rule number 3 but more closely resembles a unipolar situation: one state controls 45 percent or more but less than 50 percent and no other state controls as much as 25 percent. From a deconcentration perspective, this is a situation that is plausible at some midpoint in the transition from unipolarity to bipolarity or multipolarity. It might be tempting to adjust the 50 percent threshold, but such a move would sacrifice that benchmark's conceptual meaning. A compromise position, reflected in rule 1c, is to treat this situation separately as a case of highly asymmetrical multipolarity or near unipolarity.

    1c. in a near-unipolar system, one state controls more than 45
           percent but less than 50 percent of the relative capabilities
           and no other state possesses as much as 25 percent.

Ideally the next step would involve the construction of indexes that match the types of capabilities both approaches stress as most significant. Regrettably, no series that taps Waltz's seven dimensions is currently available. A 1494–1983 index of global reach capabilities is available, fortunately, and will be utilized in this examination. Although some of the steps taken in construction this index require considerable elaboration (an outline is provided in table 3.2), the basic assumption is that ocean-going naval power has been, and continues to be, decisive in achieving global reach in the modern world system. Certainly, the establishment and maintenance of global-scale naval power is dependent on the presence of other factors such as adequate financing and a sufficient industrial infrastructure. But it is further assumed that it is sufficient to measure sea power as one of the most salient and essential outcomes of globally competitive economic and military strength.[5]

Applying the polarity codification rules to the sea-power capability shares yields the polarity array listed in table 9.4. Each year, in consecutive order, is coded according to the type of capability distribution associated with it. Additional information on the identity of the leading global-power contenders in the order of their relative capability rank, is also provided in the third column. The list is surprisingly long. It seems almost as if system structure changes on an annual basis. But that is not quite the case. If one matches the information in columns 2 and 3, the impression that emerges is one of strings of one state in the lead among the global-powers ensemble, as isolated in table 9.5. It is a combination of the lead state's proportional fortunes—rising, falling, or maintaining its place—and the jockeying for position among the other global powers that accounts for the shifts in the overall capability distribution. The more marginal the lead state's position, the more likely the

Table 9.4

Polarity and Leading Contenders, 1494–1983

Years	Type of Polarity	Leading Contenders
1494	unipolar	England
1495–96	multipolar	England, France, Spain, Portugal
1497–1501	bipolar	England, Portugal
1502–16	unipolar	Portugal

* * *

1517–44	unipolar	Portugal
1545–50	bipolar	Portugal, England
1551	near unipolar	Portugal
1551–53	bipolar	Portugal, England
1554	unipolar	Portugal
1555–59	near unipolar	Portugal
1560–78	bipolar	Portugal, England
1579	multipolar	England, Netherlands, Portugal

* * *

1580–86	multipolar	Spain, Netherlands, England
1587–88	bipolar	Spain, Netherlands
1589–92	multipolar	Spain, Netherlands, England
1593	bipolar	Spain, Netherlands
1594–97	unipolar	Spain
1598–1607	multipolar	Spain, Netherlands, England
1608	unipolar	Netherlands

* * *

1609–20	unipolar	Netherlands
1621–23	bipolar	Netherlands, Spain
1624–26	unipolar	Netherlands
1627–29	near unipolar	Netherlands

Table 9.4 (*continued*)

Years	Type of Polarity	Leading Contenders
1630–36	unipolar	Netherlands
1637–39	near unipolar	Netherlands
1640–42	unipolar	Netherlands
1643–44	near unipolar	Netherlands
1645	multipolar	Netherlands, England, Spain
1646–67	bipolar	England, Netherlands
1668–70	multipolar	Netherlands, England, France
1671–73	bipolar	France, Netherlands
1674–75	multipolar	France, Netherlands, England
1676–81	bipolar	France, England
1682–83	multipolar	France, England, Netherlands
1684	bipolar	France, England
1685	multipolar	France, England, Netherlands
1686–87	bipolar	France, England

*   *   *

Years	Type of Polarity	Leading Contenders
1688–89	multipolar	France, England, Netherlands
1690–99	bipolar	France, England
1700–13	multipolar	Britain, France, Netherlands

*   *   *

Years	Type of Polarity	Leading Contenders
1714–17	bipolar	Britain, Netherlands
1718	near unipolar	Britain
1719–24	unipolar	Britain
1725–43	near unipolar	Britain
1744	multipolar	Britain, France, Spain, Netherlands
1745–49	near unipolar	Britain
1750–56	multipolar	Britain, France, Spain

Table 9.4 (*continued*)

Years	Type of Polarity	Leading Contenders
1757	bipolar	Britain, France
1758–62	multipolar	Britain, France, Spain
1763–82	bipolar	Britain, France
1783–91	multipolar	Britain, France, Spain

* * *

Years	Type of Polarity	Leading Contenders
1792–1808	multipolar	Britain, France, Spain
1809–12	unipolar	Britain
1813	bipolar	Britain, France
1814–15	unipolar	Britain

* * *

Years	Type of Polarity	Leading Contenders
1816–35	unipolar	Britain
1836	near unipolar	Britain
1837	unipolar	Britain
1838–42	near unipolar	Britain
1843	unipolar	Britain
1844	bipolar	Britain, France
1845–47	near unipolar	Britain
1848	bipolar	Britain, France
1849–53	near unipolar	Britain
1854–57	unipolar	Britain
1858–60	bipolar	Britain, France
1861	unipolar	Britain
1862–67	bipolar	Britain, France
1868–69	unipolar	Britain
1870–71	bipolar	Britain, France
1872–74	near unipolar	Britain
1875–79	multipolar	Britain, France, Russia
1880–82	unipolar	Britain
1883–87	bipolar	Britain, France
1888–90	unipolar	Britain
1891–93	near unipolar	Britain
1894	multipolar	Britain, France, United States, Russia, Germany

Table 9.4 (*continued*)

Years	Type of Polarity	Leading Contenders
1895–96	near unipolar	Britain
1897–1913	multipolar	Britain, Germany, United States, France
	* * *	
1914–15	bipolar	Britain, Germany
1916–18	multipolar	Britain, Germany, United States
1919–38	bipolar	United States, Britain
1939–43	bipolar	United States, Britain
1944–45	unipolar	United States
	* * *	
1946–59	unipolar	United States
1960–62	bipolar	United States, Soviet Union
1963–68	unipolar	United States
1969–83	bipolar	United States, Soviet Union

Note: Periods of global war and nonglobal war are separated by asterisks. In the last column, order of state identification is based on the relative size of global capabilities. Also, the listing is highly mechanical and based on rigid adherence to the definitional rules. A more appealing rendition might be achieved by smoothing or eliminating some of the short-lived blips and deviations (e.g., a year of marginal bipolarity amidst 20–30 years of unipolarity). Or, sequences of alternating categories such as unipolarity and near unipolarity (see 1609–1644 period) might be viewed, more simply, as a single period.

overall structure is to move from one category to another, depending in large degree on whether one or two other states are in genuine contention. If only one other state is a viable contender, the movement tends to be toward bipolarity. If more than one other state is challenging, the structural movement is likely to be in the direction of multipolarity.

Nevertheless, table 9.5 does not seem to square with the long cycle's predicted order of succession in systemic leaders (Portugal, the Netherlands, Britain, and the United States). The explanation for this discrepancy is that it is one thing to be in the lead among the global powers by a few percentage points and still another to be the clear leader with 50 percent or more of the system's global reach capabilities. With only two exceptions—the first of which (England in 1494) is located in the first year of the series at a time when global reach capabilities were not

Table 9.5

Global Powers with the Highest Relative Capability Share

Years	Global Power
1494–1501	England
1502–1576	Portugal
1577–1581	England
1582–1601	Spain
1602–1648	Netherlands
1649–1663	England
1664	Netherlands
1665–1666	England
1667–1669	Netherlands
1670–1701	Netherlands
1702–1918	Britain
1919–1983	United States

very common and the second (Spain in 1594–97) while more meaningful reflects a short-lived advantage during global war—clear leaders and unipolar distributions emerge during or immediately after bouts of global warfare. The periods of unipolarity, therefore, are most commonly associated with the era following the preceding global war.

Unipolar and near unipolar years (minus the two exceptions) are isolated in table 9.6. Give or take a few years, one hundred years separate each of the global wars since 1494. It is worth noting then that, on the average, about 69 percent of the first fifty postglobal wars tend to be associated with either unipolar or near unipolar capability distributions. If we focus only on the first 35 postglobal war years, the average proportion of years encompassed by the two highly concentrated distributions is nearly 90 percent. Thus, as predicted by long-cycle theory, the global political system tends to be highly concentrated and either unipolar or near unipolar in the aftermath of the periodic global wars. Deconcentration into bipolar and multipolar distributions provides the structural context for the next global war.

Global Power Warfare

This discussion of the polarity data provides some definite clues about the relationship between polarity and warfare. But there is more to global-power warfare than global wars alone. The dependent variable

Table 9.6

Global War, Unipolarity, and Near Unipolarity

Global War	Unipolar Years	Near Unipolar Years	Proportion of First Fifty Post-War Years Encompassed (%)
1494–1516	1502–44, 1554	1551,1555–59	70
1580–1608	1608–20, 1624–26, 1630–36, 1640–42	1627–29, 1637–39, 1643–44	66
1688–1713	1719–24	1718, 1725–43, 1745–49	62
1793–1815	1809–12, 1814–35, 1837, 1843, 1854–57, 1861, 1868–69, 1880–82, 1888–90	1836, 1838–42, 1845–47, 1849–53, 1872–74, 1891–93, 1895–96	82
1914–1945	1944–59, 1963–68		40

in this study will consist of a weighted index of all warfare between global powers since 1494. Yet the contention that all wars are not equally important is quite explicit in long-cycle theory. The most important wars are the global wars (1494–1516, 1580–1608, 1688–1713, 1792–1815, and 1914–1945) in that they bring about the reconcentration of capabilities in the system. These wars are not defined by the number of people killed, the geographical extent of warfare, or the number of global-power participants but rather whether or not these struggles for systemic leadership are in fact resolved by one winner emerging with the sufficient lead in global reach capabilities. A special interest in wars that transform a system's structure is also clearly detectable in Waltz's analyses. Thus the wars with special theoretical significance need to be distinguished from the less significant events in some systematic fashion.

Each year of global-power warfare (table 4.7) is first weighted according to the combined proportional capability shares of the global-power war participants. Scores for nonglobal war years are then reduced by a factor of 0.5. Hence, only global-war years retain their original weights in order to highlight their special theoretical significance as structural transformers. Figure 9.2 provides a graphical illustration of this interpretation of the serial history of major-power warfare. The figure also underscores the domination of the global-war years in this series. Aggregated, the global wars constitute almost exactly two-thirds (86.293 or 67.1%) of the total weighted years of global-power warfare.

While the mean values of five of the six periodic peaks (1494–1516 = .267, 1580–1608 = .893, 1688–1713 = .885, 1793–1815 = .900, 1914–1918 = .915, 1939–1945 = .853) are roughly similar, the means of the corresponding valleys (1517–1579 = .099, 1609–1687 = .267, 1714–1792 = .167, 1816–1913 = .019, 1919–1938 = .000, 1946–1983 = .000) decline in value after the unstable seventeenth century. Taking both sets of mean values into consideration, a different answer to the perennial question (see Levy, 1983a) of whether warfare is declining is suggested. In terms of global-power warfare, a restrictive subset of all warfare to be sure, the propensity to engage in

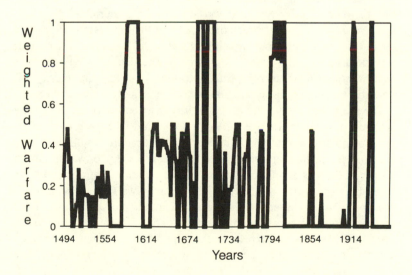

Figure 9.2   Weighted Global Power Warfare, 1494–1983

global war about once a century continues unabated. It is only in between these main events that the more preliminary bouts have declined in frequency.

TESTING THE RELATIONSHIP BETWEEN POLARITY AND GLOBAL POWER WARFARE

On one hand, we have four types of capability distributions present, in what has been described as a nonrandom fashion, across four hundred and ninety years. On the other, we have one distinctive type of behavior, warfare between the global powers, which can be discerned at numerous points in time but which noticeably clusters or peaks at roughly one-hundred-year intervals. Long-cycle theory suggests that global wars, and global warfare in general, should be less prevalent when capabilities are more highly concentrated (unipolarity and near unipolarity) than when they are less concentrated (bipolarity and multipolarity). Waltz's perspective ignores the concentration dimension altogether and argues that system-transforming warfare is more likely in a multipolar context than in a bipolar one.

In confronting these claims with empirical evidence, several testing outcomes are possible. Both viewpoints could be wrong. No association between polarity type and warfare may be discernible. One perspective may have better predictive accuracy than the other. Bipolarity could be a less dangerous systemic context, for example, than either multipolarity or unipolarity. Alternatively, the data may be interpretable as supporting both perspectives to the extent that unipolarity, bipolarity, and multipolarity are shown to increasingly more war-prone.

The most direct way to relate capability distribution types to warfare is to ask how much warfare has been associated with each of the four types of polarity conditions. However, this procedure would only have meaning if the four polarity types had been equally prevalent in the history of the global political system. Since we know that this is not the case, it is necessary to interpret the polarity-warfare association in probability terms based on the observed number of years associated with each type of capability distribution. Thus if warfare is randomly distributed, we should expect to find the sum of warfare distributed about in the same proportion as the number of years assigned to the four polarity types. Similarly, we should expect the mean of global-power warfare to be approximately the same for each type of capability distribution.

Table 9.7 provides information on the proportional distribution of polarity types and weighted warfare between the global powers, as well

Table 9.7

Polarity and Global Power Warfare, 1494–1983

Polarity Type	Number of Years	Percentage	Weighted Warfare	Percentage	Weighted Warfare Mean
Unipolar	144	29.4	26.442	20.6	.184
Near uni-polar	61	12.4	10.944	8.5	.179
Bipolar	171	34.9	34.461	26.8	.202
Multipolar	114	23.3	56.809	44.2	.498
	490	100.0	128.656	100.1	

Note: Although it is difficult to interpret the 490 years of warfare as a random sample, the observed frequency outcome is significantly different (at the .05 level with a one-tailed test) from the expected frequency outcome (χ^2 = 31.414). Outcomes associated with the unpolar and multipolar types are statistically significant; the others are not.

as the weighted warfare means by polarity type. Given the information on the proportional distribution of polarity types, less warfare than would be expected is found to be associated with the first three types of capability distributions: unipolar, near unipolar, and bipolar. Nearly twice as much warfare as anticipated is associated with multipolarity. Furthermore, the weighted warfare means rise as the polarity distribution ladder is descended into the less concentrated capability patterns. the outcome reported in table 9.7 would, therefore, seem to strongly support the long-cycle prediction while, at the same time, it does not contradict Waltz's argument.[6]

Destabilizing warfare is least common in unipolar conditions—a fact that is somewhat understated in table 9.7 due to the tendency for unipolar distributions to emerge toward the end of global wars. If one should not expect ongoing global warfare to cease abruptly with the development of a high capability concentration, it is a bit misleading to "charge" those particular unipolar years with the warfare that continues despite the skewness in capabilities. Nevertheless, table 9.7 clearly shows multipolarity to be a much more dangerous systemic context than bipolarity as well. Waltz's perspective thus would seem to be borne out as far as it goes.

Still, four hundred and ninety years is a rather large chunk of time for aggregation purposes. The analytical threat of overaggregation can be particularly troublesome when one is dealing with a system that has demonstrated evolutionary tendencies (as in the decline in global warfare between the global-war peaks). The appropriate question then is whether table 9.7's outcome is replicated when the four hundred and ninety years are broken down into more homogeneous units of time. Such an operation is carried out in table 9.8, which decomposes the 1494–1983 era into six long-cycle periods.

Long-cycle decomposition can be executed in several ways. A "long cycle" can be viewed as beginning with a formative global war and ending just before the next one begins. Contrarily, a long cycle can be said to begin at the end of the global war, when the reconcentration clock begins anew, and ends at what is usually the nadir of systemic concentration at the end of the next global war. The latter approach is pursued in table 9.8. The first period (1494–1516) is the first particular approach to interpreting long cycles. The next four periods are more comparable, each lasting from 92 to 130 years, with the fifth period reflecting the contemporary era, which is, of course, still unfolding. To aid the comparison, the distributions for the full time period are reported at the bottom of the table.

Strictly speaking, only the 1517–1608 period exactly matches the 1494–1983 outcome. Yet the deviations in the 1609–1713, 1714–1815, and 1816–1945 periods do not seem to be of equal significance. In the 1609–1713 period, the major deviation is located in the Near Unipolar column. Warfare was slightly more prevalent than expected but then there were very few years of near unipolarity. In the 1714–1815 period, the deviation is found in the Unipolar column. In this case, the greater-than-expected amount of warfare associated with unipolarity is easily explicable in terms of the high sea-power capability concentration enjoyed by Great Britain toward the end of the Napoleonic Wars. It is really only the 1816–1945 period that cannot be explained away. This time deviation from the general pattern is found in the Bipolar column. Interestingly, this is one of only two periods in the global system's history in which bipolarity was the most frequent structural context. After a long period of unbroken unipolarity, intervals of bipolarity (Britain and France, Britain and Germany, the United States and Britain) predominated. Of the three bipolar pairs in the late nineteenth and early twentieth centuries, it is the British-German combination which proved to be the most deadly contest as manifested in World War I.

Consequently, the most important outcome of table 9.8 is not that the general 1494–1983 pattern is an artifact of aggregation. This is only partially the case. What is most significant is that the general pattern obscures the fact that bipolarity can, at times, be just as destabilizing as multipolarity. Bipolarity between Britain and France in the late nineteenth century and between Britain and the United States in the years

Table 9.8

Consistency of the Polarity-Global War Relationship

Periods		Unipolar	Near Unipolar	Bipolar	Multi-polar	Total
1494–1516	Weighted warfare	3.737	0.0	1.604	.800	6.141
		(60.9)	(0.0)	(26.1)	(13.0)	(200.0)
	Years	16	0	5	2	23
		(69.6)	(0)	(21.7)	(8.7)	(100.0)
1517–1608	Weighted warfare	9.593	1.26	4.709	18.551	32.113
		(23.6)	(3.9)	(14.7)	(5.78)	(100.0)
	Years	34	6	30	22	92
		(36.9)	(6.5)	(32.6)	(23.9)	(99.9)
1609–1713	Weighted warfare	5.41	3.547	18.161	16.644	43.762
		(12.4)	(8.1)	(41.5)	(38.0)	(100.0)
	Years	25	8	47	25	105
		(23.8)	(7.6)	(44.8)	(23.8)	(100.0)
1714–1815	Weighted warfare	6.304	6.137	3.966	17.859	34.266
		(18.4)	(17.9)	(11.6)	(52.1)	(100.0)
	Years	12	25	26	39	102
		(11.8)	(24.5)	(25.5)	(38.2)	(100.0)
1816–1945	Weighted warfare	3.398	0.0	6.021	1.955	12.374
		(27.5)	(0.0)	(48.7)	(23.9)	(100.1)
	Years	37	22	45	26	130
		(28.5)	(16.9)	(34.6)	(20.0)	(100.0)
1946–1983	Weighted warfare	0.0	0.0	0.0	0.0	0.0
		(0.0)	(0.0)	(0.0)	(0.0)	(0.0)
	Years	20	0	18	0	38
		(52.6)	(0.0)	(47.4)	(0.0)	(100.0)
1494–1983	Weighted warfare	26.442	10.955	34.461	56.809	128.656
		(20.6)	(8.5)	(26.8)	(44.2)	(100.0)
	Years	144	61	171	114	490
		(26.4)	(12.4)	(34.5)	(23.3)	(100.0)

Note: Proportions in parentheses.

between World Wars I and II were not particularly dangerous in and of themselves thanks presumably in part to the long histories and learning experiences of these particular dyads. Warfare was never impossible to contemplate, but it was not regarded as very likely. France had been defeated too many times in the past. The United States and Britain had their "special" relationship, a relationship which was augmented by Britain's full appreciation for the United States' capability edge in the twentieth century.

The same cannot be said of the bipolar rivalries between England and the Netherlands and between France and England in the seventeenth and eighteenth centuries, nor of the Anglo-German rivalry in the early twentieth century. Their competitions were far more zero sum in perspective. Neither side desired, nor was content to accept, a bipolar stand-off, both sides worked to assert their capability leadership.[7] A number of wars, some of a preliminary nature and some of a global-war nature, were the result. Based on a combination of theory and on the historical record then, one can acknowledge that multipolarity tends to be more dangerous to system stability than bipolarity. But the relative virtues of bipolarity per se seem to be dependent on nonsystemic factors such as whether the bipolar dyad is prepared, or forced, to live with bipolarity. Apparently, one side or both must be prepared to make concessions to the other side. Otherwise, bipolarity, from a long-term vantage point, is simply another way station on the road to higher or lower levels of capability concentration.

While this conclusion may seem to fit the pre-World War II era, some will no doubt express reluctance to see it applied to the present and immediate future. The current bipolarity—recognizing the fact that we may disagree on when it came about—seems permanent and, in some respects, even desirable (at least in comparison to multipolarity or Soviet unipolarity). Just how durable it proves to be remains to be seen. There are at least three possible sources of new or renewed entrants to the global elite: Japan, China, and a united West Europe. None of the three potential sources seems likely to make a bid for elite membership today or tomorrow but twenty or so years in the future is another matter entirely.

Whether the present bipolarity proves to be endurable, as noted, will depend on the extent to which the United States and Soviet Union learn to live in peace with their bipolar condition. The brief history of U.S.-U.S.S.R. crisis management may be seen as hopeful (see Bobrow, 1982) but the data analyzed in these pages suggests that the history of genuine bipolarity may be even briefer. Others will no doubt contend that nuclear deterrence leaves little choice but learning to coexist. Unfortunately, deterrence has a poor historical track record. German decision makers, for instance, regarded von Tirpitz's naval buildup as an exercise in deterrence as well. Nor is it clear whether the lack of global-power war since World War II, usually the evidence upon which nuclear deterrence proponents fall back, is attributable to nuclear deterrence, unipolarity, or some combination of the two factors (see Modelski and Morgan, 1985).

CONCLUSION

In sum, Waltz's appreciation for bipolarity is not particularly well founded in systemic history, and some of the most important theoretical values of a bipolar capability distribution may be due to circumstances that are not even the products of bipolarity per se. At the same time, it is possible to agree with the conclusion that bipolarity is probably less menacing in the short term to systemic stability, however defined, than multipolarity.[8] The question that remains open is whether it makes much difference which type of polarity provides a more stabilizing systemic context if, in the long run, they are both manifestations of the more general process of capability deconcentration.

A focus on polarity patterns eventually must move to the more specific process of transition from one pattern to the next and its consequences. This chapter has examined the transition process from the most macroscopic perspective conceivable. The next chapter will focus more narrowly on the destabilizing consequences of transition between a declining system leader and a rising challenger.

10

Succession Crises and the Transitional Model

It is sometimes assumed that the older literature on international politics has little to offer analysts engaged in historical-structural analysis. Given the many different sets of assumptions and models pertaining to historical and systemic development with which conventional analysts proceed, there is regrettably, some truth to the indictment. The older literature, however, is far from barren for historical-structural purposes. what is needed is careful translation and, where appropriate, cautious cooptation and incorporation of useful insights, models, and theories. This chapter will demonstrate some of the ways in which this revision task might proceed. the focus of this chapter will be placed on yet another dimension to the determinants of systemic wars by considering one of the more interesting models from the literature— Organski's (1968; Organski and Kugler, 1980) transition model. Some aspects of this model have direct utility for the study of structural crises in the global political system.[1]

THE TRANSITION MODEL

The core of Organski's transition model is linked to his conceptualization of the world's political structure. As represented in figure 10.1, Organski divides the system's state actors into essentially three levels of power—dominant, great, and middle/small—and two attitudinal categories—satisfied and dissatisfied. At the head of the power structure is the strongest state in the system, the dominant power. Since this state is either responsible for the establishment of the prevailing international order or has inherited its control from a predecessor, the dominant power is the primary beneficiary of the status quo and, therefore, not only the most satisfied member of the system.

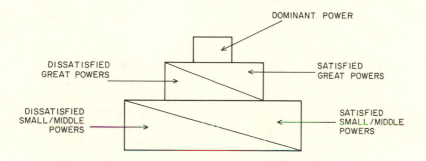

Figure 10.1   Organski's Power Structure
Source: Based on the discussion in Organski (1968)

Less influential than the dominant power, but still relatively powerful, are the great powers. Some members of this secondary grouping
cooperate or are allied with the dominant power, thereby earning a
share of the responsibilities and benefits of systemic leadership. These
great powers are considered satisfied with the international order to the
extent that they do not seek or, at least, no longer seek dominant power
status and are relatively content with the opportunities available to them
within the prevailing order. Dissatisfied great powers, on the other
hand, tend to be relatively new to great power rank. As newcomers to
power, they are confronted with a previously established order and
allocation of benefits that offer little in the way of advantages and privileges to recent arrivals. Yet the newly powerful seek and feel that they
are entitled to a position in the hierarchy that is more in accordance
with their capability attributes. Dissatisfaction is thus seen as primarily
a function of the frustration stemming from the reluctance of the status
quo supporters to surrender voluntarily some portion of their own benefits in recognition of recent and ongoing changes in the systemic distribution of power.[2]

The remainder and majority of the system are relatively weak in
comparison to the great and dominant powers. Whether satisfied or
dissatisfied with their lot in the system, small and middle powers lack
the capability to change the international order. Satisfied weak powers
either accept the status quo because it is in their interest to do so or
because they have little choice but to accept it. Dissatisfied weak

powers may cause problems for the status quo on a limited scale, but they cannot pose a true threat to the system unless they join an attempt to revise the existing order initiated by stronger and equally dissatisfied great powers.

Within this framework, the structural conditions for war and peace are fairly straightforward. Peace is likely to characterize periods in which the powerful and satisfied are much stronger than the powerful and dissatisfied. War becomes more likely when the capabilities of dissatisfied great powers begin to approximate the strength of the satisfied in general and, in particular, when a dissatisfied great power's capabilities begin to approximate the capabilities of the dominant power.[3] Moreover, the transition model is given greater specification by the consideration of five or six other factors.

The Potential Power of the Challenger

If the challenger's potential for growth is limited when it begins its rise to greater power, it is likely to be too ineffective to bring about the need for major war. Alternatively, the probability of conflict is also reduced if the challenger's potential for growth is so great that its eventual rise to dominance seems inevitable. Both the challenger and the dominant power are more likely to have time to adjust to the likelihood of transition. Inasmuch as the challenger and dominant power are respectively likely to win or lose whether or not they try to resolve the succession on the battlefield, both actors will also have ample incentive to work toward a peaceful adjustment. For Organski, it is the ambiguous intermediate situation that carries the greatest risk of war. If the power potential of the challenger is such that it may not be able to do much more than roughly match the dominant power's capabilities, the challenger will be faced with the options of waiting for the dominant power to surrender its leadership voluntarily or attempting to seize systemic leadership by defeating the dominant power in combat, other things being equal, the low probability of the first option taking place increases the probability that the second option will be exercised.

The Rate of Growth Achieved by the Challenger

Basically, the faster the ascendancy of the challenger, the greater the risk of war between the challenger and the dominant power. Four reasons are given by Organski (1968) for this expectation. A very rapid change in the distribution of capabilities leaves little time for the rising power to adjust to the greater responsibilities associated with high systemic rank. To the extent that the sudden growth of a challenger is

based on rapid industrialization and its concomitant internal disloca-
tions, moreover, challenger decision makers may be tempted to distract
attention away from internal strains and toward external causes and
enemies. Finally, extremely rapid growth may seduce challenger elites
into comparing their capability standing with their own previous standing instead of with the actual capabilities of their opponents. Overcon-
fident and impatient leaders may thus be more likely to exaggerate their
power and involve themselves in major warfare prematurely.

Flexibility, Historical Patterns, Rule Acceptance, and Developmental Sequence

The remaining factors are considered to be significant but somewhat
less crucial to the calculation of the probability of war. The more *flexible* the dominant power in adjusting to capability distribution changes,
the more likely it will be that war will be avoided. Similarly, *historical
patterns* of amicability/animosity between the dominant power and the
challenger should influence the nature of the transition, just as the
extent to which the challenger proposes to *accept the rules* of the existing international order (as opposed to plans for a radical revision)
should make some difference to how threatening the challenger is perceived to be by the supporters of the status quo. And, more recently,
Organski and Kugler (1980:21) apparently have added a sixth consideration by noting that the *nature of the developmental sequence* should
make some difference as well. The transition model tends to assume
that the rise of the challenger is based on gains in economic productivity, which, in turn, lead to the improved effectiveness of the governmental organization. But, twentieth-century developments have
suggested that the sequence can be reversed with improvements in political effectiveness leading to gains in economic productivity. While
the direct implications of this factor for the probability of war in the
transition period are not explicitly stated, the reverse sequence might
presumably indicate a slower rate of growth for the challenger and,
therefore, a more drawn-out transition process.[4]

The Timing of the Transitional Challenge

These six qualifications appear to be useful elaborations/qualifications
of the transition model's central theme. Warfare between the most powerful members of the international system is predicated on uneven patterns of growth and disequilibrating shifts in the distribution of
capabilities. All of the model's elaborations, however, do not contribute
equally to the model's clarity and potential utility. An important exam-

ple involves certain generalizations made about the timing of the transitional challenge. Organski (1968:371) writes that

It might be expected that a wise challenger, growing in power through internal development, would wait to threaten the existing international order until it was as powerful as the dominant nation and its allies, for surely it would seem foolish to attack while weaker than the enemy. If this exception were correct, the risk of war would be greatest when the two opposing camps were almost equal in power, and if war broke out before this point, it would take the form of a preventive war launched by the dominant nation to destroy a competitor before it became strong enough to upset the existing international order.

In fact, however, this is not what has happened in recent history . . . [World Wars I and II involved challengers attacking] the dominant nation and its allies long before they equaled them in power and the attack was launched by the challengers, not by the dominant camp.

Organski does not compare the two twentieth-century cases with less recent history, but we are left with the impression that challengers tend to attack the status quo group prematurely. This tendency to miscalculate could be related easily to the transition model's observations on the linkages among rapid growth, overconfidence, and impatience. Organski and Kugler, however present us with an entirely different generalization about the timing of the transitional challenge.

There is a period during which both dominant and challenging nations are roughly equal in power. The challenger has finally caught up with the dominant country, passage is a reality, and the elites on both sides view the shifts in power as threatening. The model insists that it is an attempt to hasten this passage that leads the faster-growing nation to attack. At the same time, it is a desperate attempt on the part of the still-dominant nation to intercept the challenger's progress that leads to war. Moreover, the passage may not be quick—it may take several decades—and the period may thus be punctuated by a number of armed conflicts. In addition, the model insists that attempts to arrest the gains of the faster-growing nation will fail. Whatever the fortunes of war, the challenger will probably "win" sooner or later (1980:26).

Juxtaposing the two passages may be unfair. After the passage of more than a decade, authors certainly are entitled to change their minds. The problem remains, nevertheless, that both elaborations are compatible with the basic transition model. Challengers may attack the dominant power prior to attaining rough equality (the early Organski position), or challengers and dominant powers may be most likely to fight, for various reasons, near the point of interception or when the ascending challenger attains approximate parity with the descending dominant power (the later Organski and Kugler position). The logic of the model does not permit us to choose between these two rival hypotheses. Both could find some support in the historical record, which would suggest that we need further specification about the circumstances characterizing the different timing patterns. Alternatively, neither the earlier nor the later prediction might find sufficient support if indeed World Wars I and II are contemporary aberrations in a more general pattern of challengers wisely biding their time and assuming leadership at some prudent point well after the point of interception— when the challenger's capabilities are superior to the once dominant power.

The three possibilities depicted in figure 10.2 are worth investigating in their own right. But they also possess pertinence for the study of interstate political crises. By and large, the voluminous literature on international crises tends to focus either on specific crises of some apparent significance (for example, the extensively examined 1914 and

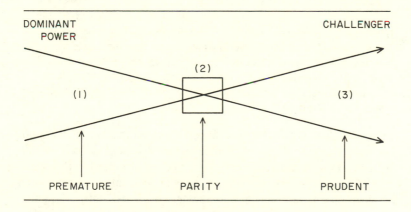

Figure 10.2   Three Different Expectations Concerning the Probability of War and Transition Process
Source: Based on the discussion in Organski (1968)

Cuban missile crises) or on crises in general, as if they all more or less belong to a general category of similar political phenomena. If Organski's emphasis on the dangers of transition is correct (and similar ideas can be found in every variety of historical-structural analysis even though the terminology may differ), all crises are not of equal significance. In itself, this statement is probably not very controversial. The point that needs to be made, however, is that the significance for the global political system and its functioning may be dependent on when they occur in terms of system time.

More specifically, interstate crises that occur outside one or more of the three transition zones in figure 10.2 may be less dangerous, regardless of their nature, than crises that take place within one or more of the transition zones. This observation follows from an interpretation of the period of transition as a structural crisis of the global political system. The issues are to what extent the world system's leadership structure and the global order associated with the leadership structure will change given significant changes in the distribution of capabilities. the crisis element hinges on whether the structural changes will be achieved through global warfare or peaceful accommodation. Once the global political system has entered the transition zone(s) and a period of structural crisis, relatively trivial incidents such as the Sarajevo assassination or a string of seemingly minor crises may serve to tilt the structural crisis in favor of global war.

Bell (1971:17) aptly refers to these preglobal war periods as "crisis slides" toward general war:

> The essence of a crisis slide . . . is not merely that crises come thick and fast, and from several angles, and that the crisis management increases the probability of war between the main adversaries, but that the process of events backs one or more of the states concerned into a corner from which its decision-makers see no way out except war.[5]

Someone with a historical-structural perspective might add that it is not only the "process of events" but also the structural context within which events take place that backs the system's more powerful states into global war corners. Yet similar types of incidents at another time and place may have few repercussions and even less political significance. Accordingly, to better understand the threats inherent to interstate crises, we need to place them within a framework of structural transition. But first, we need to improve our understanding of the nature and timing of structural transition within the world system.

PROBLEMS IN THE THE NATURE AND TIMING OF STRUCTURAL TRANSITION

To ascertain which, if any, of the three transition zones is more critical to the outbreak of global war, a number of preliminary assumptions must be made explicit. Most critically, this examination will proceed as if the question is still an open one, for while Organski and Kugler (1980) do conduct their own empirical test of the transition model, the validity of their analysis is very much open to different interpretations due primarily to a number of debatable operationalization choices.

Organski (1968:375), for instance, restricts the applicability of his transition scheme to the post-1750 period. This questionable restriction stems from his emphasis on the role of industrialization in bringing about unequal rates of growth. Prior to 1750, according to Organski, all states were preindustrial. Only after 1750 are some states preindustrial, some industrializing, and, eventually, some industrially advanced, thereby creating a context of uneven upward mobility and transition. Once all states are industrially advanced, the circumstances presumably would once again preclude the possibility of transition struggles since "great and sudden shifts in national power" would be less likely.

While there is little need to speculate about the prospects for universal industrialization, this examination will assume contrarily that the structures of the world system and the global political system were well in place prior to 1750. Nor does there seem to be any compelling reason to assume that the uneven growth of national power, the rise of global challengers, and the relative decay of world leaders required some degree or threshold of industrialization as a prerequisite, for similar processes, it is asserted, can be observed in the earlier agrarian and trade-oriented phase of the development of the modern (post-1500) world system.

A second area of contention involves Organski and Kugler's decision to focus on gross national product as their sole capability indicator and the subsequent and rather curious identification of major systemic actors involved in the transition process. It is fairly easy to take issue with their argument that gross national product is the single best capability indicator, especially in an era in which military and economic strength are no longer synonymous. For that matter, it is debatable whether economic and military strengths have even been perfect covariants within the elite subset of global powers.[6] But even if Organski and Kugler are correct about the superiority of GNP, reliance on this indicator restricts an analyst roughly to the post-1850 period, during which comparable economic data for the most important actors become available. If the transition process precedes by a substantial interval (i.e., several hundred years) the availability of a specific indicator, it behooves us to find an indicator or indicators capable of encompassing longer stretches of world-system structural history.

In any event, it is difficult to avoid misgivings about the Organski and Kugler identification of major actors outlined in table 10.1. Although minimum GNP attributes are not stated, nine states are granted central status in the 1860–1970 period. From this initial list, which more or less conforms to the usual identification of great powers, a smaller group of "contenders" is isolated. This subset, to which the transition model is said to be particularly applicable, is determined by first picking the strongest state in the system, adding any other states with 80 percent of the strongest state's capabilities, and, when this criterion is not met, including the next two most powerful states.

The procedure for identifying contenders and the reliance on the GNP indicator yields an awkward set of principal adversaries. Russia/Soviet Union remains a contender throughout the post-1860 period, while France drops out in 1890. Most odd, Japan and the United States emerge as contenders only in the post-War II era. If one has problems accepting these identifications, any subsequent data analysis that is restricted to this particular subset will also be difficult to accept.

Table 10.1

Organski and Kugler's Identification of
Major Powers and Contenders

	Central System	
Major Powers	**Members**	**Contenders**
Austria-Hungary	1860–1918	
France	1860–1970	1860–1890
Prussia/Germany	1860–1970	1890–1945
Russia/USSR	1860–1970	1860–1975
United Kingdom	1860–1970	1860–1945
Italy	1870–1970	
Japan	1900–1970	1950–1975
United States	1940–1960	1945–1975
China	1950–1970	

Source: Based on Organski and Kugler (1980:43, 45).

Organski and Kugler (1980) compound their design problems further by deciding that, within their 1860–1975 time frame, they could best examine the possibility of movement toward transition by looking at changes within six roughly twenty-year test periods (1860–1880, 1880–1900, 1900–1913, 1920–1939, 1945–1955, 1955–1975). For the authors, this temporal partitioning means that four wars (Franco-Prussian, Russo-Japanese, World War I, and World War II) require prediction. How they arrive at this conclusion is not clear, for somewhere along the way the idea that dissatisfied challengers and the dominant power contest the transition is lost. Unfortunately, it is precisely this element of the transition model that is most appealing to world-system analysis.

Be that as it may, the transition model has very little to say about preliminary bouts between potential challengers (e.g., the Franco-Prussian and Russo-Japanese wars) except that it is noted that they may occur. The appropriate match would involve wars between the dominant power (the identities of which are never revealed in Organski and Kugler, 1980) and members of the subset of contenders. Thus only the world wars of the twentieth century are legitimate subjects of inquiry for the 1860–1975 period. A war N of 4 causes enough problems; the situation is only made worse when half of the war N represent inappropriate cases for analysis. As a consequence of these and the earlier noted design problems, it is extremely difficult to evaluate the validity of the Organski and Kugler (1980) findings in a positive light.

A LONG CYCLE TEST OF THE TRANSITION MODEL

In view of the various criticisms that have been offered, a fresh start at examining the transition process seems warranted.[7] The current examination will be conducted from the long cycle perspective. Utilizing the long cycle criteria for global power status, several of the traditional great powers do not qualify while others qualify at different times than the dates suggested by Organski and Kugler.

As in the analysis performed by Organski and Kugler (1980), it is possible to delineate more narrowly the principal disputants within the global-power group. For purposes of explicit contrast, table 10.2 repeats the long-cycle perspective's identification of the principal contenders for the past five hundred years and provides dates for the periods of end-of-cycle global-succession warfare.

The auxiliary historical information associated with long-cycle theory specifies at least five periods of global warfare (1580–1608, 1688–

Table 10.2

Global Power Status by Long Cycle

Global Powers	Cycle				
	I (1517–1608)	II (1609–1713)	III (1714–1815)	IV (1816–1945)	V (1946–)
Portugal	X				
Spain	X	X	X		
Netherlands	X	X	X		
England/Great Britain	X	X	X	X	
France	X	X	X	X	
Russia/Soviet Union			X	X	X
United States				X	X
Germany				X	
Japan				X	

Source: Based on Modelski and Thompson (1981).

1713, 1792–1815, 1914–1918, 1939–1945) that may have been preceded by the transition process. Two empirical questions are of direct interest. Are the structures of the preglobal war periods characterized by a system leader with relatively declining naval capabilities and a challenger with relatively improving naval capabilities? If so, it is possible to generalize about which transition process zone (premature, parity, prudent) is most susceptible to the outbreak of war?

The test to be conducted here will deviate from the Organski and Kugler (1980) procedures by taking advantage of the longer historical scope afforded by focusing on the distribution of global naval capabilities as sanctioned by long-cycle theory. A parity situation will be defined operationally as a situation in which the challenger has achieved approximate equality with the system leader, give or take 10 percent.[8] If the challenger possesses less than 90 percent of the system leader's naval capabilities immediately prior to the outbreak of global war, the transition process will be regarded as still in the premature stage or zone. Alternatively, a challenger with more than 110 percent of the system leader's naval capabilities will be considered as evidence that the transition process has entered the prudent zone. As in Organski and Kugler (1980), the temporal focus on the transition process will be restricted somewhat arbitrarily to the twenty-five years prior to the outbreak of global war. These procedures admittedly are not particularly complicated, but then neither are the questions to be addressed. Visual examination of plots and capability distribution percentages should suffice for our immediate purposes.

ANALYZING THE TRANSITION DATA

Figures 10.3 through 10.7 plot the prewar, relative naval capability trajectories of the principal contenders for each of the five global war cases. In every case, the answer to the first question, not surprisingly, is clear-cut. The preglobal war period is characterized by the decline of the system leader and the ascendancy of a challenger subject to certain qualifications. The first sequence (1517–1608) represents an early departure from a more general pattern. Portugal, the first world power in long-cycle terms, can best be described as the first European state to take advantage of the global opportunities available to ocean-going naval powers in the sixteenth century. Because Portugal was the first, many of its accomplishments were achieved and consolidated in the absence of much competition from other global powers of the period. Its collapse and absorption by Spain in 1580 after a period of declining relative capability mark the only time that a world power has lost its status prior to the outbreak of global war.

In any event, the disappearance of an independent Portugal created a structural situation that might best be described as a three-way competition (Spain, the United Provinces of the Netherlands, and England) for the succession prize.[9] Contrary to popular impression, Spain only

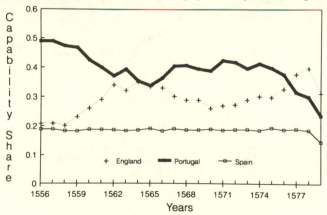

Figure 10.3   Transition Process, 1556–1579
Data Source: Modelski and Thompson (1988:115)

began to build an ocean-going navy shortly before its conquest of Portugal, and real progress was made only after 1580 and the acquisition of the Portuguese fleet. as a consequence, much of the naval rise of the challengers (for in many respects, it would not be inaccurate to regard all three of the principal contenders as challengers in the absence of a leader) takes place shortly before and, more important, during the ensuing global-war period.

The second qualification that needs to be advanced concerns the French challengers in long-cycles II and III. In both cases, the more or less consistent decline of the world power was not matched by a continuous rise on the part of the principal challenger.[10] France improved its relative naval position a great deal in the 1660s and 1670s and only marginally in the late 1770s, but its naval standing failed to improve after 1676 and 1779. Hence, it is not entirely accurate to portray the last decade or so of these two twenty-year transition phases as periods of rising challengers.

Finally, a most interesting departure from the expected transition pattern emerges in each of the plots except for the one for the 1768–

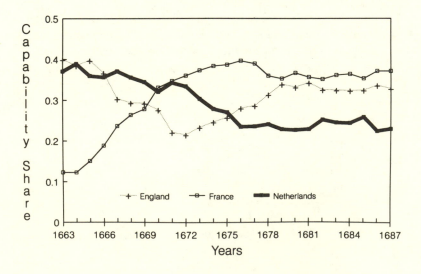

Figure 10.4   Transition Process, 1663–1687
Data Source: Modelski and Thompson (1988:117–118)

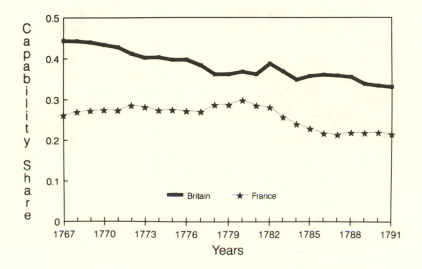

Figure 10.5   Transition Process, 1767–1791
Data Source: Modelski and Thompson (1988:120–121)

1792 period. Contrary to the relatively simple image of an intersection between a declining leader and an ascending challenger, four of the five plots show a more complicated pattern. In the 1556–1579 and 1663–1687 periods, England's naval capabilities surpass the declining world power's capability trajectory—once in the first long cycle and twice in the second cycle. Granted, it might be possible to discount the 1556–1579 situation as representative of an embryonic era for the emergence of the world system's political structure and processes. But the 1663–1687 English-Dutch capability intersections are more difficult to ignore since they are associated with conflict in the form of the generally inconclusive Anglo-Dutch wars. The point is not that there were preliminary bouts fought prior to the main event, but rather that these wars did not become global wars even though they were linked to capability transitions. A few years later, two of the disputants in the Anglo-Dutch wars entered into coalition against a sometime disputant, France. Clearly, there is something else taking place besides the decline of the satisfied and the rise of the dissatisfied.

While the incorporation of naval expenditures in the post-1816 period may exaggerate the naval strength of the United States in the 1919–1938 period, the situations depicted in figures 10.6 and 10.7, in conjunction with those of figures 10.3, 10.4, and 10.5, also suggest something is definitely missing in the transition model. Aside from whether or not the primary challenger is rising in a convincing fashion, the image of second-place challenger contesting predominance in the world system with the holder of the first-place or (former first-place) position is supported only in the less complicated 1768–1792 period (figure 10.5).

In the first long cycle, the Spanish rose from fourth place to an exceedingly shaky first place. Defeating the second-ranked naval power entailed fighting the third-ranked power as well. Emerging from third place in the 1663–1687 period, France might have been more than a match for the third-ranked Dutch if it had not been for the second-ranked English. In long-cycle IV, the Anglo-German confrontations twice began as if the United States belonged to another world system. In both cases, the German decision makers discovered that this as-

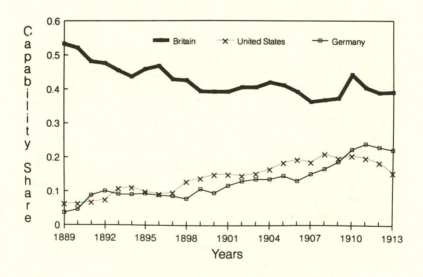

Figure 10.6   Transition Process, 1889–1913
Data Source: Modelski and Thompson (1988:123)

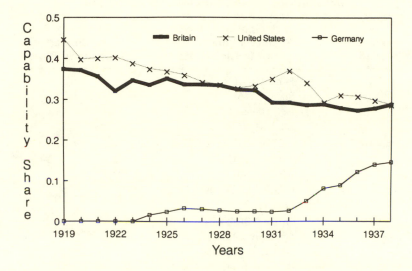

Figure 10.7   Transition Process, 1919–1938
Data Source: Modelski and Thompson (1988:124)

sumption has been a very serious miscalculation, one that it is difficult to attribute to the poor judgment brought on by rapid growth alone.[11]

The discussion of figures 10.3–10.7 has hinted at the answer to the second question concerning the point in the transition process at which global war tends to begin. Table 10.3, however, provides a more concise response. The transition period at the end of the first long cycle already has been described as something of a structural anomaly. None of the three main disputants enjoyed a decisive naval advantage. In 1584, Spain held a slight lead over the rebellious Netherlands and England but not in terms of their combined forces.[12] By the end of the global war period, both the Dutch and the English were much stronger than Spain at sea. By 1688, France had pulled ahead of the deteriorating Dutch naval effort placing its second long cycle challenge nominally in the prudent zone. But if one combines the naval strengths of the Dutch and English (something that occurred, albeit imperfectly and unanticipated by the French, in the wars of the League of Augsburg and Spanish Succession), the French position appears to have been substantially less than prudent.

Table 10.3

Transition Zones and Outbreaks of Global War

Transition Period	Principal Contender Positions Immediately Prior to Global War	Capability Ratio of Challenger to World Power
1556–1579	PORTUGAL (.236) Spain (.146) Netherlands (.281) England (.315)	n.a.
1663–1687	NETHERLANDS (.229) *France* (.371) England (.329)	1.62
1768–1792	GREAT BRITAIN (.332) *France* (.219)	.66
1889–1913	GREAT BRITAIN (.319) *Germany* (.221) United States (.156)	.57
1919–1938	GREAT BRITAIN (.285) *Germany* (.146) United States (.288)	.51

Note: World power's name in capital letters. Principal challenger indicated by italics. Proportional naval capabilities in parentheses.

CONCLUSION

The transition model possesses some utility as a guide to unraveling the capability changes that precede periods of global war. But its emphasis on a challenger overtaking the system leader, the grievances of the dissatisfied versus the inflexibility of the satisfied, and miscalculations due largely to rapid growth-induced overconfidence and impatience are insufficient to capture the full complexity of the transition process. The basic problem is that Organski's transition model envisions a one-step process: A dissatisfied great power improves its capability position to some impressive although unspecified extent and challenges the relatively declining strength of the system's leader. Yet it is the gross prematureness of the challenge and, equally if not more important, the frequent miscalculation of the identity and strength of its ultimate opposition that are not accounted for by the transition model. To account for these elements, a two-step model is necessary.

Absent from the one-step transition model is the recognition of a fundamental geopolitical distinction between the winners and losers in the global-succession struggles. The winners are maritime powers—hence, truly globally oriented—while the losers are essentially continental powers and thus relatively regionally or, in the historical context, Eurocentrically oriented. From this viewpoint, it is not the immediate threat or prospects of the emergence of a new world power and global order that precipitates global war, but rather the near-future threat (the "second step") of such a possibility. Global wars do not begin as global wars. They become global wars only after the leading maritime powers determine that the challenger's success in continental expansion/control will or could create a capability base from which a truly global challenge might be mounted. The Dutch may have had relatively little choice in opposing first their Spanish overlords and then Louis XIV in the first two long cycles, but English participation in these wars was neither inevitable nor immediate. The same generalization can be applied to British intervention in the ongoing French Revolutionary wars and belated U.S. participation in World Wars I and II.

It is most unclear, moreover, whether the primary challenger's decision makers realize, at the outset, the full extent to which their regional activities will be viewed as threatening by either the "reigning" system leader or its eventual successor. How else are we to account for the repeated surprise with which the primary challengers confront the intervention of English, British, and U.S. military forces? How else are we to explain, especially in the twentieth century, war breaking out before the primary challengers have achieved the capability base that they themselves have projected as necessary for global competition? Thus, in some respects, the challengers may not be entirely responsible for the prematureness of their challengers. Not fully understanding or appreciating how to succeed in the world system, the "challengers" watch their inherently regional or local expansion efforts slowly or quickly escalate into global wars once the system leader and/or its successor choose to enter the fray.

The reality and the threat of transition in the world system cannot be denied. But more frequently than not, it is the threat of transition, and not its accomplishment, that creates a crisis for the global political system. Within such a context, relatively insignificant, or seemingly so, local crises and conflicts may trigger global war—if the system time vis-à-vis the source and threat of structural transition is right.

Organski's transition model is not the only historical-structural model that has problems in interpreting the behavior of challengers.

Chapter 11 will raise some similar questions in the context of Chase-Dunn's world-economy model linking world wars to uneven economic growth and the functional needs of a capitalist system. Once again, the advantages of a two-step approach (as opposed to the one-step approach) to explaining systemic warfare will be emphasized.

11

Uneven Economic Growth and Systemic Challenges

One of the more frequent criticisms of the world-economy perspective, outlined in chapter three, is that it tends to submerge or subordinate international politics to the status of a by-product or resultant of the processes of capitalistic economic development. Christopher Chase-Dunn (1981) has responded to several such critiques (Skocpol, 1977; Modelski, 1978; Zolberg, 1981) by arguing that the multicentric structure of the interstate system is necessary for the continued expansion of capitalist accumulation processes and, in turn, that this structure is dependent on processes of uneven economic development for its own survival. Thus, according to Chase-Dunn, it is unprofitable to conceptualize the modern world system in terms of separate or even partially autonomous political and economic subsystems. They are far too intertwined to be able to differentiate them along artificial "political" and "economic" lines.

Chase-Dunn's defense of this world-economy position is buttressed by a summary discussion of the operations of the system's principal processes since the sixteenth century. Particular emphasis is placed on the relationships between uneven economic development, systemic challenges, and world wars. In brief, uneven economic growth is primarily responsible for the increases and decreases in relative strengths and competitive pressures that lead to world wars. World wars, moreover, represent something more than extraordinary periods of widespread combat. They demonstrate that rapid changes in the distribution of productive capabilities outstrip the political framework designed in the context of an earlier distribution of economic power. World wars thus serve the function of destroying out-moded political rules and establishing new frameworks, very much as in Gilpin's structural realist model (see chapter three), which facilitates the expansion of the capitalist accumulation process.

While this argument is articulated in a most cogent fashion, it remains less than fully persuasive. Some of the objections raised in the preceding two chapters, especially those pertaining to the interpretation of multipolarity, challenger behavior, and the double-gaited onset of system warfare, will prove to be applicable to the world-economy framework as well. Of even greater concern, however, is the question of whether functional explanations of systemic war are either necessary or all that desirable. The availability of more straightforward interpretations, it will be argued, restrict the appeal of functionalist approaches. Moreover, the intertwined status of "political" and "economic" factors should never be in doubt. What is debatable is the extent to which some systemic processes are more likely to be slighted in a world economy than may be warranted. After briefly outlining Chase-Dunn's model, some questions about crucial assumptions, interpretations, and generalizations will be raised in this chapter as part of the ongoing effort to comprehend the role of global wars and other processes in the world-system puzzle.

THE CHASE-DUNN MODEL

In the first place, the dependence of the world economy on the interstate system is established almost by definition in Chase-Dunn's model. Only two types of world systems are given consideration in the world-economy perspective: world empires and world economies. In a world empire, the economic division of labor is encompassed by the political structure of a single state. A world economy's division of labor, by contrast, exists within a system of multiple centers of political power and cultures. Consequently, in order to have a world economy (as opposed to a world-empire), there must also be a multicentric interstate system.

Needless to say, there is more to Chase-Dunn's argument than mere definitional stipulation. The primary economic significance of the multicentric structure lies in its facilitation of the mobility of capital and the expansion of capitalistic development. In a system with multiple political sovereignties, capital may be moved from areas offering relatively poor return on investment to areas promising higher marginal rates of profit or lower production costs. In the final analysis, it is argued, states can do little to constrain these migratory tendencies. Nor can states or their competing domestic groups do much to channel investment decisions away from the profit calculus and into the realm of collective/societal goods. Hence, capital accumulation and, therefore, capitalism requires a multicentric political environment in which to thrive.

The extent to which the interstate system is dependent on the world economy is a bit more complicated. If one assumes, as does Chase-Dunn, that there are two main characteristics of the interstate system that need to be sustained—the multicentricity and rivalry of the core actors and the maintenance of a network of exchange among the states—it then follows that there are three ways in which the interstate system might be fundamentally transformed (all of which Chase-Dunn equates with system disintegration):

1. The dissolution of the states in the system,
2. The complete elimination of economic exchanges between nation-states in the system,
3. The imposition of system domination by a single state.

Transformations 1 and 3 clearly would eliminate both key characteristics while transformation 2 certainly would mean the end of the second exchange network characteristic. Nevertheless, for Chase-Dunn, the fact that all of these extreme fundamental transformations have been avoided indicates that the interstate system possesses the ability to weather periodic crises that threaten its existence. This ability of the system to reproduce itself is attributed to the nature of the world economy via the uneven process of capitalistic economic development.

The unevenness of the development process suggests three major implications to Chase-Dunn. First, uneven growth obviously sustains the key characteristic of multicentric rivalries. Second, as the system's most powerful state, the "hegemonic core power" proceeds to lose its competitive advantage in economic production, the question arises as to why the declining core leader does not seize this opportunity to impose a political imperium (i.e., a world empire) while it still possesses the capabilities to do so. Chase-Dunn's response argues that the spread of technological skills and the equalization of labor costs, which are said to be at the root of the leader's relative decline, lead to changes in profit-rate differentials and the concomitant export of capital from the hegemonic core power to areas where marginal return is greater. One of the outcomes of this process is to reduce the incentives, at least on the part of the leading state's capitalists, to support economic nationalism within the declining hegemonic core power. As the capital investments of the hegemonic power are spread throughout other core states, so too are the economic and political interests of capitalists operating from financial bases in the former leading state. To the extent that states are oriented toward advancing the interests of their capitalist groups, an important assumption of the world economy school, the incentives for imperial expansion and even for defensive wars against the imperialism of core competitors are thereby rendered less than compelling.

Yet, as Chase-Dunn notes, the declining hegemonic core power and the interstate system are challenged eventually by ascending "second runners" that do attempt to impose politico-economic imperium. How is it that the challengers are consistently unsuccessful? The answer is again linked to the uneven nature of capitalist economic development. Historically, Chase-Dunn (1981:36) identifies four sets of challengers to the hegemonic power:

1. The Hapsburgs of the "long" sixteenth century
2. France's Louis XIV of the later seventeenth and early eighteenth centuries.
3. Napoleon, primarily an early nineteenth-century threat.
4. The repeated German challenges culminating in the two world wars of the twentieth century.

Each case Chase-Dunn sees as a response to the competitive pressures of uneven development in which the challengers irrationally attempt to conquer vast land areas through military force. Their repeated failures are explained in terms of the weakness of their strategy (i.e., politico-military domination unaccompanied by a strategy of competitive production for the world market), the lack of resources of capacity for executing overly ambitious goals, and the failure to augment their resources by generating necessary support for allies. This last explanation is elaborated briefly and simply. Potential allies perceive the greater political and economic gains associated with the historical pattern of decentralized growth and expansion as opposed to the less attractive possibilities offered by the challenger's proposed imperium.

From an explicitly systemic point of view, Chase-Dunn (1981:23) synthesizes these various arguments in the following way:

> The accumulation process expands within a certain political framework to the point where that framework is no longer adequate to the scale of world commodity production and distribution. Thus world wars and the rise and fall of hegemonic core powers can be understood as the violent reorganizations of production relations on a world scale, which allows the accumulation process to adjust to its own contradictions and to

begin again on a new scale. Political relations among core powers and the colonial empires which are the formal political structure of core-periphery relations are reorganized in a way which allows the increasing internationalization of capitalist production.

Chase-Dunn's perspective on world-system processes raises a number of central questions, interesting propositions, and theoretically intriguing conclusions, yet it does not constitute the only way in which the functioning of the world system may be understood. Alternative perspectives, not surprisingly, are likely to lead to different (and sometimes overlapping) emphases, interpretations, and conclusions. More specifically, a number of significant implications, outlined in figure 11.1, are attributed to the crucial variable of uneven economic growth in the Chase-Dunn model. If, however, the role of uneven economic growth is deemphasized as but one of several sources of systemic change and strife, markedly different interpretations of the repeated sequences of systemic challenges and world wars emerge.

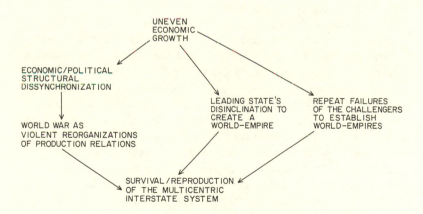

Figure 11.1   Consequences of Uneven Economic Growth in Chase-Dunn's Model
Source: Based on the discussion in Chase-Dunn (1981)

It is worth reexamining Chase-Dunn's uneven economic growth-based generalizations with an eye toward formulating rival hypotheses about the dynamics of structural change and linkages between uneven development and, first, the survival of the multicentric political system; second, the leading state's reluctance to establish a world empire in the Wallersteinian sense; third, the repeated failures of the challengers to transform the world system by creating world empires; and finally, the role of world war and imperial reorganizations in facilitating adjustments to, and expansions of, the capital accumulation process. Wherever possible, equal emphasis will be placed on exposing the apparent explanatory inadequacies of the uneven economic development factor and on proposing alternative generalizations based upon a long cycle of global politics perspective.

A DIFFERENCE OF PERSPECTIVE

The Role of Multicentricity

1. *The multicentric structure of the interstate system is necessary for the continued expansion of capitalist accumulation processes just as the multicentric system's structure is dependent on processes of uneven economic development for its survival.*

It is difficult to disagree with the idea that the capitalist world economy is and has been dependent upon the world's politically multicentric structure for its development and the nature of its historical expansion. An economy rarely exists, as Gilpin (1981:133) has observed, "in an autonomous sphere governed solely by economic laws." Indeed, it is possible to go even further and suggest that fluctuations in the character of the multicentric structure (i.e., the ebb and flow of political power concentration) correspond to, and may well cause, fluctuations in important economic processes. Kindleberger's (1973) argument that the Great Depression of the interwar years was in part due to the absence of a system leader offers one example. Chapter eight's discussion of various interpretations on the linkages between Kondratieffs and warfare provides other examples.

Chase-Dunn's arguments for the dependence of the interstate system on certain economic processes are much more debatable. Some of the grounds for disagreement are traceable to a variety of assumptions associated with Chase-Dunn's single logic. For example, Chase-Dunn attributes the reproduction or survival of the political system to the maintenance of its two chief characteristics—multicentric core rivalries and an interstate exchange network—which, in turn, are said to be dependent upon uneven economic development. Since a structural transformation from multicentricity to unicentricity would involve a major change for an initially multicentric system, it is not difficult to accept the idea that multicentricity is a key characteristic of the political system. Granting the same status to maintaining an interstate exchange network is a different matter. Of course, if nothing—signals, bullets, commodities, or PingPong teams—was exchanged, one would be hard pressed to find any semblance of interaction between the members of the system and equally hard pressed to justify the term *system*. Chase-Dunn, however, appears to restrict his conceptualization of exchange network to economic exchanges. Therefore, whatever is necessary to maintain the economic system becomes necessary for the political system by implicit and somewhat circular assumption.

Yet if the members of an interstate system choose or are forced to develop exclusively autarchic national economies (as opposed to the normal tendency toward some degree of national autarchy), it is difficult to see how or why this must be equated with the demise of all interstate relations and, therefore, the interstate system itself. Multicentric interstate politics presumably would continue, albeit, perhaps with fewer restrictions than before. Again the short-term impact of the late 1920s/early 1930s world depression on interstate trade and the consequent autarchic tendencies might serve as a less than perfect illustration of this point as well.

These minor quarrels over abstract assumptions not withstanding, other, more telling, grounds for disagreement are traceable to differences of opinion on how best to interpret the dynamics of change during the past 500 years.

The Disinclination toward Empire

2. *Uneven economic development accounts for the system's leading state's disinclination to create a world empire.*

Chase-Dunn asks why the world-system's leading state does not attempt to impose imperium or politico-military domination as the leader begins to lose its competitive edge in production. An equally pertinent and more revealing question is why the world leader does not create a world empire when it is at the peak of its competitive edge. A partial answer to both questions stems from the observation that while a European empire, as well as various imperial or partial world empires, may have once appeared to be conceivable, a true world empire administered by a single state in the Wallersteinian sense has yet to appear feasible—especially to those states with the best chance of accomplishing such a task.

There are at least two major classes of what the world-economy school refers to as "core powers." One group is composed of states that are relatively globally oriented or more involved in expanding and exercising political and economic influence on a global scale in contrast to their varying interests in the continental affairs of Europe. This group has supplied the world-system's lead state, or in long-cycle theory's terms, the world power (Portugal, the United Provinces of Netherlands, Great Britain, and the United States) during the past five centuries. A second group is composed of states that have focused much of their expansionary energies within their own immediate region (e.g., Spain, France, and Germany), usually at the expense of their ongoing but intermittent global activities. This second group has provided the system's unsuccessful challengers.[1]

These global versus regional orientations need not be viewed as fixed constants. Some level of global activity is not inconsistent with a high regional profile. And even in globally oriented states, factions have quarreled over the advantages and liabilities of continental versus global strategies. An illustration of this phenomenon may be found in the sectional cleavages associated with support for the state navy in seventeenth-century Dutch and nineteenth-century American political history. The naval historian, Padfield (1979:8–18), offers still another approach to the subject by promoting a threefold categorization of sea powers, land powers, and hybrids—the last of which encompasses states in which the sea and territorial orientations are fairly evenly balanced and the "drives wobble."

Nevertheless, the basic reason for the emergence of at least two types of orientation appears to be traceable primarily to developments in the economic sphere—but more to the development of a world-market economy than to uneven economic growth as Chase-Dunn suggests. If one accepts the idea that territorial expansion provided the principal path to growth and expansion in wealth and power in the agrarian based, pre-1500 world (Gilpin, 1981:112, 132), the gradual development of a world-market economy enabled certain states to gain more (and to expand more effectively) through specialization and long-distance trade than through the traditional mode of territorial conquest.

While the advantages of a commercial orientation are not new, as the experiences of Athens and Venice demonstrate, the post-1500 emergence of a worldwide market gave those states with the resources, need, and appreciation to exploit it fully a tremendous advantage in the world economy as well as in world politics. These same states developed the sea power essential to the realization of the advantages of world trade and the exercise of global influence. The seventeenth-century Dutch leadership in maritime trade represented a substantial improvement on the Portuguese attempt to forge a spice trade monopoly in the sixteenth century. And this Dutch commercial leadership eventually gave way to British leadership in the eighteenth century—an economic transition later enhanced greatly by the productive predominance bestowed upon Great Britain by the Industrial Revolution.

Three consequences of these transformations are most significant. First, the European region's Mediterranean center of economic and political gravity gave way to the world system's Atlantic center. Second, a global political system emerged for the first time, and although this political system has retained close ties to Europe to the present day, its political implications have frequently transcended the local politics of the European continent. Third, entry into the global political system's elite required ocean-going naval strength to advance extra-continental political and economic interests and provide protection from rivals abroad and at home. While it is certainly true that naval strength is dependent upon economic strength (Kennedy, 1976:xvi), naval strength was required first to facilitate the very creation of much of the global elite's newfound wealth.

Nevertheless, the point to be stressed is that globally oriented system leaders have been in a better position to avoid the limitations inherent in creating a formally unicentric or single-state world system because of their global trade orientations. Underscoring the very real limitations of world power, it is doubtful that the unicentric goal has ever been attainable in the past 500 years, nor, one could argue, was it ever really necessary. The rewards flowing from powerful (while informal) political, economic, and cultural influence on a world scale have been enormous. The associated problems have also seemed sufficiently difficult to manage without taking on more. In this respect, it is difficult to quarrel with Chase-Dunn's (1981:39) assertion that the

> overhead costs of purely geopolitical expansion . . . cannot effectively compete with the low overhead strategy of allowing a more decentralized political system to bear the costs of administration while surplus extraction is accomplished by trade.

As the leader's position erodes, attempts to achieve a unicentric world empire become even less likely than when the potential opposition was much weaker, although growing competitive pressures may cause the waning leader to deviate from the low-cost course, as in the territorial scramble for partial world empires in the late nineteenth century (see Thompson and Zuk, 1986).

The Challenger's Threat

3. *Challengers threaten to fundamentally transform the multicentric structure of the interstate system and world economy. Nevertheless, uneven economic development accounts for the repeated failure of the challengers to establish world empires.*

The best opportunity for a unicentric transformation along the lines Chase-Dunn has in mind is found in the late sixteenth century. After Portugal's Moroccan debacle in 1578, Spain was able to conquer its Iberian neighbor fairly easily in 1580. If Spain had also been able to suppress the Dutch revolt, invade and occupy England, and absorb civil-war-prone France, the interstate system and the fledgling world economy might have possessed something approximating a unicentric structure for as long as the Spanish could have held on to their conquests.[2] But this "best opportunity" came at a time when the interstate system and the world economy were both still emerging from Europe's feudal era. After Phillip II, it seems even less likely that a triumphant postsixteenth-century challenger would have created a unicentric system. Nor is it clear that postsixteenth challengers were seeking to establish world empires in the Wallersteinian/Chase-Dunn sense.

In a rather curious footnote, Chase-Dunn (1981:36) remarks that it is possible that one or more of the challenges did not constitute an attempt at world imperium and, consequently, may not have represented threats to the survival of the interstate system and world economy. He then states that it is the structural consequences of a challenger's victory and not the challenger's admittedly often disputed intentions (c.f., Nelson and Olin, 1979:92–183) that are at issue.

This contention seems to imply that the revolutionary consequences of a challenger's victory are somewhat independent of the challenger's intentions. While this possibility is not implausible, Chase-Dunn then proceeds to argue that even if none of the challenger's hypothetical victories would have been likely to change the multicentric character of the interstate system, one must still credit uneven capitalist development for the structural ability or absence of a challenge to the system's multicentricity. If this is the case, however, a different argument presumably must be developed to establish the dependence of the interstate system on certain economic processes. The idea of the challenger's structural threat is too central to Chase-Dunn's model to have the single logic work both ways.

The challenges definitely constituted threats—but probably not to the survival of the multicentric interstate system or the world economy. Rather, they should be seen as threats to the hierarchical structure of at least one and sometimes both subsystems—although not necessarily to the same extent. This assertion reflects in part a disinclination to accept another critical assumption of the world-economy school. The initial continuum point—world empire (unicentric state system) versus world economy (multicentric state system)—are treated as if they are exhaustive categorical dichotomies with few or no intermediate points worth considering. Aspiring conquerors may well have dreamed (and certainly have been accused by their opponents) of seeking a unicentric world empire. But in reality most, if not all, of the past five centuries of global conflict have revolved around variations on or toward the multicentric end of the continuum.

These variations have appeared in the form, demonstrated in chapter ten, of multipolar, bipolar, or unipolar power distributions (either political and/or economic). They must all still be considered multicentric systems. In the long-cycle framework, the world power's initial position of preponderance is evidence of a highly concentrated distribution of power and unipolar structure for the global political system. As the leading power's capability lead gradually erodes, the system returns to a multipolar structure as contenders prepare for another world leadership succession struggle.

As the system moves from multipolarity to unipolarity, the system may seem to give the appearance of moving toward a unicentric world empire. Historically, however, the movement has always stopped well short of reaching anything resembling the unicentric end point of the structural continuum. Thus, a challenger seeking to rearrange a multicentric system's hierarchical arrangement to its own advantage, therefore, need not mean that the challenger is seeking to create the multicentric system's opposite—a unicentric world empire.

Contrary to Chase-Dunn's emphasis on the challenger's threat to system survival, it can be argued, as in chapter ten's two-step model, that the challengers sought only continental or European expansion and predominance. In this view, the threat that is created by the aspirants to regional predominance is directed not so much at the system itself as at the positions of the leading, more globally oriented powers of the world system.

Whether or not control of Europe is viewed as the ultimate goal of the challenger, it becomes clear (although not always immediately) that the challenger's continental expansion will entail a dangerous and unacceptable revision of what has already become an uncertain pecking

order among the major powers. Not only could such a revision interfere with access to the historically important European markets, it also
would constitute an impressive increase in the challenger's capacity to
make future world leadership bids. In this respect, and from the perspective of the more globally oriented states, global wars possess an
often reluctant, frequently belated, preemptive quality.

Doubts have already been expressed about the full extent of the challenger's goals. It is also conceivable that the challenges are less than
fully premeditated. Invariably, the challenger appears to act on the
hope, belief, or mistaken assumption that one or more of the globally
oriented powers will not oppose its continental activities. In both of the
German challenges of the twentieth century, for example, German decision makers entertained peculiar views about the likelihood of American entry into the war.

These misperceptions may be mixed with impatience and/or the
overconfidence stemming from a challenger's occasionally rapid capability improvements and encouraged by a system characterized by declining order and increasing strife. But in any event, global wars tend to
begin as relatively localized affairs, becoming global in scope only
after the globally oriented power(s) decides to participate. Thus, what
we see in retrospect as a major challenge may not have been fully
intended as one by the challenger's decision makers.

From the challenger's perspective, the global war often tends to
break out somewhat prematurely in the sense that the challenger has
not clearly surpassed the system's former leading state or the eventual
successor either in terms of key economic or military capabilities.[3] One
could probably say that warfare becomes global in scope, in part, because it is in the perceived interest of the globally oriented state(s) to
ensure that the challenger does not achieve a vastly improved position
through continental expansion.[4] Relevant data in support of this observation, in addition to the material presented in chapter ten are provided
in table 11.1.

The world-economy perspective (Wallerstein, 1980) emphasizes productive, trade, and financial predominance as the triangular foundation
of the hegemonic core power status. Long-cycle theory stresses the
significance of relative naval capabilities (Modelski and Thompson,
1987b) and lead economies (chapter six). While data on all of these
criteria are not available for each global succession struggle, some
information is available for most of the categories in the cases of the
two most recent contests.

Table 11.1

British, German, and American Percentage Shares of Relative Capabilities

Year	Industrial Production			Leading Sector Position			Trade			Gross National Product			Naval Expenditures			Battleships		
	GB	Ger	USA	GB	Ger	USA	GB	Ger	USA	GB	Ger	USA	GB	Ger	USA	GB	Ger	USA
1870	38	16	27	52	14	18	40	13	16	22	15	27	39	6	15			
1875							39	14	14	20	17	27	36	9	14			
1880	32	17	34	43	15	26	36	15	17	20	13	30	38	8	10	58	0	0
1885				33	18	35	34	19	16	18	13	31	34	7	9	50	0	0
1890							35	19	17	17	13	34	39	8	12	51	0	0
1895							34	20	18	16	13	35	41	8	12	40	8	6
1900	24	21	36	25	19	36	34	20	19	16	13	37	36	10	16	39	9	14
1905							32	20	19	15	13	39	35	12	24	44	16	12
1910	19	20	43	15	18	50	30	23	18	14	12	41	33	17	19	53	26	21
1913	17	20	44				27	24	19	12	12	41	30	14	16	46	29	14
WWI																		
1920				10	11	69	40	5	34	11	11	46	23		53	47	0	22
1925							29	14	25	11	9	48	32	5	40	33	0	29
1930	11	15	53	8	12	62	37	11	18	11	9	47	26	5	37	33	0	25
1935							38	13	27	11	11	42	22	12	28	28	4	28
1938	11	13	39	8	13	57	36	17	29	11	13	42	27	20	27	26	7	26
WW II																		
1946							30		50	11		64						
1950	9	7	64	9	7	64	28	2	41	9	5	54						

Source: Industrial production—Rostow (1978); leading sector position—see chapter 6; trade—based on percent of world trade data in Banks (1971) and Rostow (1978); gross national product—based on GNP per capita data in Rostow (1980) and population data in Banks (1971); naval expenditures—Modelski and Thompson (1988); battleships restricted to first class predreadnoughts between 1880 and 1905 and dreadnought after 1906 (Modelski and Thompson, 1988).

Note: Percentage shares based on a six-state group: Great Britain (GB), France, Russia/USSR, Germany (Ger), Japan, and United States (USA).

Prior to World War I, Germany's economic position only approximated the waning leadership position of Great Britain (Kindleberger, 1978). The same can hardly be said of the German-American economic comparison. Especially clear is Germany's inadequate preparation for global warfare at sea. As a consequence, Germany has twice been isolated from non-European resources by naval blockades of the continent—a consistent antichallenger strategy introduced in the late sixteenth century by attempts to intercept Spanish treasure fleets from the New World and naval stores from the Baltic.

The challenger has yet to defeat the coalition brought together to oppose its expansionary behavior. But the challenger's "irrationality" is displayed not so much by its attempt to conquer adjacent territory. In most cases, the challenger demonstrated the capability to accomplish these local conquests. Rather, the error surfaces in the misperceptions and mistaken estimations about the identity and strengths of the opposition. Leaving a great deal of room for the study of decision-making pathologies, this reflects a basic and curiously consistent misunderstanding of the nature of politico-economic developments in the history of the modern world system. Not only have unsuccessful challengers been less than appreciative of the virtues of world marketing strategies (requiring a more global orientation) emphasized by Chase-Dunn, challengers have failed repeatedly to develop the naval capabilities necessary for achieving a global reach and, more pragmatically, confronting the Dutch, the British, or the Americans at sea.

The successful system leader's global orientation leads to the low overhead strategy while the contintentally oriented challengers have attempted the high overhead, catch-up-by-brute-strength route—with a singular lack of success. Accordingly, it can be argued that it is not so much the lack of resources or the lack of appeal for potential allies that causes the second-runners to fail. Both factors play a role, but they are direct derivatives of the defective policy/strategy choices. Challengers may control the resources to dominate Europe in the short run but, so far, they have lacked the resources to simultaneously control continental Europe and engage globally oriented maritime powers. And despite frequently wishful thinking by challengers, territorial expansion on the European continent has repeatedly led to global conflict.

The challengers do attract allies, but the ones that are attracted are apt to prove—as in the cases of eighteenth-century Spain, early twentieth-century Austria-Hungary, or Mussolini's Italy—to be far more trouble than their assistance is worth. The problem is that the allies that are essential to victory in the long run are likely to see their position directly or indirectly threatened by continental expansion. Either they are globally oriented states that have an opportunity to retain, to regain, or to succeed to the system leader position without pursuing the challenger's high overhead strategy. Or they are regionally oriented land powers that find themselves in the way of the challenger's expansion. Russia/the Soviet Union has assumed this role in the last three global wars. Again, all system leadership aspirants have not pursued the continental expansion path—only the unsuccessful ones. In the long run, it is not uneven growth that accounts primarily for the challenger's repeated failures but more how challengers choose to apply their relative gains in economic and political power.[5]

The Functions of World Wars

4. *World wars may be understood as violent reorganizations of production relations which allow the accumulation process to adjust to its contradictions and to expand on a larger scale. Internationalization of capitalist production is facilitated by the reorganization of political relations among core powers and colonial empires.*

The economic functions of world or global wars suggested by this generalization appear to clash with Chase-Dunn's dissynchronization interpretation and the actual outcomes of world wars. The economic growth of the challenger(s) and the relative decline of the leading power are said to create a new distribution of economic strength that does not correspond to the political structure established in an earlier "hegemonic" era. Global violence is necessary to realign an out-dated political structure with a newly emerged economic structure. Global violence is also said to overcome inherent contradictions and geographical restraints on the capital accumulation process. Yet for global wars to perform all of these functions, one would think that the wars would have to be contests fought between a former leader and its eventual successor. This pairing has yet to occur. In the sixteenth century, the primary disputants were all challengers from a long-cycle perspective—a declining Spain versus the ascending powers of Elizabethan England and the rebellious United Provinces of Netherlands. Since the seventeenth century, the former leader has successfully opposed a continentally oriented challenger and the eventual successor has twice joined the struggle as an ally of the former leader.

If the challengers have always lost, it is rather awkward to attribute a reorganization function to their challenges. Yet the system's political and economic structures do tend to experience fundamental change in that one member of the winning coalition emerges from these global wars as the leading politico-military and lead economic power of the world system. Power capabilities are highly concentrated initially along unipolar, as opposed to unicentric, lines during the immediate postwar period. As the concentration erodes so too does the capability base for system leadership and the global order maintained by the world power—until a new world power emerges in a future global war fought to determine whose version of global order will prevail in the postwar era. Uneven economic growth—particularly to the extent that it is predicated on the types of technological change discussed in chapter six—may be an important factor in this rhythm of political, military, and economic power erosion, but it does not tell the whole story.

Finally, the extent to which formal core-periphery or imperial relations are reorganized by the global wars seems less clear-cut than the pattern implied by Chase-Dunn. Major reorganizations might have been more likely if the challengers had ever won the succession struggles. Instead, formal empires have tended to have been acquired and extended between the global succession struggles—not during or even immediately after the succession contests. Part of the reason for this development is that more recent challengers have been imperially poor (and, therefore, control relatively few spoils of war to reallocate), while earlier global winners often were more interested in global bases (or too weak to penetrate the interiors of Africa and Asia) than in acquiring extensive territories. The more recent exceptions to these generalizations about imperial reorganizations (e.g., the Spanish colonies after the Napoleonic wars, the Ottoman empire after World War I, and portions of the British, French, and Dutch empires after World War II) tend to involve centers of empire whose decline or weakness is accelerated, but not essentially caused, by their participation in the global wars. In this case, ironically, it is uneven economic growth and decline that may provide the more powerful explanation.

CONCLUSION

This chapter constitutes a debate about how the world system and its variably interdependent economic and political subsystems have evolved over the past 500 years. The debate does not concern the utility of a historical-structural vantage point or a theoretical focus on the significance of structural changes in the distribution of power. The ultimate point of contention, however, does center on the extent to which one can defend the claim that changes in the system's capitalistic power structure constitute the roots of systemic challenges and war and

the repetitive dynamic of concentration, deconcentration, and reconcentration of power.

This point of departure is, of course, an important theoretical and
empirical question for historical-structural studies and one that is unlikely to be resolved merely by verbal argument. Nevertheless, it is
possible to take issue with the proposition that the system's multicentric
structure is dependent on processes of uneven economic growth and
development for its survival and reproduction. While there may be
differences of opinion concerning some aspects of the logical consist-
ency of the Chase-Dunn model, the crux of the present disagreement
revolves around the interpretation of the historical relationship between
uneven economic growth and the goals and conflict behavior of the
world system's most powerful states. Contrary to Chase-Dunn's specific arguments, the following threefold set of countergeneralizations
have been advanced:

Uneven economic development cannot account for the system leader's disinclination to create a world empire because a world empire in
the strict world-economy perspective sense has yet to appear feasible,
attractive, or particularly necessary to the respective system leaders.
These globally oriented states have been able to gain far more through
specialization and long-distance trade than through the traditional mode
of territorial conquest and centralized control.

Uneven economic development cannot account for the repeated failures of the challengers to establish world empires and fundamentally
transform the multicentric structure of the political system and world
economy. On the one hand, it is not clear that postsixteenth-century
challengers have in fact sought to establish unicentric world empires.
Nor is it likely that their challenges have constituted genuine threats to
the survival of a multicentric interstate system or world economy. Instead, globally oriented states seem to react to the challenger's threat of
continental expansion and predominance in terms of its immediate impact as a regional problem and, if left unchecked, in terms of its near-
future implications as a global problem. On the other hand, the
mistakes challengers make in identifying their likely opposition and
their inadequate readiness for global combat raises intriguing questions
about the extent to which the challengers' threats are both recognized
and premeditated.

If world wars are to be viewed as violent, yet functional, realign-
ments of production relations and dissynchronized economic and political structures, it would lend credence to the interpretation if the war
took the form of combat between a declining leader and an ascending

successor. Yet it is globally oriented states that oppose the more continentally oriented challengers, and it is the challengers who, so far, have always lost. Since the seventeenth century, the eventual postwar successor has either joined the global combat as an ally of the former leader, or the former leader has regained its leadership role. While the rites of succession are intensely bloody, the actual assumption of leadership by a new world power reflects something of a *fait accompli* that the exhausted former leader has little choice but to accept. Alternatively, one might say that the attempts at reorganization and structural reconcentration that actually takes place follows in the aftermath of the violence. Thus, fundamental structural changes are indeed associated with world or global wars, but the changes brought about are as much in spite of the challengers' efforts as they are due to them.

The historical-structural study of the modern world system, nevertheless, is still developing. Differences of interpretation concerning how to decipher the past 500 years of world-system history should be expected and welcomed to the extent that they help sharpen rival explanations and lead eventually to tests of competing hypotheses.[6] In the interim, we can all agree that a tremendous amount of theoretical and empirical analysis remains to be accomplished in unraveling the central processes of the world system.

12

Structural Change and Global War: Back to the Future—1914? 2030? 2050?

Previous chapters have examined the global-war question from a number of angles. Different frameworks of analysis have been considered as have some of the implications for an understanding of global war that stem from these differences. More concretely, an empirical basis for making generalizations about a number of the properties of global war and the processes that lead up to these infrequent tests of systemic strength has also been created. The every-hundred-years-or-so timing of the wars after 1494 that facilitate capability reconcentration has been established. The consensually critical role of leading technological sectors has been explicated in the theoretical sense and charted from 1780 to the present. The possession of data on the concentration of naval power and technological innovation provides the opportunity to examine the interaction and temporal sequencing of economic and military leadership-capability foundations. Precisely where global war enters these processes of capability concentration can also be determined.

Similarly, the role of long economic waves in the nexus of capability concentration/deconcentration and war can at least be reviewed, if not fully specified. Somewhat more susceptible to analysis over the last half millennium is the contextual role played by structural shifts in the distribution of military power. Finally, there is much to be gained by considering the relative capability positions of the challengers, the declining system leaders, and their ultimate successors at the onset of global war and the implications of these positions for our understanding of not only the process of leadership transition but also the role of uneven development in driving the processes of structural transformation.

The preceding eleven chapters do not provide answers for all of the questions about global wars that might be raised or even the ones that most deserve responses. For example, little has been said about the consequences of global war. Far too little is known about the processes fueling systemic leadership decline—obviously one of the central processes leading to global war. There is a great deal more to be learned about the similarities and dissimilarities in the roles played by the grand strategies of global-war participants—both prior to and during the years of combat. But precisely because these topics are both worthwhile and complex, they must be postponed for future consideration.[1]

Instead of plunging into the development of these topics, the principal purpose of this concluding chapter is to summarize many of the arguments and much of the evidence that have been presented in the preceding chapters. Of course, there are a variety of ways in which this task might be executed. But if we really do know a considerable amount about global war already, as is being asserted in this study, one of the more challenging ways to engage in summarization and to continue probing into what we think we know in contrast to what we clearly do not yet know is to contemplate the future of global war.

As Modelski (1987e:219) has commented:

> . . . the spelling out of a scenario is a way of testing theory. As
> global politics unfolds on its course, the weaknesses of this
> analysis will stand revealed and its strengths will be reaffirmed.
> A theory that emerges from such a trial unscathed in its
> essentials will have literally withstood the test of time.

The basic question then is: do we know enough to predict the probability of a future outbreak of global war? Alternatively, do we know enough to be able to assess other scholars' analytical predictions about the advent of a Third World War? After all, a forecast pertaining to the likelihood of World War III hardly represents an excursion into virgin territory.

In the past few years the prospect of a Third World War has become an increasingly fashionable topic of discussion. Novels develop scenarios on how such a war will be fought and who, if anyone, would win (see, for example, Hackett, 1982; Clancy, 1986). Television and movies tend to specialize in the lower budget, postwar consequences of global war. Academic discussions, such as this one, attempt to theorize about the timing and etiology of such wars. Several books are published each year on how best to prevent nuclear war (e.g., Allison et al., 1985; Nincic, 1985). Scientists argue over the extent of destruction expected from nuclear winter (Sagan, 1983/84). Meanwhile, military planners continue to practice conventional global-war techniques, such as North Atlantic convoy operations and South Pacific amphibious landings, learned in earlier wars. The Soviet navy escalates the scale of its Pacific operations and searches for bases in the South Pacific—where British, German, and American navies once competed for similar prerogatives a century earlier.

People thinking, writing, and talking about World War III are not necessarily likely to make such wars more probable. Yet the upswell in interest may well signify some movement in system time toward the greater likelihood of the outbreak of global war. Some observers certainly think this is the case. One argument of particular interest in this vein is the contention that the global system is presently approaching a situation evoking the years immediately preceding the outbreak of World War I.

After surviving 1984 must we now anticipate the return of 1914? To pursue this question further, we need to first consider the points of view advanced by Miles Kahler (1979) and Albert Bergesen (1983). The former author can be located in or near the structural realist camp. Bergesen is closely linked to the world-economy school. Despite the differences in paradigmatic outlook, the degree of overlap in their arguments for our approaching or reapproaching a 1914-like state of affairs is considerable. But, by now, the overlap should not be all that surprising. Equally overlapping, and again in what should be in a less than surprising way, are the counterarguments put forward by the two leading spokesmen for the leadership long-cycle and world-economy schools of thought (Modelski, 1987e and Wallerstein, 1986). Neither of these two scholars anticipate a global war prior to roughly the middle of the next century. However, both individuals also advance arguments for anticipating the possibility of avoiding altogether another global war. We will turn to these more optimistic arguments after first reviewing the case for the "return-of-1914" perspective.

TWO 1914 SCENARIOS

Kahler's 1914 Analogy

Kahler's interest in the onset of World War I is not specifically predicated on a commitment to tracing structural change. Although some of his observations are expressed in structural terms, Kahler's point of departure is based on the twentieth century's two outbreaks of world war and the apparent differences in causal contexts. Europeans in general are said to be more sensitive to the possibility of the recurrence of

a World War I—a war that emerged with little warning after a long
period of peace.[2] Americans are described as being obsessed or at least
being more attuned to the repetition of a Munich-like (1938) appease-
ment in a conflict-prone era and its presumed consequence—World
War II. In part rhetorically, Kahler (1979:374) asks: "It is assumed [in
Europe] that we could recognize another Hitler, but could we discern a
second Sarajevo?"

To facilitate the discernment process, Kahler proceeds to discuss the
similarities of the present era with the period immediately preceding
1914. As indicated in table 12.1, the similarities Kahler sees are numerous. They are also quite amenable to, or at least compatible with,
historical-structural interpretation. Despite one of the more obvious
differences between the earlier and contemporary eras—the polarity
structure—Kahler considers the current period to possess significant
potential for movement toward multipolarity. Evidence for this potential
is discussed largely in terms of continuing post-World War II military
capability advances made by the Soviet Union and the more recent
steps taken to begin Chinese military modernization. This incipient
shift toward a more genuinely multipolar power distribution, assuming
the persistence of Sino-Soviet antagonisms, increases both flexibility
and insecurity. One way to respond to perceptions of increased insecurity is to create new alliance bonds. Yet the new commitments that tend
to accompany the new alliance partners work to reduce the flexibility
that initially emerges with a more diffused power distribution.

Returning to the present bipolar confrontation, Kahler also acknowledges the the U.S.-U.S.S.R. competition bears some resemblance to
the British-German rivalry prior to 1914. Both the United States and,
earlier, Britain represent established system leaders with pronounced
commitments to sea power. Germany and, now, the Soviet Union can
also be described as continental challengers, each "seeking its place in
the sun through a Weltpolitik based European world" (Kahler,
1979:375).

Even so, Kahler is uncomfortable with this aspect of the analogy. He
points out that the Soviet Union has not justified the development and
expansion of its fleet in terms of the risk theory advanced by the German admiral von Tirpitz. The stated German objective was not to out-
build the British navy. Rather, it was argued, given the worldwide
dispersal of British naval forces, all that was necessary was to build a
fleet sufficiently large to make the British think twice before attacking
through the North Sea.

Table 12.1

Kahler's 1914 Analogy Elements

1. Multipolarity or movement toward multipolarity.
2. The tendency to search for new alliance partners.
3. Rivalry between a maritime hegemon and a continental challenger
4. Policy disputes within the hegemonic elite over the challenger's intentions and the most appropriate measures to combat them.
5. The tendency to superimpose and/or to confuse the hegemonic/challenger rivalry with local quarrels.
6. Increased sensitivity to perceived attacks on bloc structures accompanied by the tendency to impute meddling and malevolence on the part of the main rival.
7. Renewed competition outside the established spheres of influence.
8. The potential for mixing the threat of an unfavorable military balance with domestic political problems.
9. Declining internationalism and increasing nationalism.
10. Renewed interest in geopolitics.
11. The revival of arguments for the advantages of preemptive warfare.

Source: Based on the discussion in Kahler (1979).

Kahler also notes that the Soviet navy has not assumed the same symbolic functions performed by the German imperial navy within the German political system—an embodiment of national unity and middle-class nationalism. Moreover, it is argued that Germany's naval challenge became the major bone of contention with Britain. In contrast, the Soviet Union and the United States had been at loggerheads long before the Soviet Union initiated its most recent naval expansion.

It is certainly appropriate to draw attention to these differences between the Anglo-German and Soviet-American rivalries. One wonders, however, whether they are really all that important. Von Tirpitz's risk theory, for example, can be taken at face value as a peculiar deterrence scheme that failed to deter the adversary. In this respect, it is not too surprising that the Soviets have not publicly emulated it. But it is also possible to interpret the risk theory as a governmental rationale intended for legislative consumption in order to best extract financial commitments for continued fleet expansion purposes (Kennedy, 1983:129–160). To the extent that this interpretation can be defended, the parallel to the Soviet case should not be expected. Different types of bureaucratic strategies would be necessary in the Soviet political system to elicit sustained naval support. Similarly, Soviet geographical and geopolitical opportunities for naval expansion are vastly different than in the earlier German case.

Much the same can be said about the differences in political symbolism. Whether the Soviet Union has class conflict problems or not, the structure of domestic group antagonisms in the USSR is not one of agrarian Junkers versus an emerging, urbanized middle class. Thus one should not expect to find the same political myths operating in dissimilar political contexts.

As for the timing and saliency of the naval expansion issue, it seems rather difficult to sustain the argument that the issue was central and emerged early in one case and was peripheral and late to develop in the second case. In both cases, challengers appreciate to some extent the need to compete with the system leader at sea. Precisely when a challenger chooses to initiate its naval expansion may not be all that significant (except perhaps to its chances of success). At the very least, the challenger's timing may not be as significant as the likely consequences of the naval expansion effort—increases in the perception of threat and hostility toward the challenger on the part of the system leader.

Kahler's reservations about the maritime/continental dimension of rivalry notwithstanding, he appears to be more than prepared to resume the structural analogy. The challenger's policies are apt to provoke disputes within the system leader's decision-making elite. What are the challenger's real intentions? What strategies are best suited to respond? Not surprisingly, different points of view about ultimate intentions lead to different responsive strategies. One camp is likely to advise some amount of accommodation while another will insist upon a militant vigilance against any acts of aggression.

There is also a tendency to interpret local conflicts and disputes through the lenses of the leader-challenger rivalry. The propensity to misinterpret takes on a self-fulfilling character. A dispute that began as genuinely local can be escalated to a systemic-level dispute. Similarly, the established powers will be likely to see the challenger's hand behind all threats to the stability of the status quo, particularly in those spheres of influence, often contiguous, in which the pattern of dominance-subordination has been resolved some time earlier. The possibility of political change and unrest in the absence of the provocation of outside agitators is simply denied. Whether or not these perceptual tendencies, long familiar to students of group conflict, prove to be responsible for the outbreak of overt hostilities, the general sense of insecurity is heightened. The urge to compete throughout the system is also likely to be accentuated. Peaceful accommodation of challenger goals also becomes less likely. If, as Kahler argues, smaller states are in a better position, now as opposed to the immediate pre-1914 period, to drag the strongest powers into their quarrels, the social psychology of leader-challenger relations have become even more dangerous over time.

In most respects, the last four elements in Kahler's 1914 analogy (see table 12.1) are less central than the first seven. It is tempting to compare Austro-Hungarian imperial problems—even if that state was not the systemic challenger—with the seemingly chronic potential for the disintegration of the Soviet Union's federal unity or the collapse of its economic system. The argument, an old one, is that serious domestic problems can provide additional incentives for aggressive foreign policy behavior that may divert attention away from the internal difficulties. The normal aversions to risk-taking may be lowered even further if it appears probable that the challenger's future military position will be less advantageous. The temptation is to fight now while the possibility of victory is presumably better than if the fighting is postponed to some future date.

In the last three points, Kahler draws attention to the relaxation of several attitudinal restraints on full-scale warfare. Nationalism is thought to be on the rise as is interest in geopolitical arguments. One could argue that it is the maritime leader-continental challenger confrontation that helps to restimulate interest in geopolitics. Kahler's point, however, is that geopolitical doctrines are inherently nationalist and conservative, that they justify endlessly expanding competition throughout the world, and that such doctrines can be used to justify the suppression of domestic welfare spending as a resource diversion. Finally, a parallel is drawn for the pre-1914 and the contemporary period in terms of a revival of interest in the perceived advantages of preemptive-war strategies. The prospects for short and winnable conflicts, nearly unthinkable in earlier days, begins to appear more attractive.

Many of these observations seem appropriate. Yet the question that is left entirely open-ended, however, is precisely where in the pre-1914 context does the present period fit? Are we closer to "1870" than to "1914"? For a more specific fix on this question, Bergesen's (1983) analysis is helpful.

Bergesen's Four-Phase Model

Bergesen's perspective is easily located within the world-economy perspective. His rendition of system time, nevertheless, is unorthodox by that perspective's standards and, ironically, resembles the chronology attributed to Gilpin in chapter three. Based on his perceptions of the timing of systemic cycles of war and peace (see Bergesen and Schoenberg, 1980; Bergesen, 1985), Bergesen divides the post-1500 era into three phrases of international instability/conflict (1500–1815, 1870–1945, and 1973–) separated by brief periods of hegemonic stability (1815–1870 and 1945–1973). This cyclical process of stability and instability is regarded as a characteristic of a capitalistic world system that periodically reorganizes the way in which it functions—as in the uneven development argument developed by Chase-Dunn (chapter 11).

A hegemonic economy rises to supremacy based on its technological innovations. The failure to maintain its hegemonic dominance triggers a round of competition and conflict among core powers for reasons that would seem familiar to Kahler.[3]

> As the hegemonic power declines, the major core states become more equal. Power is pluralized. This creates an increasingly unstable situation, as there is no dominant state to underwrite international agreements or enforce international order. Instability grows. States reach out to each other through treaty and alliance in an effort to halt the growing friction but that fails. The instability increases. Competition and rivalry become more open, resulting in international incidents and eventually open conflict. The core moves from the order of hegemonic dominance to international anarchy. The cycle thus begins again with the appearance of a new hegemonic state and another period of peace and economic expansion (Bergesen, 1983:258).

This explanation of course is hardly unique. What Bergesen does differently, however, is to identify four stages in the transition from the alternating phases of hegemonic order and general disorder. Figure 12.1 summarizes the basic flow of this model.

The transition to general warfare begins with hegemonic decline and the rise of new economic competitors. The new competition can take more than one form according to Bergesen. In the mid to late nineteenth century, competition to Britain developed in the form of new and strong states (Germany) or newly stronger states (the United States). In the twentieth century, Japan is an example of the newly stronger type of competitor. The field of competition is extended even further by the emergence of the newly industrializing countries or NICs. The outcome is similar in both centuries—a more polycentric core and greater pluralization of world industrial production.

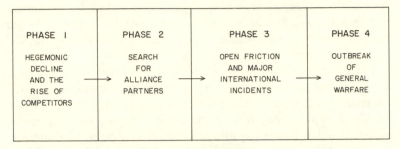

Figure 12.1   Bergesen's Four-Stage Model of the Onset of General Warfare

Source: Based on the discussion in Bergesen (1983)

Bergesen also ties this first phase to Kondratieff waves essentially along the lines reviewed in chapter four. The new competitors first emerge during upswings that create openings for upward mobility. The subsequent overproduction leads to a downturn that serves to weed out the old hegemonic power. To be competitive in the next upswing, the former hegemon must take this opportunity to restructure its economy but is unlikely to do so successfully.

As in Kahler's 1914 analogy, the second phase represents an attempt to recreate the order formerly associated with the phase of hegemonic dominance. As power becomes more equal, uncertainty and instability increase. States respond by creating security arrangements with other states. The major power alignments are mirrored by the gradual disintegration of the hegemon's bloc. Client states of the former hegemon (e.g., Iran, Nicaragua), in particular, are likely to become less stable as the old and largely external source of regime legitimacy decays.

Phase two's increased instability is not ameliorated by the efforts to arrange new alliances. Phase three is a period of open conflict and crisis confrontations, primarily between core powers attempting to defend or expand their spheres of influence in the world economy's periphery. Bergesen identifies the great-power crises of 1906–1913 as the earlier manifestation of phase three. The current phase three is said to be ongoing and is loosely depicted as the 1980s–1990s.

In phase four, the frictions of phase three break out into overt warfare. Among the telltale signs of war preparations are changes in military strategy, naval races, new-weapons paranoia, and the rearmament of all the core powers. The consequent period of general warfare then functions to restructure and "rejuvenate" the world economy. A new hegemon emerges. Another bout of innovation and capital accumulation then begins. Presumably, the resumption of this process would depend, as in the case of a future global war, on whether anything was left to accumulate.

The arguments and observations of Kahler and Bergesen seem quite compatible. Both see symptoms of incipient multipolarity—increased uncertainty and insecurity, the search for stabilizing pacts, and the likelihood of increasing friction and confrontations among the major powers. Neither author is particularly taken with the usual counterarguments advanced against the possibility of another global war. These include increasing interdependence and the unprecedented scale of devastation associated with the use of contemporary weapon systems. Both of these counterarguments have been heard before, not coincidentally, in the years immediately prior to the outbreak of World War I. Both counterarguments assume some form of decision-maker rationality—expressed in economic-cost benefit terms or in terms of military capability calculations. Yet the literature on decisions to go to war are replete with multiple irrational elements (e.g., Jervis, 1976; Lebow, 1981; Levy, 1983b, 1985b, 1986). An extraordinary amount of optimism is required to think that these pathologies of decision making have somehow disappeared or will be suppressed conveniently in the future.

One wonders, nonetheless, how close we really are to the types of contextual conditions that hint that global war may be just around the structural corner. Kahler is rather ambiguous on this score. Most of the factors to which he draws attention could be found in varying forms at any point in a forty-year, pre-1914 interval. Bergesen, on the other hand, is more specific. If we are now in his third phase, phase four, it is implied, cannot be too far away—perhaps beginning around the turn of the century.

Many, if not all of the similarities/analogies suggested by Kahler and Bergesen seem quite, appropriate and equally compatible with the general thrust of historical-structural analysis of international relations. There are other features of contemporary systemic change, however, that suggest 1914 or at least another global war may not yet be all that imminent.

More "optimistic" historical-structural scenarios do exist. In keeping with one of the underlying themes of this study, it is fortuitous that a "2030 plus" long-cycle scenario exists, as does a "2050" world-economy forecast. Nevertheless, it is far from coincidental that these longer-range predictions share certain common denominators even though, in the end, they diverge fundamentally in the natures of their envisioned futures.

A 2030-PLUS SCENARIO

Modelski (1987e) begins the construction of his scenario by projecting the four-phased, generational length, long-cycle chronology some forty-five years into the future. As depicted in table 12.2, the last quarter of the twentieth century is identified as a period of delegitimation. What is to be expected in this and the next phase is the continuing but very gradual erosion of U.S. leadership.

Several reasons are advanced for the prediction of a slow rate of deconcentration. First, the very strong position attained by the United States in 1945 was much more impressive than the postwar peaks achieved by earlier world powers. These gains in the initial capability foundation for leadership might be expected to dissipate more slowly than the earlier, comparatively weaker foundations. In any event, the historical deconcentration pattern (in terms of naval power) from the middle of the delegitimation to the middle of the deconcentration phases, established in the first four cycles, is only a few percentage points.

Moreover, the likelihood of substantial gains in terms of global reach capability positions on the part of other states does not seem great. The Soviet Union was able to achieve a semblance of nuclear parity in the 1970s, but the structural weaknesses of its economic base are likely to constrain further positional improvements. Of the other possible contenders—Japan, Western Europe, China, and India—there is considerable evidence of improvement in terms of their economic foundations and even some signs of marginal enhancements in military

Table 12.2

A Long-Cycle Phase Forecast

Phase	Years
Global War	1914–1945
World Power	1945–1973
Delegitimation	1973–2000
Deconcentration	2000–2030

Source: Based on Modelski (1987c:4).

global-reach capabilities. Yet none of the potential contenders are advancing in both areas simultaneously. As a consequence, there is little reason to expect dramatic changes in the global political system's distribution of power.

A slowly deconcentrating political system means that the effectiveness of the system will decline and that unresolved political problems will proliferate. Conflict should increase in terms of frequency and intensity and should be particularly evident in the Third World—along the lines of the protracted Iranian-Iraq War. Multinational corporations and other users of world transportation routes will be confronted with increased risks and uncertainty. At the same time, the Kondratieff consolidation/contraction in world trade, finance, investment, and aid that is associated with the delegitimation phase should give way to the emergence of new industries (information, telecommunications, bioengineering, or space) and a new phase of prosperity. Just where these new industries will emerge will determine the location of the world economy's active zone and, consequently, the most likely source of leadership in the twenty-first century.

If the long cycle plays itself out as it has in the past, a global war to resolve the system's need for leadership and to make systemic policy choices could be anticipated sometime after 2030. The main problem with this scenario, however, is that it overlooks a substantial change in one of the major circumstances upon which it is predicated. Namely, the nature of the tests of strength that punctuated the long-cycle course of events over the past five centuries can no longer be tolerated. The advent of nuclear weapons has made the global war institution a dangerous anachronism in the sense that a nuclear war, to put it mildly, would be unlikely to facilitate the reconcentration of leadership capabilities. It is doubtful, indeed, that any global political system would survive.

Accordingly, Modelski contends, the world system's most pressing political problem is the search for new, less destructive ways to provide leadership and global decision making. Four embryonic possibilities are visible currently. Two involve the insitution of summitry—either the ostensibly economic summits of the United States, Canada, Britain, France, Germany, Japan, and Italy or the more sporadic encounters of the two military superpowers. The other two possible avenues to look for changes in policy making can be traced to the chances of increased autonomy for decision making in international organizations—both at the regional level and more encompassing United Nations network.

Different observers will no doubt disagree about the likelihood of any of these alternative avenues of political decision making becoming sufficiently efficacious to ameliorate the pressures for another global war. Modelski, of course, offers no guarantees that these four are the only possibilities or even the most appropriate alternatives. What he does suggest, however, is that deterrence policies, at best, offer only a temporary deferral of a macrodecision that, historically, has relied upon intensive uses of force. A forecast of the future probability of a global war, therefore, hinges on the limited time remaining to devise and, subsequently, to learn to live with an alternative decision-making forum.

> By 2016, it should be fairly clear whether there will or will
> not be a "next" global war. If the world will have begun to build
> an alternative mechanism for global decision making, then the
> likelihood of it occurring will decline. . . . [If the prospects are
> not visible,] pressures for a return to the traditional, and more
> primitive, methods of the past might well become irresistible.
> (Modelski, 1987e:240).

A 2050 SCENARIO

Wallerstein's (1986) forecast is couched in two different temporal frames of reference. One type of scenario emerges when the point of reference is restricted to middle-run, cyclical processes. A much different outcome is produced by considering only long-term, secular trends. The analytical trick, for Wallerstein, is to attempt to predict what might happen when middle- and long-run processes interact with one another.

The cyclicality of the middle-run processes renders them easier to predict. They also have been the primary theoretical preoccupation of world-economy analysts and, therefore, should be fairly familiar to readers. The three interrelated processes that serve the predictive purposes best are the tightening and loosening of core-periphery ties, the expansion/contraction of the world economy, and the movement toward and away from hegemony.

Currently, we are depicted as experiencing a phase of hegemonic decline (circa 1970–1995). With the end of U.S. hegemony in the late 1960s and the onset of a Kondratieff-B-economic contraction phase, intense competition between the United States, Western Europe, and Japan is the order of the day. The principal goals of the competition are twofold. In the short term, the idea is to export losses and unemployment to other parts of the industrialized world. In the slightly longer term, the main prize is to capture monopolistic control over the industries (i.e., microprocessing, biogenetics, and new energy sources) that will galvanize the next Kondratieff upturn sometime in the decade after 1990.

Corporations are preparing for this upturn by engaging in research and product development, industrial espionage, and organizational changes (e.g., mergers and cartels). Governments are playing their part by providing various types of public subsidization of the corporate activities. Of the major participants in this competition, Wallerstein favors the prospects of the Japanese enterprises that are described as "inching steadily ahead" because they are less burdened by public and private consumption drains than the Americans and the West Europeans.

Wallerstein further assumes that the principal contenders for hegemonic succession will be Japan and a revitalized Western Europe. A reshuffling of alliance commitments is expected to accompany the geographical shift in the production of the leading sector industries. Closely adhering to the historical script described in chapter three, Japan, the sea/air-based contender, will ally with the former hegemon, the United States. Initially the senior partner, the United States will gradually be transformed into the junior partner as were the Dutch and the British in earlier successions. China may also join this grouping.

If China should join the trans-Pacific alliance, the land-based contender, Western Europe, should be expected to enter into an arrangement with the Soviet Union and Eastern Europe. In the associated struggle over control of the periphery, the Middle East would probably be captured by the more proximate Euroasians. Latin America would most likely stay within the trans-Pacific orbit. All other things being equal, these conflicts could be expected to lead to a fourth world war in the middle of the twenty-first century (circa 2050).

But all other things are not seen by Wallerstein as being equal. Rather, he argues that the world system is in the midst of a long-term structural crisis that has been ongoing since 1914. This structural crisis has been brought about by the very great success of the capitalist world economy which, paradoxically, tends to undermine its own primary accumulation function. The increasing degree of commodification in the economic system leaves little room for the traditional approach to the overproduction problems associated with the cyclical middle-run processes. The resulting gradual squeeze on the accumulation process will lead to an intensified struggle among elites and, eventually, a breakdown of political order and ideology. These developments, in turn, should pave the way for the emergence of a new historical system presumably along the lines of the European transition from feudalism to capitalism.

What shape this new historical system will take is left unclear. Wallerstein cautiously limits his prediction to a binary choice. The new system will either continue to be inegalitarian as is the current system or it will become more egalitarian.

> I am firmly convinced that moments of transition from one historical system to another are those rare moments in which human will has wide scope and in which therefore historical choices are real and not manipulated. The successor historical system or systems circa 2050 or 2100 will be the one we construct. But it is not clear which one we will chose to construct (Wallerstein, 1986:16).

What is also left unclear, besides the source of Wallerstein's optimism about the wide scope of choice that will emerge in "the moments of transition," is whether, or to what extent, the availability of real historical choices will depend on the intensive and extensive destructuration that would follow in the wake of a fourth world war.

1914? 2030? 2050?

We have now seen four different approaches to forecasting a future global war. Kahler employs the 1914 metaphor as a structural analogy for comparing current developments with pre-Sarajevo parallels. Bergesen's use of the 1914 metaphor is more theoretically based. For him, the 1914 term merely signifies the most recent outbreak of global war in a recurring process. Modelski and Wallerstein, on the other hand, avoid the attention riveting practice of equating a future global war with a previous one. Yet, at the same time, they are unequivocal in their belief that another global war could occur sometime between 2030 and 2050 if other factors (the construction of alternative decision-making forums or the resolution of a long term structural crisis in capital accumulation) do not intervene.

Who is "right"? Or, at least, who seems closest to the mark? Ultimately, we will of course have to wait and see how events develop in order to determine whose forecast proves to be the most accurate. In the interim, however, we can only evaluate these predictions in light of the information on structural change and global war that is currently available.

What do we know? We know that global wars are a recurring phenomenon. Over the past five hundred years, global wars have broken out on five occasions (1494–1516, 1580–1608, 1688–1713, 1792–1815, and 1914–1945). Each time, it has taken some twenty-five to thirty years to resolve the issues at stake. Ultimately, a system leader emerges from the fighting, at the head of the winning coalition, and enjoying a substantial lead in the capabilities necessary for global reach. An initial near monopoly in ocean-going naval/air power constitutes one component of the capability foundation. Another important component is the lead power's status as the world system's most active economic zone. This status places the system leader squarely at the center of the world economy in terms of the innovative development of leading sectors, but also in terms of investment, trade, and credit.

Metaphorically, the postglobal war reconcentration of political-economic and military capability can be compared to a wind-up toy that has had its key turned several revolutions or its batteries replaced or recharged. Gradually, though, the key winds down. The batteries lose their charge. So too do the political-economic frameworks and structures that were imposed on the global political system and the world economy in the aftermath of a global war fought to decide systemic leadership and consequent macropolicy orientations. On the average, this process of reconcentration and deconcentration has required about one hundred years or three to four generations to complete the cycle.

One of the more obvious implications of this interpretation of global war is that we need not be too concerned with Sarajevo assassinations or the rise of risk-takers such as Adolf Hitler. These factors, no doubt, made some contribution to the onset of global war fighting in earlier periods. But, from a structural point of view, these precipitating elements were not the most significant causal factors. What is far more critical is whether the structural context has evolved and eroded to the point at which the probability of a new struggle over systemic governance becomes great.

We know something about the timing of this erosion process. It is a simple task to compute the intervals of time (63, 79, 78, and 98 years, respectively) that elapsed between the earlier global wars. The intervals may be increasing somewhat over time, but the average interwar period is about 80 years. If we look 80 years beyond the end of the last global war in 1945, the year 2025 appears to represent a reasonable projection of the historical evidence. Nevertheless, such a projection can only be regarded as a crude first cut suggesting merely that information on the timing of earlier wars would indicate that the probability of a global war in the very near future is not all that high. More time ordinarily is required for deconcentration to proceed sufficiently.

The term *ordinarily* in the last sentence should be highlighted. Forecasting into the future assumes that the important parameters have remained roughly unchanged or else that we know how to adjust the model for important changes that have taken place. In this case, there is always the possibility that the tempo of deconcentration has accelerated as has the tempo of so many other processes in the twentieth century. Table 12.3 is intended to address this possibility. One way to look for acceleration is to compare the system leader's current relative position (in terms of sea power) to its predecessors' positions in earlier centuries.

Focusing on the forty to fifty years after the preceding global war, table 12.3 lists the average relative position (for the forty-first to fiftieth year decade) for each successive system leader. The positions clearly are not identical. The two-power nature of the post-1945 era also complicates the numerical comparison process. The proportional change (decline) in the leader's naval position since the end of the last global war, therefore, may provide a more interpretable indicator. In this respect, the 1985–1993 interval is associated with the greatest proportional amount of decline—although it is not greatly different in some

Table 12.3

Comparing Positional and Distributional Changes over Time

40 to 50 Years After the Previous Global War	System Leader's Relative Position*	Proportional Change in the System Leader's Position**	Global Distribution of Naval Power
1557–1566	.408	–24.2	predom. bipolar
1649–1658	.342	–35.0	bipolar
1753–1762	.419	– 7.7	predom. multipolar†
1856–1865	.477	–27.7	predom. bipolar
1985–1993	.623	–37.7	bipolar

*Relative position represents an average for the decade.

**Comparison period for computing proportional change is the relative position in the first postglobal war year to the average position forty to fifty years later.

†The twenty years after 1762, however, were bipolar years.

ways from the extent of Dutch decline in the seventeenth century. But even this comparison is not without its problems. The Dutch lead never quite compared to the extraordinary position attained by the United States for a period of time after World War II. Hence, considerable proportional decline was almost inevitable in the U.S. case given the unusual relative peak achieved on the sea-power dimension.

The American lead in naval power, based on information on ships currently under construction or planned, is expected to be retained at least through 1993, and quite likely beyond that date as well. There is to be sure a difference between a lead in a multipolar world as opposed to the current bipolar world. Yet it is interesting to observe, as recorded in table 12.3's last column, that bipolarity, with only one exception (1753–1762), is in fact the characteristic nature of the naval distribution of global power at the approximately half-century juncture. Even the exception is only partial for the predominant multipolarity of the 1753–1762 decade quickly gave way to two decades of bipolarity.

The United States' lead in naval global reach capabilities, as a consequence, does not appear to be evaporating any more quickly than the rates experienced by its predecessors. While less historical information is available on leading-sector decline, the United States' index position in 1980 was comparable to the British position in the 1870s, just as its climacteric period was commencing. Between 1870 and 1910 (see table 6.6), the British leading-sector position literally melted away (.519 to .146). But another leadership meltdown is not inevitable and perhaps not even all that likely. The preliminary data available for 1985, for example, suggest a slight upturn for the United States position rather than continued decline. While further positional decline, particularly in terms of the older leading sectors, seems probable, it is conceivable that the pace of leading-sector deconcentration will be much more moderate than was the case in the less technologically complex nineteenth century. Whether this prediction is borne out by events will depend of course on what happens in the newest sectors over the next two to three decades. Simply because the British proved themselves unable to catch the next wave of industrial innovation does not mean that history need repeat itself exactly. It is also possible to catch some portion of the wave without dominating it. But to be in a position to make more informed predictions about this issue, we will need to improve our understanding of just how the processes of industrial decline work. Generally, analysts continue to function in the speculative mode on these matters. Until that state of affairs changes, we will have to wait and see what happens in such sectors as computer technology, biogenetics, and aerospace.

There can be little doubt that the current system leader has experienced relative decline. Still, the prospects for the continued relative decline of the system leader constitute only one side of the forecasting coin. Nor is it particularly difficult to identify challengers or at least potential challengers. Even so, we need to be careful not to exaggerate the extent to which the leader has declined, a point argued forcefully by Russett (1985). Alternatively, as Modelski (1987e) points out, we need to be careful not to exaggerate the positional gains achieved by the various candidates for future systemic leadership. Figure 12.2 plots the post-1945 positional developments of the system's two leading military powers, according to the global reach indicators advocated by long-cycle analysts (aircraft carriers, ballistic missiles at sea attributes, and nuclear attack submarines—see table 3.3).

Figure 12.2 demonstrates the relative decline of the United States and the rise of the Soviet Union. But it also depicts a large gap between the positions of the two states. And while their trajectories appear to be moving toward the possibility of transitional convergence, the rate of movement is not all that rapid. Between 1960 and 1985, the average annual positional rate of change was 0.3 percent. Perhaps of equal

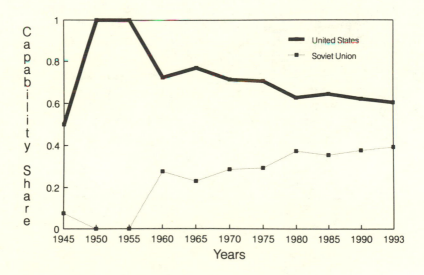

Figure 12.2   Contemporary Positional Change in Naval Power
Data Source: Modelski and Thompson (1988:92)

significance is that no other state has yet crossed the minimal ten percent capability threshold for global competitiveness. Nor are those states in the best position to do so—Britain, France, China, or Japan—very likely to exceed the minimal threshold in this century.[4] Multipolarity in terms of naval, global reach capabilities has not yet descended upon us.

Naval capabilities are only part of the structural change picture. Figure 12.3 plots the economic equivalent to figure 12.2 by comparing the post-1945 positional changes experienced by the system's two leading economic powers—the United States and Japan.[5] Again, the system leader's relative position has definitely declined. The position of the hypothetical economic challenger has clearly improved. But the ascending and descending trajectories appear to have some way to go before they cross. As in the case of naval power, it may not be that the direction of change depicted in figure 12.3 will continue unchecked. Japan is unusually vulnerable to raw-material shortages. It faces a rapidly aging population and also must deal with its own competitive chal-

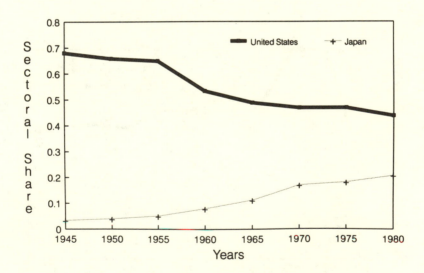

Figure 12.3   Contemporary Positional Change in Leading-Sector Production
Data Source: See footnote 5, Chapter 6

lenges from Asian neighbors such as South Korea and eventually China. Presumably, the United States remains in a position to improve its competitive leading-sector position—even if the historical odds are not encouraging.

There is also the historical-structural anomaly evidenced by the need for two charts to portray the decline of the systemic leader and its most likely challengers. There is an obvious military challenger candidate that appears most unlikely to become a serious economic challenger in the foreseeable future. There is an obvious leading economic rival that, so far, appears unlikely to become a serious military challenger in this century. This novelty of structural change in the modern world system encourages restraint in forecasting any imminent struggle for leadership succession. Since it is something of a novelty, the development might be interpreted in more than one way. But if there were two full-fledged challengers to the current American leadership, the predictions of imminent conflict would seem more plausible and in line with the recurring patterns in the global political system. Since neither the Soviet Union nor Japan can be construed as a full-fledged challenger in the 1980s, one would think that a new, albeit quite possibly temporary, restraint on global competition has emerged.

While we are on the subject of possible challengers, however, the Wallerstein prediction of a Japanese-West European competition does not appear to fit the historical pattern very well. The Soviet Union currently best fits the more regionally oriented challenger image as established by the earlier behavior of Spain, France, and Germany. A united Western Europe might be expected to be as globally/maritime oriented as the Japanese despite the fact that both actors could be faced with serious threats from within their immediate geopolitical regions. A united Western European navy probably could also qualify more quickly as a global power than could the Japanese navy. At the same time, the prospects for Western Europe becoming once again the location of the world system's most active economic zone seem less than good.

The Western Europe-Japan match-up would violate the historical pattern in another way. The pattern has been that the winning coalition fractures. One member subsequently changes sides and becomes the primary challenger. The principal members of the last winning coalition were the United States, the Soviet Union, and Britain. A united Western Europe would, most likely, be a composite of members from both the previous winning and losing coalitions. Japan was a member of the losing coalition as well. In this respect and others, the Soviet

Union, a prototypical example of a state attempting to catch up in the systemic competition by brute strength, remains the best candidate to become the primary challenger in the early midtwenty-first century.

Yet it needs to be kept in mind that the evidence also suggests that the challenge tends to be a premature one. The primary challenger errs in estimating the identity and strengths of the eventual opposition in what is typically an initially regional level war. Some ostensibly regional wars thus become global wars when the system leader and its allies (perhaps including the leader's eventual successor) perceive the systemic framework that they have established earlier and benefited from for several generations is now in jeopardy. It is the threat of a future power transition and not its accomplishment that creates the showdown crisis for the global political system. The two-step nature of the outbreak of global war suggests some caution in feeling comfortable with the prospects of having some thirty-five to forty (2025–2030) to sixty (2050) years to construct a viable alternative to the now too dangerous global war institution. Since the outbreak of global war historically is predicated in part on fundamental strategic misperceptions and other decision-maker pathologies, it may prove grossly misleading to trust too much in a projected timetable—no matter how well justified it appears to be in historical and theoretical terms.

To the extent that a thirty-five- to sixty-year predicted breathing space encourages complacency, the prospects for a future global war will be all the more self-fulfilling. To break free of the global system's most primitive mechanism for leadership succession and to construct some alternative approach will require not only the widespread recognition of the basic cyclical patterns underlying the outbreak of global way—no mean task in itself—but also a sense of urgency. If these prerequisites are satisfied, the odds are that there could be sufficient time to learn how to do things differently. Otherwise, the continuities displayed by five hundred years of structural change and systemic political history are less than encouraging.

Notes

Chapter One. An Introduction to Structural Change and Global Wars

1. A wide range of views on the subject of the recent relative decline of the United States may be found in Bolling and Bowles (1982), Bowles and Gintis (1982), Calleo (1982), Chase-Dunn (1982), Magaziner and Reich (1982), Olson (1982), Abernathy et al. (1983), Bowles et al. (1983), Goldfrank (1983), Reich (1983), Philips (1984), Rupert and Rapkin (1985), Russett (1985), Scott (1985a, 1985b), Thurow (1985), Dumas (1986), Krieger (1986), Cohen and Zysman (1987), Kegley and Wittkopf (1987), and Silk (1987).

2. Based on Levy's (1983a) battle-death data, Modelski (1984:7) links 25.5 million battle-deaths (from a total of 32.2 million in great power warfare) to five global wars fought between 1494 and 1945. The specific wars are identified in chapter three (table 3.2).

3. Some analysts view many, if not all, of the interactions that go on between states as inherently "systemic" (e.g., McClelland, 1966; Choucri and North, 1975). The analytical problem then becomes one of differentiating theoretically between dyadic systems, regional subsystems, and the world system. Others aggregate "external" behavior and label these activities as systemic. Singer and Small (1968), among many others, provide an example when they aggregate all interstate alliances operative in any given year in order to create indexes of systemic alliance structure. Yet adding the local alliances of Latin America or Southeast Asia to those of NATO or the Warsaw Pact, without any semblance of weighting, tends to distort the nature of the world system's alliance structure(s). Still other analysts believe that the nation-state is a or the most real or tangible actor in international politics and that any talk of a higher order system is too intangible to be meaningful. Many of the "structural realists" who are discussed in chapter two and three give this impression. Inasmuch as both the "state" and the "system" are nothing more than conceptualizations for various types of entities and relationships, though, it is not clear why one concept should be viewed as any more or any less tangible than the other.

4. Bueno de Mesquita (1975, 1978, 1980), for instance, utilizes a type of systemic-level analysis. However, this work precedes the emphasis on expected utility that continues to ignore systemic contextual considerations in published work (Bueno de Mesquita and Lalman, 1986). Bueno de Mesquita and Lalman (1987), however, do attempt to contrast the explanatory power of some systemic and dyadic variables but find little support for the systemic arguments that they choose to consider. For other critiques of the expected utility approach, see Majeski and Sylvan (1984) and Wagner (1984).

5. I have borrowed these structural conflict principles from Tilly's (1975) application of them to domestic systems.

Chapter Two. Systemic Structure and the Development of International Relations Theory

1. Keohane (1986:7), among others, argues that the key assumptions of realism can be found in Thucydides' (1954) discussion of the causes of the Peloponnesian Wars.

2. Masterman (1970) demonstrates that there are at least twenty-one different meanings for the paradigm term.

3. See Lijphart (1981) and Puchala (1981) for different views on this alternative paradigm. It might be more accurate to refer to Holsti's global society group as an antirealist coalition that neither functions explicitly as a coalition nor that has much in common other than a shared opposition to classical assumptions. However, the rejection of the realist assumptions is rarely complete. Classical realpolitik elements can be detected in both global society and neo-Marxist analyses.

4. A prominent example is the eagerness with which international political economy has been embraced by analysts operating out of the classical framework—despite the classical paradigm's traditional low priority assigned to economic relations.

Chapter Three. Three Models of Structural Change

1. For related conceptual distinctions, see Braudel's (1973) "long durée," Skocpol's (1979:23) "world time" and Allan's (1980) "diplomatic time." Wilcox (1987) offers a general philosophy of history analysis of the problems that stem from what he refers to as Newtonian absolute time.

2. See the discussion in Krasner (1976), Lake (1983), Cowhey and Long (1983), Lawson (1983), McKeown (1983), Stein (1984), Gallarotti (1985), Snidal (1985), Frederick (1986), and Yarbrough and Yarbrough (1987).

3. One of the ironies associated with hegemonic stability analyses is that several of the scholars most closely associated with its development go to some lengths to distance themselves from the model. Kindleberger (1973) and Keohane and Nye (1977), for instance, are often credited as important "founding fathers." Yet both Kindleberger (1986) and Keohane have stated on occasion that they do not consider themselves hegemonic stability theorists.

4. Carr (1946) and Aron (1966) would certainly fit into this group as having pronounced structural interests within the general classical realist paradigm. Gilpin (1972) credits Thucydides as an early precursor of the structural realist position.

5. This section will concentrate on Gilpin (1981), but Gilpin (1975) is certainly of interest as well. For recent critiques of Gilpin's analysis, see Rogowski (1983) and Pearson (1987).

6. An annotated list of some of this work may be found in Modelski (1987f). See, in particular, Modelski (1987d) for his most systemic statement to date. Partial critiques of the long-cycle approach may be found in Rapkin (1983), Zolberg (1983), Kumon (1987), Chase-Dunn and Sokolovsky (1983), Levy (1985), Holsti (1985b), and Rosecrance (1987).

7. Precisely where one breaks into a cycle and labels it as a beginning point is an arbitrary matter. Modelski's current preference is to begin each long cycle with the global war phase. But it is also possible to argue that a new cycle begins only when a new world power appears on the global scene after the global war has ended.

8. Chapter eight will pursue this topic further.

9. Wallerstein's principal world-economy studies include Wallerstein (1974, 1979,

1980, and 1984). For various types of critiques of Wallerstein's approach, see Brenner (1977), Skocpol (1977), Brewer (1980), and Zolberg (1981).

10. More attention is given to Wallerstein's approach to hegemony in chapter six.

Chapter Four. System Time and Its Phases: Conflicting Images

1. Yet there is also a perverse tendency to give the hegemonic leader too much credit for stabilizing the system when it is at its peak.

2. Cipolla (1970) is another imperial behavior source favored by Gilpin.

3. For comparative analyses of historical systems, see Walker (1953), Modelski (1964), Wesson (1978), Ekholm and Friedman (1982), and Chase-Dunn (forthcoming).

4. This issue is likely to be contested as scholarly interests in empires appear to be reviving (see, for example, Doyle, 1986).

5. Keep in mind that Wallerstein (1984) regards the Thirty Years' War (1618–1648) as the first world war whereas the first global war from the long-cycle perspective ended over one hundred years before 1618. The two frameworks overlap only on the French Revolutionary/Napoleonic and World Wars I and II succession struggles.

6. The Research Working Group is identified as being composed of eleven members in 1977–1978 with Terence K. Hopkins and Immanuel Wallerstein serving as coordinators.

7. The propensity to specialize on the upward or downward theoretical slopes is not carved in stone. Modelski (1987a), for example, is beginning to give more attention to the prewar rise of the eventual system leaders.

8. See Raymond and Kegley's (1987) analysis of internationalized civil wars for another comparison of the two approaches' powers of conflict prediction. See Kowalewski (1987) for a related examination of peripheral election riots.

Chapter Five. Looking for Cycles of War and Peace

1. The impact analysis involved longitudinal statistical techniques discussed in Box and Tiao (1975) and McCleary and Hay (1980). In this case, the main point of the analysis is to look for evidence of abrupt, relatively permanent versus temporary changes in the mean level of a time series.

Chapter Six. Toward a Partial Explanation of the Roots of Global War

1. See Rapkin (1987) for an examination of the concept of leadership in world politics.

2. To be fair to Keohane, he neither considers himself to be a hegemonic stability analyst nor is hegemony his principal concern in the 1984 study. Rather, his primary interests have to do with what he prefers to refer to as "post-hegemonic" problems.

3. A rise in system leadership on the part of Japan would clearly invalidate this statement. Although Japan does not seem as likely a candidate as is commonly thought, see the discussion in Vogel (1986).

4. Additional decline hypotheses and models, frequently less comprehensive than the four described in their book, may be found in the following literature: Sprout and Sprout (1968), Hobsbawm (1969), Melman (1974), Smith (1977), Gamble (1981), Kaldor (1981), Szymanski (1981), Olson (1982), Tylecote (1982), Thompson and Zuk (1986),

and Rasler and Thompson (1987). Needless to say, these citations do not exhaust the pertinent literature.

5. The bulk of the data may be found in Mitchell (1980, 1982); U.S. Department of Commerce (1975); Reagan (1984), and various United Nations yearbooks. Hammond (1897), Hammond and Hammond (1926), Plummer (1937), Svennilson (1954), Lamar (1957), Nutter (1962), Koh (1966), Deane and Cole (1967), Aldcroft (1970), Banks (1971), Price (1981), Clarke and Matko (1983), Motor Vehicle Manufacturers Association (multiple volumes), and Linz (1985) were most useful for filling certain holes in the series. *The Economist* (1985) supplied the airframe data and information reported in Malerba (1985), and OECD (1985) facilitated the estimation of the semiconductor series. For an earlier data collection thrust in a similar vein, see Chase-Dunn (1976).

6. Ironically, the more qualitative-oriented leading-sector measurement stumbles into the same inflationary problem encountered when using army size as an indicator of military strength. The significance of early nineteenth-century Russia is exaggerated in the same way Chinese capabilities are overstated when population is used as an indicator in the late twentieth century. Doran and Parson (1980) encounter a version of this problem. A slightly different question is how much bias is introduced by ignoring the production of the Asian NICs? The six states that provide the country focus in the leading-sector index have tended to monopolize the world's production in these spheres. The extent to which this is the case, however, is in the process of changing. The ability to contrast Asian NIC production with their exports of leading-sector goods certainly would speak to the question of indicator-system distortion in several ways—something which is likely to become more significant in future years than it has in the years covered by table 6.6.

Chapter Seven. Leading Sectors, Naval Power, and Global War

1. In between these very general positions are scholars who focus on the benefits and liabilities associated with specific wars (e.g., Small, 1980). Stein and Russett (1980) provide a very useful overview of the war evaluation literature.

2. This view runs counter to Organski and Kugler's (1980) Phoenix Factor, which argues that the losers tend eventually to catch up to and surpass the ostensible winners. However, the historical evidence is less than fully supportive of this assertion (see Siverson, 1980; Rasler and Thompson, 1985b).

Chapter Eight. Long Economic Waves and Global War

1. There is a subset of the long-wave literature that will not be dealt with in this chapter. Work pertaining to psychological moods (Klingberg, 1952; Holmes, 1985; Elder and Holmes, 1985), debt (Pfister and Suter, 1987), or cultural values (Weber, 1981, 1983; Namenwirth and Weber, 1987) are certainly interesting. They tend, however, to introduce complications that would take us away from this chapter's focus on global war. The linkages between short-term economic fluctuations and war (Thompson, 1982; Russett, 1983) will also be ignored.

2. Discussions of the early work done on the Kondratieff wave can be found in Garvey (1943), Eklund (1980), Tinbergen (1981), and van Duijn (1983).

3. Vayrynen also introduces an alliance variable, but its impact on the conflict predictions is not entirely clear.

4. The Korean War problem is discussed in Thompson (1983).

5. The European price data are taken from Mitchell (1981). The American data are from U.S. Department of Commerce (1975). The series have been converted to constant 1913 values.

6. Wartime military spending levels did not end abruptly in 1918. Instead, they were gradually reduced in 1919 and 1920.

7. Alternatively, American prices were greatly inflated during the Revolutionary War. If Kondratieff's American price series had encompassed values for the 1770s and early 1780s, another major price spike would have been quite evident and in violation of the long-wave pattern.

8. Observers disagree on how to treat the post-World War II phases of the long wave. An extensive review of the various interpretations is provided by Goldstein (1986).

9. The biasing problem of the first and last observations in computing linear trends is discussed in McCleary and Hay (1980) and Rasler and Thompson (1985b).

10. Namenwirth and Weber (1987:131) disagree with Goldstein's treatment of British economic fluctuations in the eighteenth century (1689–1790) as well.

Chapter Nine. Polarity and Global Power Warfare

1. Recent reviews of the pertinent literature may be found in Siverson and Sullivan (1983) and Sabrosky (1985).

2. An earlier and briefer comparison of these approaches may be found in Rapkin (1983).

3. This assumption is reasonably common within the literature of classical realism.

4. Polarity refers to the distribution of capabilities while polarization addresses the tendency for actors to cluster around the poles (Rapkin et al., 1979). In contrast to Waltz's preoccupation with polarity, however, polarization should be viewed as just as much a systemic attribute as polarity.

5. The emphasis on naval power at the expense of other types of resources, of course, is derived from long-cycle theory's concentration on the global political system and its primary actors, the global powers. In this respect, the maritime bias of the sea-power indexes utilized here is no greater than is appropriate for a system that is perceived to be equally biased toward maritime resources.

6. For readers who are uncomfortable with the double weighting given to global warfare, the outcome reported in table 10.7 changes when the war-weighting scheme is dropped but perhaps not as much as one might expect. The proportional distribution of unweighted warfare (unipolar, 21.7%; near unipolar, 12.8%; bipolar, 29.0%; multipolar, 36.6%) is very similar to the weighted warfare distribution. More change, however, is registered in the unweighted warfare means (unipolar, .257; near unipolar, .359; bipolar, .290; multipolar, .548). Nevertheless, and whether or not one accepts the justification for the weighting, it is clear that more warfare is associated with multipolar conditions than is the case with unipolar and bipolar contexts.

7. Interestingly, Waltz assumes that actors will seek to maintain their positions. The problem with bipolarity is that some actors seek not only to maintain but also to improve their relative positions.

8. See Deutsch and Singer (1964) for a classical statement of the advantages of multipolarity over bipolarity. Needless to say, their argument is not supported by the evidence presented in this chapter either.

Chapter Ten. Succession Crises and the Transitional Model

1. There is more than one model of the transition process. Each of the three schools of thought discussed in chapter three could be said to have its own interpretations of transition. Doran's work (Doran and Parsons, 1980; Doran, 1983a, 1983b, 1985) offers still another interpretation. Care should be taken, however, in distinguishing between structural transition at the peak of the systemic pyramid and the more ordinary positional transitions any two states might experience vis-à-vis one another. The first type refers to a systemic process. The second type does not. Analyses pertaining to the nonsystemic variety are reviewed in Siverson and Sullivan (1983).

2. Organski's dissatisfied great powers would seem to be the most fruitful area in which to apply status-discrepancy or frustration-aggression models (Galtung, 1964; Wallace, 1972; East, 1972; Ray, 1974; Midlarsky, 1975) rather than attempting to account for all interstate conflict with these types of models.

3. Unfortunately, there is a tendency for the model to waver as to whether one should contrast the coalition strengths of the satisfied and dissatisfied or the comparative strengths of the dominant power and the primary challenger. Since the precise identities of the global-war coalitions frequently are not known until after the wars are under way, a point to which we will return later in this chapter, the latter focus would seem to be preferable.

4. The emphasis on novel developments in the twentieth century (i.e., the communist model) may be misleading. Is it indeed safe to assume that growth in economic productivity and wealth have been the root of all capability gains in the sixteenth through nineteenth centuries? Contrary evidence and arguments may be found in Dickson and Sperling (1970), Mathias and O'Brien (1976), O'Brien and Keyder (1978), and Rasler and Thompson (1983, 1985a).

5. Unfortunately, for our purposes, Bell (1971) does not develop the structural implications of crisis slides.

6. Organski and Kugler (1980:34–38) regress a number of other types of capability against GNP and find a strong linear relationship. It is not clear, nevertheless, to what extent this positive relationship is based simply on the presence of similar longitudinal trends.

7. For an overlapping critique of some aspects of Organski and Kugler's analysis from a nonworld-system perspective, see Siverson (1980).

8. Organski and Kugler (1980) adopt 80 percent as their criterion of equality, but this seems a bit too generous.

9. The French were involved as well, but internal warfare reduced their effectiveness.

10. Something similar occurs in the 1909–1913 German case, but the brevity of the relative decline suggests caution in interpreting its significance.

Chapter Eleven. Uneven Economic Growth and
Systemic Challenges

1. It may be somewhat premature but the Soviet Union in the fifth long-cycle (1946–   ) appears to fit readily into this second category as well. On the other hand, see Rosecrance (1986) for a vastly different sort of dichotomization of major actors.

2. For an imaginative fictional treatment of this imperial Spanish scenario, see Brunner (1969). Parker (1979) offers a historian's slant on this scenario.

3. One exception to this postsixteenth-century generalization is the rapid naval capability improvements made by France, under Colbert's direction, in the latter part of the seventeenth century. Even so, the French had too little time and not enough global inclination to learn how to exploit their briefly held lead in naval power. This subject is also discussed in chapter ten.

4. This viewpoint leads one to a fairly distinctive perspective on the classical "balance of power" concept as an eighteenth-century doctrine designed to explain and justify the British world power's behavior vis-à-vis regional European politics.

5. A similar observation, confined to what he refers to as Germany's distorted view of world politics based on continental perspectives, serves as Dehio's (1962:3–15) rationale for tracing "four centuries of the European power struggle." In this vein, see also Wight (1978:68–80).

6. Chase-Dunn and Sokolovsky (1983) constitutes a response to an earlier version of this chapter.

Chapter Twelve. Structural Change and Global War

1. With Karen Rasler, I have been working on the state-building consequences of global war. Rasler and Thompson (forthcoming) is one outcome of this 1982–1985 NSF-funded project. We are also engaged in a second NSF-funded project (1985–1987) on the causes of systemic leadership decline. Posen (1984) is suggestive of what could be done in terms of grand strategy. I hope to pursue the grand-strategy question from a historical-structural perspective in coming years.

2. The diplomatic history literature on the outbreak of World War I is immense. For social science treatments of the outbreak process, see Holsti et al. (1968), Zinnes (1968), Holsti (1971), Nomikos and North (1976) and Lebow (1981).

3. The theoretical scenario is also quite compatible with the model put forward by Choucri and North (1975).

4. Modelski and Thompson (1988) specifically review the naval power prospects of Britain, France, and China.

5. Unlike the two-power military competition depicted in figure 12.2, the relative positions charted in figure 12.3 are based on the six-power production total (the United States, the Soviet Union, Japan, France, Britain, and West Germany) utilized in chapter 6.

References

Abernathy, William J., Kim B. Clark, and Alan M. Kantrow (1983). *Industrial Renaissance: Producing a Competitive Future for America.* New York: Basic Books.

Abrams, Philip (1982). *Historical Sociology.* Ithaca: Cornell University Press.

Aldcroft, Derek H. (1970). *The Inter-War Economy: Britain, 1919–1939.* London: B. T. Batsford.

Alker, Hayward R., Jr., and Thomas J. Biersteker (1984). "The Dialectics of World Order: Notes for a Future Archeologist of International Savoir Faire." *International Studies Quarterly* 28 (June): 121–142.

Allan, Pierre (1980). "Diplomatic Time and Climate: A Formal Model." *Journal of Peace Science* 4 (Spring): 133–150.

Allison, Graham T. (1971). *Essence of Decision.* Boston: Little, Brown.

Allison, Graham T., Albert Carnesale, and Joseph S. Nye, Jr. [eds.] (1985). *Hawks, Doves, and Owls: An Agenda for Avoiding Nuclear War.* New York: W. W. Norton.

Aron, Raymond (1966). *Peace and War.* New York: Doubleday.

Ashley, Richard K. (1986). "The Poverty of Neorealism," pp. 255–300 in Robert O. Keohane (ed.), *Neorealism and Its Critics.* New York: Columbia University Press.

Banks, Arthur S. (1971). *Cross-Polity Time-Series Data.* Cambridge, MA: MIT Press.

Barbera, Henry (1973). *Rich Nations and Poor in Peace and War.* Lexington, MA: Lexington Books.

Barr, Kenneth (1979). "Long Waves: A Selective Annotated Bibliography." *Review* 2 (Spring): 675–718.

Beer, Francis A. (1974). *How Much War in History: Definitions, Estimates, Extrapolations, Trends.* Beverly Hills, CA: Sage.

Bell, Coral (1971). *The Conventions of Crisis: A Study in Diplomatic Management.* London: Oxford University Press.

Bennett, Douglas C., and Kenneth E. Sharpe (1985). *Transnational Corporations Versus the State: The Political Economy of the Mexican Auto Industry.* Princeton: Princeton University Press.

Bergesen, Albert (1981). "Long Economic Cycles and the Size of Industrial Enterprise," pp. 179–189 in Richard Rubinson (ed.), *Dynamics of World Development.* Beverly Hills, CA: Sage.

——— (1982). "Economic Crises and Merger Movements: 1880s Britain and

1980s United States," pp. 27–39 in Edward Friedman (ed.), *Ascent and Decline in the World-System.* Beverly Hills: Sage.

—— (1983). "1914 Again? Another Cycle of Interstate Competition and War," pp. 255–273 in Patrick J. McGowan and Charles W. Kegley, Jr. (eds.), *Foreign Policy and the Modern World-System.* Beverly Hills, CA: Sage.

—— (1985). "Cycles of War in the Reproduction of the World Economy," pp. 313–331 in Paul M. Johnson and William R. Thompson (eds.), *Rhythms in Politics and Economics.* New York: Praeger.

Bergesen, Albert, and Chintamani Sahoo (1985). "Evidence of the Decline of American Hegemony in World Production." *Review* 8 (Spring): 595–611.

Bergesen, Albert, and Ronald Schoenberg (1980). "Long Waves of Colonial Expansion and Contraction, 1415–1969," pp. 231–277 in Albert Bergesen (ed.), *Studies of the Modern World-System.* New York: Academic Press.

Blainey, Geoffrey (1973). *The Causes of War.* New York: Free Press.

Bobrow, Davis B. (1982). "Uncoordinated Giants," pp. 23–49 in Charles W. Kegley, Jr., and Patrick J. McGowan, eds., *Foreign Policy: USA/USSR.* Beverly Hills: Sage.

Bolling, Richard, and John Bowles (1982). *America's Competitive Edge.* New York: McGraw-Hill.

Boulding, Kenneth E. (1962). *Conflict and Defense.* New York: Harper and Row.

Bousquet, Nicole (1979). "Esquisse D'une Theorie de L'alternance de Concurrence et D'hegemonie Au Centre de L'economie-monde Capitaliste." *Review* 2 (Spring): 501–517.

—— (1980). "From Hegemony to Competition: Cycles of the Core?" in Terence K. Hopkins and Immanuel Wallerstein (eds.), *Processes of the World-System.* Beverly Hills: Sage.

Bowles, Samuel, and Herb Gintis (1982). "The Crisis of Liberal Democratic Capitalism: the Case of the United States." *Politics and Society* 11:51–93.

Bowles, Samuel, David M. Gordon, and Thomas E. Weisskopf (1983). *Beyond the Waste Land.* Garden City, NY: Anchor/Doubleday.

Box, George E. P., and G. C. Tiao (1975). "Intervention Analysis with Applications to Economic and Environmental Problems." *Journal of the American Statistical Association* 70 (March): 70–92.

Braudel, Fernand (1973). *The Mediterranean and the Mediterranean World in the Age of Philip II,* vol. 2, translated by Sian Reynolds. New York: Harper and Row.

—— (1984). *The Perspective of the World,* translated by Sian Reynolds. New York: Harper and Row.

Brenner, Robert (1977). "The Origins of Capitalist Development: A Critique of Neo-Smithian Marxism." *New Left Review* 104 (July): 25–81.

Brewer, Anthony (1980). *Marxist Theories of Imperialism: A Critical Survey.* London: Routledge and Kegan Paul.

Brunner, John (1969). *Times Without Number.* New York: Ace Books.

Brzezinski, Zbigniew (1986). *Game Plan: How to Conduct the US-Soviet Contest*. Boston: Atlantic Monthly Press.

Bueno de Mesquita, Bruce (1975). "Measuring Systemic Polarity." *Journal of Conflict Resolution* 19:187–216.

—— (1978). "Systemic Polarization and the Occurrence and Duration of War." *Journal of Conflict Resolution* 22:241–267.

—— (1980). "Theories of International Conflict: An Analysis and an Appraisal," pp. 361–398 in Ted R. Gurr, ed., *Handbook of Political Conflict: Theory and Research*. New York: Free Press.

—— (1981). *The War Trap*. New Haven: Yale University Press.

Bueno de Mesquita, Bruce, and David Lalman (1986). "Reason and War." *American Political Science Review* 80 (December): 1113–1129.

Bueno de Mesquita, Bruce, and David Lalman (1987). "Empirical Support for Systemic and Dyadic Explanations of International Conflict." Paper delivered at the annual meeting of American Political Science Association, Chicago, September 3–6.

Burton, John W. (1972). *World Society*. Cambridge: Cambridge University Press.

Calleo, David (1982). *The Imperious Economy*. Cambridge, MA: Harvard University Press.

Carr, E. H. (1946/1962). *The Twenty Years' Crisis*. London: St. Martin's Press.

Chase-Dunn, Christopher K. (1976). "Toward a Formal Comparative Study of the World-System." Unpublished paper. Binghamton, NY: Fernand Braudel Center Working Paper.

—— (1981). "Interstate System and Capitalist World-Economy: One Logic or Two?" *International Studies Quarterly* 25 (March): 19–42.

—— (1982). "International Economic Policy in a Declining Core State," Pp. 77–96 in William Avery and David P. Rapkin (eds.), *America in a Changing World Political Economy*. New York: Longman.

—— (forthcoming). *The Structure of World-Systems*. Berkeley: University of California Press.

Chase-Dunn, Christopher K., and Joan Sokolovsky (1983). "Interstate Systems, World-Empires and the Capitalist World-Economy: A Response to Thompson." *International Studies Quarterly* 27 (September): 357–367.

Choucri, Nazli, and Robert C. North (1975). *Nations in Conflict: National Growth and International Violence*. San Francisco: W. H. Freeman and Co.

Cipolla, Carlo (1965). *Guns, Sails and Empires: Technological Innovation and the Early Phases of European Expansion, 1400–1700*. New York: Minerva Press.

—— (1970). *The Economic Decline of Empires*. London: Methuen.

Clancy, Tom (1986). *Red Storm Rising*. New York: G. P. Putnam's.

Clarke, Roger A., and Dubravko J. I. Matko (1983). *Soviet Economic Facts, 1917–81*. New York: St. Martin's Press.

Cohen, Stephen S., and John Zysman (1987). *Manufacturing Matters: the Myth of the Post Industrial Economy.* New York: Basic Books.

Cowhey, Peter F., and Edward Long (1983). "Testing Theories of Regime Change: Hegemonic Decline or Surplus Capacity?" *International Organization* 37 (Summer): 385–424.

Cox, Robert (1987). *Production, Power and World Order: Social Forces in the Making of History.* New York: Columbia University Press.

Deane, Phyllis, and W. A. Cole (1967). *British Economic Growth, 1688–1959: Trends and Structure.* 2d ed. London: Cambridge University Press.

Dehio, Ludwig (1962). *The Precarious Balance: Four Centuries of the European Power Struggle,* translated by C. Fullman. New York: Random House.

Denton, Frank H., and Warren Phillips (1968). "Some Patterns in the History of Violence." *Journal of Conflict Resolution* 12 (June): 182–195.

Deutsch, Karl W., Sidney A. Burrell, Robert A. Kann, Maurice Lee, Jr., Martin Lichteman, Raymond E. Lindgren, Francis L. Loewenheim, and Richard W. Van Wagenen (1957). *Political Community and the North Atlantic Area.* Princeton: Princeton University Press.

Deutsch, Karl W., and J. David Singer (1964). "Multipolar Power Systems and International Stability." *World Politics* 16 (April): 390–406.

Dickinson, F. G. (1940). "An Aftercost of the World War to the United States." *American Economic Review* 30 Supplement, Part 2 (March): 326–339.

Dickson, P. G. M., and J. Sperling (1970). "War Finance, 1689–1714," in J. S. Bromely (ed.), *The New Cambridge Modern History: The Rise of Great Britain and Russia, 1688–1725,* vol. 6. Cambridge: Cambridge University Press.

Doran, Charles F. (1983a). "Power Cycle Theory and the Contemporary State System," pp. 165–182 in William R. Thompson (ed.), *Contending Approaches to World System Analysis.* Beverly Hills, CA: Sage.

——— (1983b). "War and Power Dynamics: Economic Underpinnings." *International Studies Quarterly* 27 (December): 419–441.

——— (1985). "Power Cycle Theory and Systems Stability," pp. 292–312 in Paul M. Johnson and William R. Thompson (eds.), *Rhythms in Politics and Economics.* New York: Praeger.

Doran, Charles F., and Wes Parsons (1980). "War and the Cycle of Relative Power," *American Political Science Review* 74 (December): 947–965.

Doyle, Michael W. (1986). *Empires.* Ithaca: Cornell University Press.

Duijn, Jacob J. van (1983). *The Long Wave in Economic Life.* London: George Allen and Unwin.

Dumas, Lloyd J. (1986). *The Over-Burdened Economy.* Berkeley: University of California Press.

Dupuy, Robert E., and T. N. Dupuy (1977). *The Encyclopedia of Military History,* revised edition. New York: Harper and Row.

East, Maurice A. (1972). "Status Discrepancy and Violence in the International System: An Empirical Analysis," Pp. 299–319 in James N. Rosenau, Vincent Davis, and Maurice A. East (eds.), *The Analysis of International Politics.* New York: Free Press.

The Economist (1985). *The Big Six: A Survey of the World's Aircraft Industry.* (June 1)

The Economist (1986). "Japan v. America: A Survey of High Technology." 300 (August 23): 3–18.

Ekholm, K., and J. Friedman (1982). " 'Capital' Imperialism and Exploitation in Ancient World-Systems." *Review* 6:87–110.

Eklund, Klas (1980). "Long Waves in the Development of Capitalism?" *Kyklos* 33, fasc. 3:383–419.

Elder, Robert E., and Jack E. Holmes (1985). "International Economic Long Cycles and American Policy Moods," Pp. 239–264 in Paul M. Johnson and William R. Thompson (eds.), *Rhythms in Politics and Economics.* New York: Praeger.

Elvin, Mark (1973). *The Pattern of the Chinese Past.* Stanford: Stanford University Press.

Falk, Richard, and Samuel S. Kim (1983). "World Order Studies and the World System," Pp. 203–237 in William R. Thompson (ed.), *Contending Approaches to World System Analysis.* Beverly Hills, CA: Sage.

Farrar, L. L., Jr. (1977). "Cycles of War: Historical Speculations on Future International Violence." *International Interactions* 3:161–179.

Forrester, Jay W. (1981). "Innovation and Economic Change." *Futures* 13 (August): 323–331.

Frank, Andre Gunder (1978). *World Accumulation, 1492–1789.* New York: Monthly Review Press.

Frederick, Suzanne Y. (1987). "The Instability of Free Trade: Power, Order and Trade Policy Patterns in the World System," Pp. 186–217 in George Modelski (ed.), *Exploring Long Cycles.* Boulder, CO: Lynne Rienner.

Freeman, Christopher, John Clark, and Luc Soete (1982). *Unemployment and Technical Innovation.* London: Frances Pinter.

Gallarotti, Giulio M. (1985). "Toward a Business-cycle Model of Tariffs." *International Organization* 39 (Winter): 155–187.

Galtung, Johan (1964). "A Structural Theory of Aggression." *Journal of Peace Research* 1:95–119.

Gamble, Andrew (1981). *Britain in Decline: Economic Policy, Political Strategy and the British State.* Boston: Beacon Press.

Garvey, George (1943). "Kondratieff's Theory of Long Cycles." *Review of Economic Statistics* 25 (November): 203–220.

Gilpin, Robert (1972). "Has Modern Technology Changed International Politics?," Pp. 166–174 in James N. Rosenau, Vincent Davis, and Maurice A. East (eds.), *The Analysis of International Politics.* New York: Free Press.

——— (1975). *US Power and the Multinational Corporation.* New York: Basic Books.

—— (1981). *War and Change in World Politics*. Cambridge: Cambridge University Press.

—— (1987). *The Political Economy of International Relations*. Princeton: Princeton University Press.

Goldfrank, Walter L. (1983). "The Limits of Analogy: Hegemonic Decline in Great Britain and the United States," Pp. 143–154 in Albert Bergesen (ed.), *Crises in the World-System*. Beverly Hills: Sage.

Goldstein, Joshua S. (1985). "War and the Kondratieff Upswing." *International Studies Quarterly* 29 (December): 411–441.

—— (1986). "Long Cycles in War and Economic Growth." Unpublished Ph.D. dissertation. Cambridge, MA: MIT.

Gordon, David M. (1980). "Stages of Accumulation and Long Economic Cycles," Pp. 9–45 in Terence K. Hopkins and Immanuel Wallerstein (eds.), *Processes of the World-System*. Beverly Hills, CA: Sage.

Guetzkow, Harold (1957). "Isolation and Collaboration: A Partial Theory of InterNation Relations." *Journal of Conflict Resolution* 1 (March): 48–68.

Haas, Ernst B. (1964). *Beyond the Nation-State*. Stanford: Stanford University Press.

Haas, Ernst B. (1975). *The Obsolescence of Regional Integration Theory*. Berkeley: Institute of International Studies, University of California.

Hackett, John (1982). *The Third World War: The Untold Story*. New York: Bantam Books.

Hammond, M. B. (1897). *The Cotton Industry*. New York: Macmillan.

Hammond, J. L., and Barbara Hammond (1926). *The Rise of Modern Industry*. New York: Harcourt, Brace and Co.

Hansen, Roger D. (1969). "Regional Integration: Reflections on a Decade of Theoretical Efforts." *World Politics* 21 (January): 242–271.

Harbottle, T. (1975). *Dictionary of Battles*, revised and updated by G. Bruce. New York: Stein and Day.

Hobsbawm, Eric J. (1969). *Industry and Empire*. London: Pelican.

Holmes, Jack (1985). *Mood/Interest Theory of American Foreign Policy*. Lexington: University Press of Kentucky.

Holsti, Kalevi, J. (1985a). *The Dividing Discipline: Hegemony and Diversity in International Theory*. Boston: Allen and Unwin.

—— (1985b). "The Necrologists of International Relations." *Canadian Journal of Political Science* 18:675–695.

Holsti, Ole (1971). *Crisis Escalation War*. Montreal: McGill-Queen's University Press.

Holsti, Ole R., P. Terrence Hopmann, and John D. Sullivan (1973). *Unity and Disintegration in International Alliances: Comparative Studies*. New York: Wiley.

Holsti, Ole R., Robert C. North, and Richard A. Brody (1968). "Perception and Action in the 1914 Crisis," Pp. 123–158 in J. David Singer (ed.), *Quantitative International Politics: Insights and Evidence*. New York: Free Press.

Hopkins, Raymond, and Richard W. Mansbach (1973). *Structure and Process in International Politics.* New York: Harper and Row.

Jervis, Robert (1976). *Perception and Misperception in International Politics.* Princeton: Princeton University Press.

Job, Brian L. (1981). "Grins Without Cats: In Pursuit of Knowledge of Internation Alliances," Pp. 39–63 in P. Terrence Hopmann, Dina A. Zinnes, and J. David Singer (eds.), *Cumulation in International Relations Research.* Denver: University of Denver Monograph Series in World Affairs.

Kahler, Miles (1979). "Rumors of War: The 1914 Analogy." *Foreign Affairs* 47 (Winter): 374–396.

Kaldor, Mary (1981). *The Baroque Arsenal.* New York: Hill and Wang.

Kegley, Charles W., Jr. (1986). "Assumptions and Dilemmas in the Study of America's Foreign Policy Beliefs: A Caveat." *International Studies Quarterly* 30 (December): 447–471.

Kegley, Charles W., Jr., and Eugene R. Wittkopf (1987). *American Foreign Policy: Pattern and Process,* Third edition. New York: St. Martin's Press.

Kelly, Regina (1977). *The Impact of Technological Innovation on Trade Patterns.* Washington, D.C.: Bureau of International Economic Policy and Research, U.S. Department of Commerce.

Kennedy, Paul (1976). *The Rise and Fall of British Naval Mastery.* New York: Scribner's Sons.

—— (1983). *Strategy and Diplomacy, 1870–1945.* London: George Allen and Unwin.

Keohane, Robert O. (1984). *After Hegemony: Cooperation and Discord in the World Political Economy.* Princeton: Princeton University Press.

—— (1986). "Realism, Neorealism and the Study of World Politics," Pp. 1–26 in Robert O. Keohane (ed.), *Neorealism and Its Critics.* New York: Columbia University Press.

Keohane, Robert O. and Joseph S. Nye, Jr., eds. (1972). *Transitional Relations and World Politics.* Cambridge, MA: Harvard University Press.

—— (1977). *Power and Interdependence: World Politics in Transition.* Boston: Little, Brown.

Kindleberger, Charles P. (1973). *The World in Depression, 1929–1939.* Berkeley: University of California Press.

—— (1978). *Economic Response: Comparative Studies in Trade, Finance and Growth.* Cambridge, MA: Harvard University Press.

—— (1986). "Hierarchy Versus Inertial Cooperation." *International Organization* 40 (Autumn): 841–847.

Klingberg, Frank L. (1952). "The Historical Alternation of Moods in American Foreign Policy." *World Politics* 4 (January): 239–273.

Koh, Sung Jae (1966). *Stages of Industrial Development in Asia.* Philadelphia: University of Pennsylvania Press.

Kondratieff, Nicolai D. (1935). "The Long Waves in Economic Life." *Review of Economic Statistics* 17 (November): 105–115.

—— (1979). "The Long Waves in Economic Life," *Review* 2 (Spring): 519–562.

Kowalewski, David (1987). "Peripheral Revolutions in World-System Perspective." Paper delivered at the annual meeting of the International Studies Association, Washington, D.C., April.

Krasner, Stephen D. (1976). "State Power and the Structure of International Trade." *World Politics* 28 (April): 317–347.

Krieger, Joel (1986). *Reagan, Thatcher and the Politics of Decline*. New York: Oxford University Press.

Kuhn, Thomas S. (1970). *The Structure of Scientific Revolutions*. Chicago: University of Chicago Press.

Kumon, Shumpei (1987). "The Long Cycle Theory Examined," P. 56–84 in George Modelski (ed.), *Exploring Long Cycles*. Boulder, CO: Lynne Rienner.

Kurth, James R. (1979). "The Political Consequences of the Product Cycle." *International Organization* 33 (Winter): 1–34.

Kuznets, Simon S. (1964). *Postwar Economic Growth*. Cambridge, MA: Harvard University Press.

—— (1971). *Economic Growth of Nations: Total Output and Production Structure*. Cambridge, MA: Harvard University Press.

Lakatos, Imre (1970). "Falsification and the Methodology of Scientific Research Programmes," Pp. 91–196 in Imre Lakatos and Alan Musgrave (eds.), *Criticism and the Growth of Knowledge*. Cambridge: Cambridge University Press.

Lake, David A. (1983). "International Economic Structures and American Foreign Economic Policy, 1887–1934." *World Politics* 35 (July): 517–543.

—— (1984). "Beneath the Commerce of Nations: A Theory of International Economic Structures." *International Studies Quarterly* 28 (June): 143–170.

Lamar, Mirko (1957). *The World Fertilizer Economy*. Stanford: Stanford University Press.

Landes, David S. (1969). *The Unbound Prometheus*. Cambridge: Cambridge University Press.

Lawson, Fred (1983). "Hegemony and the Structure of International Trade Reassessed: A View from Arabia." *International Organization* 37 (Spring): 317–338.

Lebow, Richard N. (1981). *Between Peace and War: The Nature of International Crisis*. Baltimore: Johns Hopkins University Press.

Levy, Jack S. (1983a). *War in the Modern Great Power System, 1495–1975*. Lexington: University Press of Kentucky.

—— (1983b). "Misperception and the Causes of War." *World Politics* 35 (October): 76–99.

—— (1985). "Theories of General War." *World Politics* 37 (April): 344–374.

—— (1986). "Organizational Routines and the Causes of War." *International Studies Quarterly* 30 (June): 193–222.

Lijphart, Arend (1974). "The Structure of the Theoretical Revolution in International Relations." *International Studies Quarterly* 18 (March): 41–74.

——— (1981). "Karl W. Deutsch and the New Paradigm in International Relations," Pp. 233–251 in Richard L. Merritt and Bruce M. Russett (eds.), *From National Development to Global Community: Essays in Honor of Karl W. Deutsch*. London: George Allen and Unwin.

Linz, Susan J. (1985). "World War II and Soviet Economic Growth, 1940–1953," Pp. 11–38 in Susan J. Linz (ed.), *The Impact of World War II on the Soviet Union*. Totwa, NJ: Rowman and Allanheld.

Mackinder, Halford (1962). *Democratic Ideals and Reality.* New York: Norton.

Macksey, Kenneth (1986). *Technology in War.* New York: Prentice-Hall.

Maddison, Angus (1982). *Phases of Capitalist Development.* New York: Oxford University Press.

Magaziner, Ira C., and Robert R. Reich (1982). *Minding America's Business: The Decline and Rise of the American Economy.* New York: Vintage.

Mahan, Alfred T. (1890). *The Influence of Sea Power Upon History, 1660–1783.* New York: Hill and Wang.

Majeski, Stephen J., and David J. Sylvan (1984). "Single Choices and Complex Calculations: A Critique of the War Trap." *Journal of Conflict Resolution* 28:316–340.

Malerba, Francis (1985). *The Semiconductor Business: The Economics of Rapid Growth and Decline.* Madison: University of Wisconsin Press.

Mandel, Ernst (1980). *Long Waves of Capitalist Development: The Marxist Interpretation.* Cambridge: Cambridge University Press.

Mansbach, Richard W., Yale Y. Ferguson, and Donald E. Lampert (1976). *The Web of World Politics: Nonstate Actors in the Global System.* Englewood Cliffs, NJ: Prentice-Hall.

Mansbach, Richard W., and John A. Vasquez (1981). *In Search of Theory: A New Paradigm for Global Politics.* New York: Columbia University Press.

Masterman, Margaret (1970). "The Nature of a Paradigm," Pp. 59–89 in Imre Lakatos and Alan Musgrave (eds.), *Criticism and the Growth of Knowledge.* Cambridge: Cambridge University Press.

Mathias, P., and Patrick O'Brien (1976). "Taxation in Britain and France, 1715–1810: A Comparison of the Social and Economic Incidence of Taxes Collected for the Central Governments." *Journal of European Economic History* 5 (Winter): 601–650.

McCleary, Richard, and R. A. Hay, Jr. (1980). *Applied Time Series Analysis for the Social Sciences.* Beverly Hills: Sage.

McClelland, Charles A. (1966). *Theory and the International System.* New York: Macmillan.

——— (1972). "On the Fourth Wave: Past and Future in the Study of International Systems," pp. 15–40 in James N. Rosenau, Vincent Davis, and Maurice A. East (eds.), *The Analysis of International Politics.* New York: Free Press.

McGowan, Patrick J. (1980). "Problems of Theory and Data in the Study of World-System Dynamics." Presented at the joint annual meetings of the International Studies Association/West and the International Studies Association, Los Angeles, California.

McGowan, Patrick J., and Howard B. Shapiro (1973). *The Comparative Study of Foreign Policy.* Beverly Hills, CA: Sage.

McKeown, Timothy J. (1983). "Hegemonic Stability Theory and 19th Century Tariff Levels in Europe." *International Organization* 37 (Winter): 73–92.

McNeill, William H. (1982). *The Pursuit of Power: Technology, Armed Force and Society Since AD 1000.* Chicago: University of Chicago Press.

Melman, Seymour (1974). *The Permanent War Economy: American Capitalism in Decline.* New York: Simon and Schuster.

Mensch, Gerhard O. (1979). *Stalemate in Technology: Innovations Overcome the Depression* Cambridge, MA: Ballinger.

Midlarsky, Manus I. (1975). *On War: Political Violence in the International System.* New York: Free Press.

—— (1984). "Some Uniformities in the Origins of Systemic War." Presented at the annual meeting of the American Political Science Association, Washington, D.C.

—— (1986). *The Disintegration of Political Systems: War and Revolution in Comparative Perspective.* Columbia: University of South Carolina Press.

Miskimin, H. A. (1977). *The Economy of Later Renaissance Europe, 1460–1600.* Cambridge: Cambridge University Press.

Mitchell, Brian R. (1980). *European Historical Statistics, 1750–1975,* second rev. ed. New York: Facts on File.

—— (1982). *International Historical Statistics, Africa and Asia.* New York: New York University Press.

Modelski, George (1964). "Kautilya: Foreign Policy and International System in the Ancient Hindu World." *American Political Science Review* 58 (September): 549–560.

—— (1970). "The Promise of Geocentric Politics." *World Politics* 22 (July): 617–635.

—— (1972). *Principles of World Politics.* New York: Free Press.

—— (1974). *World Power Concentrations: Typology, Data, Explanatory Frameworks.* Morristown, NJ: General Learning Press.

—— (1978). "The Long Cycle of Global Politics and the Nation-State." *Comparative Studies in Society and History* 20 (April): 214–235.

—— (1979). *Transnational Corporations and World Order.* San Francisco: W. H. Freeman.

—— (1981). "Long Cycles, Kondratieffs, and Alternating Innovations: Implications for U.S. Foreign Policy," Pp. 63–83 in Charles W. Kegley, Jr., and Patrick J. McGowan (eds.), *The Political Economy of Foreign Policy Behavior.* Beverly Hills: Sage.

—— (1982). "Long Cycles and the Strategy of United States International Political Economy," Pp. 97–116 in William Avery and David P. Rapkin (eds.), *America in a Changing World Political Economy.* New York: Longman.

—— (1983). "Qualifications for World Leadership." *Voice* [Japan] (October): 210–229.

—— (1984). "Global Wars and World Leadership Selection." Presented at the second World Peace Science Society Congress, Rotterdam, the Netherlands.

—— (1987a). *Long Cycles in World Politics.* Seattle: University of Washington Press/London: Macmillan.

—— [ed.] (1987b). *Exploring Long Cycles.* Boulder, CO: Lynne Rienner.

—— (1987c). "The Study of Long Cycles," Pp. 1–15 in George Modelski (ed.), *Exploring Long Cycles.* Boulder, CO: Lynne Rienner. .

—— (1987d). "A System Model of the Long Cycle," Pp. 112–128 in George Modelski (ed.), *Exploring Long Cycles.* Boulder, CO: Lynne Rienner.

—— (1987e). "A Global Politics Scenario for the Year 2016," Pp. 218–248 in George Modelski (ed.), *Exploring Long Cycles.* Boulder, CO: Lynne Rienner.

—— (1987f). "A Bibliography of Long Cycles Research, 1975–1985," Pp. 249–256 in George Modelski (ed.), *Exploring Long Cycles.* Boulder, CO: Lynne Rienner.

Modelski, George, and Sylvia Modelski (1988). *Documenting World Leadership.* Seattle: University of Washington Press.

Modelski, George, and Patrick Morgan (1985). "Understanding Global War." *Journal of Conflict Resolution* 29 (September): 391–417.

Modelski, George, and William R. Thompson (1980). "Elaborating the Theory of Long Cycles in Global Politics: A Cobweb Model." delivered at the annual meeting of the American Political Science Association, Washington, D.C., August.

—— (1981). "Testing Cobweb Models of the Long Cycle of World Leadership." Presented at the annual meeting of the Peace Science Society (International), Philadelphia, Pennsylvania, November.

—— (1987). "Testing Cobweb Models of the Long Cycle," Pp. 85–111 in George Modelski (ed.), *Exploring Long Cycles.* Boulder, CO: Lynne Rienner.

—— (1988). *Sea Power and Global Politics Since 1494.* Seattle: University of Washington Press/ London: Macmillan.

Morgenthau, Hans J. (1973). *Politics Among Nations: The Struggle for Power and Peace,* Fifth edition. New York: Knopf.

Motor Vehicle Manufacturers Association (1981). *World Motor Vehicle Data.* Detroit: Motor Vehicle Manufacturers Association.

Mowat, R. B. (1928). *A History of European Diplomacy.* London: Edward Arnold.

Moyal, J. E. (1949). "The Distribution of Wars in Time." *Journal of the Royal Statistical Society* 115, Ser. A, Pt. IV: 446–449.

Namenwirth, J. Zvi, and Robert P. Weber (1987). *Dynamics of Culture.* Boston: Allen and Unwin.

Nef, John U. (1950). *War and Human Progress: An Essay on the Rise of Industrial Civilization.* Cambridge, MA: Harvard University Press.

Nelson, K. L., and S. C. Olin (1979). *Why War? Ideology, Theory and History.* Berkeley: University of California Press.

Nincic, Miroslav (1985). *How War Might Spread to Europe.* Solna, Sweden: Stockholm International Peace Research Institute.

Nomikos, Eugenia V., and Robert C. North (1976). *International Crisis: The Outbreak of World War I.* Montreal: McGill-Queen's University Press.

North, Robert (1969). "Research Pluralism and the International Elephant," Pp. 218–242 in Klaus Knorr and James N. Rosenau (eds.), *Contending Approaches to International Politics.* Princeton: Princeton University Press.

Nutter, G. Warren (1962). *The Growth of Industrial Production in the Soviet Union.* Princeton: Princeton University Press.

O'Brien, Patrick, and C. Keyder (1978). *Economic Growth in Britain and France, 1780–1914.* London: Allen and Unwin.

OECD (1985). *The Semi-Conductor Industry: Trade Related Issues.* Paris: Organization for Economic and Cultural Development.

Olson, Mancur (1982). *The Rise and Decline of Nations.* New Haven: Yale University Press.

Organski, A. F. K. (1968). *World Politics.* New York: Alfred Knopf.

Organski, A. F. K., and Jacek Kugler (1980). *The War Ledger.* Chicago: University of Chicago Press.

Padfield, Peter (1979). *Tide of Empires: Decisive Naval Campaigns in the Rise of the West, 1481–1654.* London: Routledge and Kegan Paul.

Parker, Geoffrey (1979). *Spain and The Netherlands, 1559–1659: Ten Studies.* London: Collins.

Parry, J. H. (1966). *The Establishment of the European Hegemony: 1415–1715,* 3rd rev. ed. New York: Harper and Row.

Pearson, Daniel (1987). "The Global Economic Order of the Eighteenth Century," Pp. 158–185 in George Modelski (ed.), *Exploring Long Cycles.* Boulder, CO: Lynne Reinner.

Perroux, Francois (1979). "An Outline of a Theory of the Dominent Economy," pp. 135–154 in George Modelski (ed.), *Transnational Corporations and World Order.* San Francisco: W. H. Freeman.

Pfister, Ulrich and Christian Suter (1987). "International Financial Relations as Part of the World-System". *International Studies Quarterly* 31 (September): 239–272.

Philips, Kevin P. (1984). *Staying on Top: Winning the Trade War.* New York: Vintage.

Plummer, Alfred (1937). *New British Industries in the Twentieth Century.* London: Pitman and sons.

Pollard, Robert A., and Samuel F. Wells, Jr. (1984). "1945–1960: The Era of American Economic Hegemony," Pp. 333–390 in William H. Becker and Samuel F. Wells, Jr. (eds.), *Economics and World Power: An Assessment of American Diplomacy Since 1789.* New York: Columbia University Press.

Posen, Barry R. (1984). *The Sources of Military Doctrine: France, Britain, and Germany Between the World Wars*. Ithaca: Cornell University Press.

Posthumus, Nicholas W. (1946). *Inquiry into the History of Prices in Holland*, vol. 1. Leiden: E. J. Brill.

Price, Roger (1981). *An Economic History of Modern France, 1730–1914*. New York: St. Martin's Press.

Puchala, Donald J. (1972). "Of Blind Men, Elephants and International Integration." *Journal of Common Market Studies* 10 (March): 267–284.

—— (1981). "Integration Theory and the Study of International Relations," Pp. 145–167 in Richard L. Merritt and Bruce M. Russett (eds.), *From National Development to Global Community: Essays in Honor of Karl W. Deutsch*. London: George Allen and Unwin.

Rapkin, David P. (1983). "The Inadequacy of a Single Logic: Toward an Integration of Political and Material Approaches to the World System," Pp. 241–268 in William R. Thompson (ed.), *Contending Approaches to World System Analysis*. Beverly Hills: Sage.

—— (1987). "World Leadership," Pp. 129–157 in George Modelski (ed.), *Exploring Long Cycles*. Boulder, CO: Lynne Rienner.

Rapkin, David P., William R. Thompson with Jon A. Christopherson (1979). "Bipolarity and Bipolarization in the Cold War Era: Conceptualization, Measurement and Validation." *Journal of Conflict Resolution* 23 (June): 261–295.

Rasler, Karen A., and William R. Thompson (1983). "Global Wars, Public Debts, and the Long Cycle." *World Politics* 35 (July): 489–516.

—— (1985a). "War Making and State Making: Governmental Expenditures, Tax Revenues, and Global Wars." *American Political Science Review* 79 (June): 491–507.

—— (1985b). "Global War and Major Power Economic Growth." *American Journal of Political Science* 29 (August): 513–538.

—— (1988). "Longitudinal Change in Defense Burdens, Capital Formation and Economic Growth: The Systemic Leader Case." *Journal of Conflict Resolution* 31 (March).

—— (forthcoming). *War and Statemaking: The Shaping of the Global Powers*. Boston: Allen and Unwin.

Ray, James L. (1974). "Status Inconsistency and War Involvement in Europe, 1816–1970." *Peace Science Society (International) Papers* 23:69–80.

Raymond, Gregory A., and Charles W. Kegley, Jr. (1987). "Long Cycles and Internationalized Civil War." *Journal of Politics* 49:481–499.

Reagan, Ronald (1984). *Economic Report of the President*. Washington, D.C.: U.S. Government Printing Office.

Reich, Robert B. (1983). *The Next American Frontier*. New York: Penguin.

Research Working Group on Cyclical Rhythms and Secular Trends (1979). "Cyclical Rhythms and Secular Trends of the Capitalist World-Economy: Some Premises, Hypotheses, and Questions." *Review* 2 (Spring): 483–500.

Richardson, Lewis F. (1960). *Statistics of Deadly Quarrels*. Pittsburgh: Boxwood.

Rogowski, Ronald (1983). "Structure, Growth, and Power: Three Rationalist Accounts." *International Organization* 37 (Autumn): 713–738.

Roland, Alex (1985). "Technology and War: A Bibliographic Essay," Pp. 347–379 in Merritt R. Smith (ed.), *Military Enterprise and Technological Change: Perspectives on the American Experience.* Cambridge, MA: MIT Press.

Rose, Arnold (1941). "Wars, Innovations and Long Cycles: A Brief Comment." *American Economic Review* 31 (March): 105–107.

Rosecrance, Richard (1986). *The Rise of the Trading State.* New York: Basic Books.

—— (1987). "Long Cycle Theory and International Relations." *International Organization* 41:283–301.

Rosenau, James N. (1966). "Pre-Theories and Theories of Foreign Policy," Pp. 27–92 in R. B. Farrel (ed.), *Approaches to Comparative and International Politics.* Evanston: Northwestern University Press.

—— (1971). *The Scientific Study of Foreign Policy.* New York: Free Press.

—— (1982). "Order and Disorder in the Study of World Politics: Ten Essays in Search of Perspective," Pp. 1–7 in Ray Maghroori and Bennett Ramberg (eds.), *Globalism versus Realism: International Relations' Third Debate.* Boulder, CO: Westview Press.

—— (1986). "Before Cooperation: Hegemons, Regimes, and Habit-Driven Actors in World Politics." *International Organization* 40 (Autumn): 849–894.

Rostow, Walt W. (1978). *The World Economy: History and Prospect.* Austin: University of Texas Press.

Rupert, Mark E., and David P. Rapkin (1985). "The Erosion of U.S. Leadership Capabilities," Pp. 155–180 in Paul M. Johnson and William R. Thompson (eds.), *Rhythms in Politics and Economics.* New York: Praeger.

Russett, Bruce (1983). "Prosperity and Peace." *International Studies Quarterly* 27 (December): 381–387.

—— (1985). "The Mysterious Case of Vanishing Hegemony; or, Is Mark Twain Really Dead?" *International Organization* 39 (Spring): 207–231.

Sabrosky, Alan N. [ed.] (1985). *Polarity and War: The Changing Structure of International Conflict.* Boulder, CO: Westview Press.

Sagan, Carl (1983/84). "Nuclear War and Climatic Catastrophe: Some Policy Implications." *Foreign Affairs* 62 (Winter): 256–292.

Schumpeter, Joseph A. (1939). *Business Cycles: A Theoretical, Historical and Statistical Analysis of the Capitalist Process.* New York: McGraw-Hill.

Scott, Bruce R. (1985a). "U.S. Competitiveness: Concepts, Performance, and Implications," Pp. 13–70 in Bruce R. Scott and George C. Lodge (eds.), *U.S. Competitiveness in the World Economy.* Boston: Harvard Business School Press.

—— (1985b). "National Strategies: Key to International Competition," Pp. 71–143 in Bruce R. Scott and George C. Lodge (eds.), *U.S. Competitiveness in the World Economy.* Boston: Harvard Business School Press.

Silk, Leonard (1987). "The US and the World Economy." *Foreign Affairs* 65:458–476.

Singer, J. David (1961). "The Level of Analysis Problem in International Relations," Pp. 77–92 in Klaus Knorr and Sidney Verba (eds.), *The International System: Theoretical Essays.* Princeton: Princeton University Press.

Singer, J. David, Stuart Bremer, and John Stuckey (1972). "Capability Distribution, Uncertainty, and Major Power War, 1820–1965," Pp. 19–48 in Bruce Russett (ed.), *Peace, War and Numbers.* Beverly Hills: Sage.

Singer, J. David, and Thomas Cusack (1981). "Periodicity, Inexorability, and Steersmanship in International War," Pp. 404–422 in Richard Merritt and Bruce Russett (eds.), *From National Development to Global Community.* London: George Allen And Unwin.

Singer, J. David and Melvin Small (1968). "Alliance Aggregation and the Onset of War," Pp. 247–286 in J. David Singer (ed.), *Quantitative International Politics: Insights and Evidence.* New York: Free Press.

—— (1972). *The Wages of War.* New York: John Wiley.

Siverson, Randolph M. (1980). "War and Change in the International System," Pp. 211–232 in Ole R. Holsti, Randolph M. Siverson, and Alexander L. George (eds.), *Change in the International System.* Boulder, CO: Westview.

Siverson, Randolph M., and Michael P. Sullivan (1983). "The Distribution of Power and the Onset of War." *Journal of Conflict Resolution* 27 (September): 473–494.

Skocpol, Theda (1977). "Wallerstein's World Capitalist System: A Theoretical and Historical Critique." *American Journal of Sociology* 82 (5): 1075–1090.

—— (1979). *States and Social Revolutions.* Cambridge: Cambridge University Press.

Small, Melvin (1980). *Was War Necessary? National Security and U.S. Entry Into War.* Beverly Hills: Sage.

Small, Melvin, and J. David Singer (1982). *Resort to Arms.* Beverly Hills: Sage.

Smith, Merritt Roe (1985). "Introduction," pp. 1–37 in Merritt Roe Smith (ed.), *Military Enterprise and Technological Change: Perspectives on the American Experience.* Cambridge, MA: MIT Press.

Smith, Ronald P. (1977). "Military Expenditures and Capitalism." *Cambridge Journal of Economics* 1:61–76.

Snidal, Duncan (1985). "The Limits of Hegemonic Stability Theory." *International Organization* 39 (Autumn): 579–614.

Sombart, Werner (1913). *Krieg und Kapitalismus.* Leipzig: Duncker and Hublot.

Sorokin, P. A. (1937). *Social and Cultural Dynamics: Fluctuations of Social Relationships, War, and Revolution.* New York: American Book Company.

Sprout, Harold, and Margaret Sprout (1968). "The Dilemma of Rising Demands and Insufficient Resources." *World Politics* 20 (July): 660–693.

Staniland, Martin (1985). *What Is Political Economy?* New Haven: Yale University Press.

Starr, Harvey (1974). "The Quantitative International Relations Scholar as

Surfer: Riding the 'Fourth Wave'." *Journal of Conflict Resolution* 18 (June): 336–368.

Stein, Arthur (1984). "The Hegemon's Dilemma: Great Britain, the United States, and the International Economic Order." *International Organization* 38 (Spring): 355–386.

Stein, Arthur, and Bruce M. Russett (1980). "Evaluating War: Outcomes and Consequences," Pp. 399–422 in Ted R. Gurr (ed.), *Handbook of Political Conflict: Theory and Research*. New York: Free Press.

Strange, Susan (1982). "Cave! Hic Dragones: A Critique of Regime Analysis." *International Organization* 36 (Spring): 479–496.

Svennilson, Ingvar (1954). *Growth and Stagnation in the European Economy*. Geneva: United Nations.

Szymanski, Albert (1981). *The Logic of Imperialism*. New York: Praeger.

Thompson, William R. (1982). "Phases of the Business Cycle and the Outbreak of War." *International Studies Quarterly* 26 (June): 301–311.

—— (1983). "Cycles, Capabilities and War: An Ecumenical View," Pp. 141–163 in William R. Thompson (ed.), *Contending Approaches to World System Analysis*. Beverly Hills: Sage.

Thompson, William R., and Karen A. Rasler (1988). "War and Systemic Capability Reconcentration." *Journal of Conflict Resolution* 32 (June).

Thompson, William R., and Gary Zuk (1982). "War, Inflation, and Kondratieff's Long Waves." *Journal of Conflict Resolution* 26 (December): 621–644.

—— (1986). "World Power and the Strategic Trap of Territorial Commitments." *International Studies Quarterly* 30 (September): 249–267.

Thucydides (1954). *The Peloponnesian War*, translated by Rex Warner. Harmondsworth: Pelican.

Thurow, Lester C. (1985). *The Zero-Sum Solution*. New York: Simon and Schuster.

Tilly, Charles (1975). "Revolutions and Collective Violence," Pp. 483–555 in Fred I. Greenstein and Nelson W. Polsby (eds.), *Handbook of Political Science: Macro Political Theory*. Reading, MA: Addison-Wesley.

Tinbergen, J. (1981). "Kondratiev Cycles and So-Called Long Waves: The Early Research." *Futures* 13 (August): 258–263.

Toynbee, Arnold J. (1954). *A Study of History*, vol. 9 London: Oxford University Press.

Tylecote, Andrew B. (1982). "German Ascent and British Decline, 1870–1980: The Role of Upper Class Structure and Values," Pp. 41–67 in Edward Friedman (ed.), *Ascent and Decline in the World-System*. Beverly Hills: Sage.

United Nations (multiple volumes). *U.N. Statistical Yearbook*. New York: United Nations.

United Nations (multiple volumes). *Yearbook of Industrial Statistics*. New York: United Nations.

United Nations (multiple volumes). *Yearbook of World Energy Statistics*. New York: United Nations.

U.S. Department of Commerce (1975). *Historical Statistics of the United*

States, Colonial Times to 1970. Washington, D.C.: U.S. Government Printing Office.

Vasquez, John A. (1983). *The Power of Power Politics: A Critique.* New Brunswick, NJ: Rutgers University Press.

Vayrynen, Raimo (1983). "Economic Cycles, Power Transitions, Political Management and Wars Between Major Powers." *International Studies Quarterly* 27 (December): 389–418.

Viotti, Paul R., and Mark V. Kauppi (1987). *International Relations Theory: Realism, Pluralism, Globalism.* New York: Macmillan.

Vogel, Ezra F. (1986). "Pax Nipponica?" *Foreign Affairs* 64 (Spring): 752–767.

Wagemann, E. (1930). *Economic Rhythm: A Theory of Business Cycles,* translated by D. H. Blelloch. New York: McGraw-Hill.

Wagner, R. Harrison (1984). "War and Expected-Utility Theory." *World Politics* 36:407–423.

Walker, Richard L. (1953). *The Multi-State System of Ancient China.* Hamden, CT: Shoe String Press.

Wallace, Michael D. (1973). *War and Rank Among Nations.* Lexington, MA: D. C. Heath.

Wallerstein, Immanuel (1974). *The Modern World-System: Capitalist Agriculture and the Origins of the European Economy in the Sixteenth Century.* New York: Academic Press.

—— (1979). *The Capitalist World-Economy.* Cambridge: Cambridge University Press.

—— (1980). *The Modern World-System: Mercantilism and the Consolidation of the European World-Economy, 1600–1759.* New York: Academic Press.

—— (1984). *The Politics of the World-Economy.* Cambridge: Cambridge University Press.

—— (1986). "Japan and the Future Trajectory of the World-System: Lessons From History?" Unpublished paper. Binghamton, NY: Fernand Braudel Center, State University of New York–Binghamton.

Waltz, Kenneth N. (1959). *Man, the State and War.* New York: Columbia University Press.

—— (1964). "The Stability of a Bipolar World." *Daedalus* 93 (Summer): 881–900.

—— (1967). "International Structure, National Force and the Balance of World Power." *Journal of International Affairs* 21:215–231.

—— (1979). *Theory of International Politics.* Reading, MA: Addison-Wesley.

Ward, Michael D. (1982). *Research Gaps in Alliance Dynamics.* Denver: University of Denver Monograph Series in World Affairs.

Weber, Robert P. (1981). "Society and Economy in the Western World System." *Social Forces* 59 (June): 1130–1148.

—— (1983). "Cyclical Theories of Crises in the World-System," Pp. 37–55 in Albert Bergesen (ed.), *Crises in the World-System.* Beverly Hills: Sage.

Wesson, Robert G. (1978). *State Systems: International Pluralism, Politics, and Culture*. New York: Free Press.

Wheeler, Hugh G. (1980). "Postwar Industrial Growth," pp. 253–284 in J. David Singer (ed.), *The Correlates of War II: Testing Some Realpolitik Models*. New York: Free Press.

Wight, Martin (1978). *Power Politics*. Hedley Bull and C. Holbraad (eds.), New York: Holmes and Meier.

Wilcox, Donald J. (1987). *The Measure of Times Past: Pre-Newtonian Chronologies and the Rhetoric of Relative Time*. Chicago: University of Chicago Press.

Wilkinson, David (1980). *Deadly Quarrels: Lewis F. Richardson and the Statistical Study of War*. Berkeley: University of California Press.

Wright, Quincy (1942/1965). *A Study of War*. Chicago: University of Chicago Press.

Yarbrough, Beth V., and Robert M. Yarbrough (1987). "Cooperation in the Liberalization of International Trade: After Hegemony, What?" *International Organization* 41 (Winter): 1–26.

Zinnes, Dina A. (1968). "The Expression and Perception of Hostility in Prewar Crisis: 1914," Pp. 85–119 in J. David Singer (ed.), *Quantitative International Politics: Insights and Evidence*. New York: Free Press.

Zolberg, Aristide R. (1981). "Origins of the Modern World System: A Missing Link." *World Politics* 33 (January): 253–281.

—— (1983). " 'World' and 'System': A Misalliance," Pp. 269–290 in William R. Thompson (ed.), *Contending Approaches to World System Analysis*. Beverly Hills: Sage.

Index